Organizing from the Inside Out

JULIE MORGENSTERN

Organizing
from
the
Inside Out

■ The
Foolproof
System for
Organizing
Your Home,
Your Office,
and Your Life

Hodder & Stoughton

First published in Great Britain in 2000 by Hodder and Stoughton
A division of Hodder Headline

10 9 8 7 6 5 4 3

A CIP Catalogue record for this title is available from the British Library

ISBN 0 340 79466 6 (Trade paperback edition)
ISBN 0 340 81830 1 (Hard cover edition)

Printed and bound in Great Britain by
Mackays of Chatham plc, Chatham, Kent

Hodder and Stoughton
A division of Hodder Headline
338 Euston Road
London NW1 3BH

To my daughter Jessi, whose own magnificent gift of writing
inspired me to reach for my dream. May this book,
in turn, inspire you to reach for yours.

And to my parents, whose unwavering support and belief
in me even through the messy times is a miracle.

Contents

Introduction:

The Most Important Organizing Book You'll Ever Read   3

PART ONE • LAYING THE FOUNDATION

1. A New Way of Looking at Organizing   9
2. What's Holding You Back?   16

PART TWO • SECRETS OF A PROFESSIONAL ORGANIZER

3. Analyze: Taking Stock   39
4. Strategize: Creating a Plan of Action   47
5. Attack: Getting the Job Done   59

PART THREE • APPLYING WHAT YOU'VE LEARNED

How to Use This Section   71
6. Traditional Offices and Filing Systems   73
7. Home-Based Businesses   90
8. Cubicle Workstations   102
9. Mobile Offices   110
10. Household Information Centers   122
11. Attics, Basements, and Garages   136

12. Bathrooms   149

13. Bedrooms   158

14. Closets   166

15. Kids' Rooms   179

16. Kitchens   190

17. Living Rooms   201

PART FOUR · TACKLING TIME AND TECHNOLOGY

18. Conquering the Clock   213

19. Taming Technology   228

Appendix A:

Resources for Organizing Products   241

Appendix B:

Suggested Further Reading   243

Acknowledgments   245

Index   249

Organizing
from the
Inside Out

Introduction

The Most Important Organizing Book You'll Ever Read

OK, so you've been trying for years to get organized.

You've bought tons of books, clipped magazine articles, even taken an occasional workshop.

You've enviously looked through the pages of organizing catalogs, the aisles of hardware stores, and the pristine environments of organized friends and colleagues, aching for the perfect answer to the war against clutter.

You've spent countless dollars on a myriad of baskets, bins, sorters, racks, hooks, calendars, and cubby systems you were *sure* would put your life in order.

You've even stayed home from picnics, parties, and dates to attack your clutter by applying the Organizing Credo: *"When in doubt, throw it out."*

Yet, for all your efforts, you never seem to quite cross the finish line.

You experience a moment of relief, a flash of promise, but maintaining the peaceful bliss of an organized space remains out of reach. Before long, the clutter is back, and chaos is reigning once more.

You are suffering from a condition I call "the Yo-yo Organizing Syndrome." It works—or rather, it *doesn't* work—just like yo-yo dieting, where you experiment with method after method of losing weight, making lots of enthusiastic starts, but always give up before reaching the finish line, and you wind up losing no weight or even weighing more than before. With Yo-yo Organizing, no matter how far along you get, you always end up slipping back and are forced to start from ground zero the next time you gather your willpower.

Frustrating. Maddening. Overwhelming. Demoralizing. Whether you are mildly or wildly disorganized, getting organized can often seem an impossible task.

But is it?

Absolutely not. The frustrations you experience trying to get organized are not the result of some innate inability. I contend they are due to your never having learned *how* to organize. It's not a subject taught in school. As a result, you have developed quite a few misconceptions, beliefs, and ineffective techniques that are standing in your way. The goal of this book is to radically change your thinking and approach to the organizing process. It will challenge all of your previous ideas about getting organized and cast light on what has been holding you back. It will show you specific techniques to make any organizing project simple, manageable, and attainable, rather than frustrating, overwhelming, and impossible.

A complete re-education, *Organizing from the Inside Out* teaches you how to work *with* your personality rather than against it to achieve the results you are looking for. It was designed as a permanent reference book for the twenty-first century; you can read and reread its pages to master the fundamental principles of organizing anything. This book's lessons, filled with the secrets of a professional organizer, provide you with a framework for taking advantage of all the other organizing books, articles, seminars, and products on the market.

The days of Yo-yo Organizing are over—you are about to discover how gratifying and successful organizing can be.

HOW TO USE THIS BOOK

Those of you reading this book probably fall into one of three groups:

- You've struggled your whole life to get organized, and have never quite succeeded.
- You used to be organized, but lost your grip somewhere along the way.
- You feel basically organized, but are constantly looking for ways to improve your skills and systems.

Whichever group you fall into, one thing is true: *You want quick solutions.*

You don't have much time on your hands and need to become better organized swiftly so you can get on with your life. You don't want it to take forever because organizing is only a means to an end: to live your life more fully.

To that end, this book is structured to be as reader-friendly as possible. The only requirement is that you read Parts 1 and 2. They lay the foundation, teaching you the "how to" of organizing you never learned in school. Once you have grasped the fundamental principles in them, everything else will fall into place. Then you can turn to the chapters in Parts 3 and 4 which deal with the problem areas in your home or office that are of interest to you, and apply the principles you've learned to create customized systems that work for you.

. . .

In 1989, I created Task Masters, a full-service organizing business for homes, offices, and everything in between. Since then, hundreds of clients have called me when their own attempts at getting organized have failed. It's not easy for them to make that call. Some hold on to my number for years before working up the nerve. They are embarrassed. And they are afraid.

Their biggest fears? That theirs is the worst clutter problem I've ever seen. That there is little I can do to help, and that it will take years to dig them out, if it can ever be done at all. They can't imagine where to start, and can see no light at the end of the tunnel.

Clients are always amazed that (1) I am neither shocked by nor pessimistic about what they show me, and (2) I can quickly map out a plan of action. How am I able to do this? Because nearly a decade as a professional organizer has taught me that there is a simple, reliable method that works every time, no matter how formidable the task.

Organizing from the Inside Out demystifies the organizing process by teaching you that formula, the same one I use with my clients; I promise it will help you win the war against clutter *forever*, just as it has helped them.

Most other books, articles, and seminars on organizing tend to focus on the solution rather than the problem: Here's a hot idea for organizing a bathroom; here's a cool technique for organizing your files; here's a neat tip for organizing your closets. What they ignore are the internal and external issues—the psychological quirks, hidden dissuaders, and common mistakes we all make—that stand between us and achieving our dream of a usefully arranged and organized space. And yet without understanding these all-important issues, no amount of hot ideas, cool techniques, or neat tips will work.

Organizing from the Inside Out goes beyond all these other books, articles, and seminars by exploring the entire process from the right direction. It will teach you

• How to identify the roadblocks in your path to organizing success, examine and confront these issues, and put them behind you at last

• A foolproof method for customizing your space to reflect who you are and what is important to you

• What questions to ask before buying that next organizing container, gizmo, or gadget

You will discover your own power to get organized, stay organized, and bring out your own personal and professional best.

You will actually come to enjoy the organizing process because once you understand how simple that process can be, you will experience a sense of liberation and power you've never known before.

PART 1

Laying the Foundation

A New Way of Looking at Organizing

If I asked you to describe an organized space, what would you say? From most people, I hear things like "neat and tidy," "spare," "minimalistic," and "boring."

But an organized space has nothing to do with these traits. There are people whose homes and offices appear neat as a pin on the surface. Yet, inside their desk drawers and kitchen cabinets, there is no real system, and things are terribly out of control. By contrast, there are many people who live or work in a physical mess, yet feel very comfortable in this environment and can always put their hands on whatever they need in a second. Could they be considered organized? Absolutely.

Being organized has less to do with the way an environment *looks* than how effectively it *functions*. If a person can find what they need when they need it, feels unencumbered in achieving his or her goals, and is happy in his or her space, then that person is well organized.

I'd like to propose a new definition of organization: "Organizing is the process by which we create environments that enable us to live, work, and relax exactly as we want to. When we are organized, our homes, offices, and schedules reflect and encourage who we are, what we want, and where we are going."

MISCONCEPTIONS ABOUT ORGANIZING

Misconceptions affect the way you think about any process, poisoning your attitude toward it and eroding even your best efforts to succeed by convincing you before you start that you're bound to fail.

Here are some of the most common beliefs about organizing, and the debunking facts that will change your thinking.

Misconception: Organizing is a mysterious talent. Some lucky people are born with it, while others, like you, are left to suffer.

Fact: Organizing is a skill. In fact, it's a remarkably simple skill that anyone can learn. How do I know? Because I was once a notoriously disorganized person myself. In fact, everyone who "knew me when" is amazed at the irony of how I make my living today. Two summers ago, I went to my twenty-fifth summer camp reunion. Naturally, as we all got caught up on what everyone was doing with their lives, I spoke with pride about my work. Since professional organizing is such an unusual field, all of my old friends found the concept absolutely fascinating. One brave soul dear, sweet Martin G., put his arm around me, discreetly pulled me off to the side, and whispered politely, "Uh, Julie . . . I don't remember you *ever* being particularly *organized.*"

From the day I was born until I had my own child, I lived in a constant state of disorder. I was a classic right-brained creative type, always living in chaos, operating out of piles, spending half my days searching for misplaced papers, lost phone numbers, and missing car keys. I'd permanently lost everything from little stuff to big stuff: passports, birth certificates, cameras, jewelry, shoes, and clothing. I'd lost things that belonged to other people. I once spent four hours searching for a friend's car in the parking lot at Chicago's O'Hare Airport, because I hadn't paid any attention to where I had left it.

I was one of those people who lived "in the moment": spontaneous and charming, but never planning more than one minute into the future. As a result, I was always scrambling at the last minute, and frequently didn't get things done on time, either because I forgot I had to do them or because I couldn't find whatever I needed to get the task done.

My day of reckoning came when I had a baby. When Jessi was three weeks old, I decided it'd be a beautiful day to take her for a walk by the waterfront. When she got up from a nap, my husband went to get the car and I went to get the baby. Suddenly I realized, hey, I should probably take along a few supplies. What did I need? Let's see, diapers, a blanket . . . Oh, yes, a bottle of water, and maybe a toy or two. I started running around the house, gathering items. Every time I thought I was ready, I'd think of something else to bring. The Snugli, a sweater, and how about a tape to listen to in the car on the way? By the time I was packed up, more than two hours had passed and Jessi had fallen back asleep. I realized at that moment that if I didn't get my act together, my child would never see the light of day.

I decided to organize the diaper bag. Dumping out all the items I had gathered for our outing, I began by grouping all the supplies into categories that made sense to me: things to keep her warm with in one group (blanket, change of clothes, sweater); things to feed her with in another group (water bottle, pacifier); things to change her with in another (diapers, wipes, powder); and finally things to entertain her with (toys, a tape for the car).

Then I assigned each category of items a particular section of the bag, so that I could quickly get my hands on items when I needed them and know at a glance if anything was missing. I ended by tucking an inventory of all the supplies into a special pocket in the bag as well, as a tool to make restocking the bag easy. What a victory! From that day forward I was in control, packed and ready to go at the drop of a dime, confident that I had everything I needed at my fingertips.

That diaper bag was the first thing I ever successfully organized. And though it sounds small, it was truly the beginning of my path to organization. After that, I tackled other areas of my house, my drawers, my closets, papers, and so on, always using the same basic approach I used to organize that diaper bag. The rest, as they say, is history. I had happily discovered that organizing is a very straightforward skill, learnable even by the likes of someone as once hopelessly disorganized as me.

Misconception: Getting organized is an overwhelming, hopeless chore.
Fact: No matter what you're organizing, no matter how daunting the task or how huge the backlog, getting organized boils down to the same very simple, predictable process. Once mastered, you will discover organizing to be an incredibly cleansing and empowering process—an exhilarating way of freeing yourself up and maintaining a steady life course in a complex world. You'll even consider it fun because it produces a gratifying sense of clarity, focus, and accomplishment.

Consider this reaction from newly organized speaker Connie Lagan:

> Cleaning out the clutter has magically, maybe even miraculously, released creative energy within me. The first evening after I completed my own business spring cleaning, I sat in my office chair and stared. I could not believe how energizing it was to see "white space." My eyes had places to rest and my spirit had found a home once again in the place where I spend most of my waking hours.

Misconception: It's impossible to *stay* organized.
Fact: Organizing is sustainable, if your system is built around the way you think and designed to grow and adapt with you as your life and work change. It is when your system is a poor fit for you that maintenance is a difficult chore. In addition, like eating well and staying fit, organizing is a way of life that requires monitoring and ongoing effort until it becomes satisfyingly ingrained. Instructions on how to maintain your system are an integral part of the organizing process presented in this book.

Misconception: Organizing is a nonproductive use of time. People in my workshops often say to me, "I *want* to get organized, I *try* to get organized, but I always feel like I should be doing more important things with my time—calling on customers, attending meetings, going to seminars, writing proposals, spending time with family and friends, relaxing, even catching up on my sleep."

Fact: Life today moves more rapidly than it did fifty years ago and will continue accelerating in the years ahead, presenting us with more opportunities and ever-greater demands on our time and ability to make choices. In an environment like this, those who are organized will thrive. Those who are disorganized will feel overwhelmed, unsure of which way to turn, and flounder. You can no longer afford *not* to be organized. Organizing has become a survival skill for the twenty-first century, and *Organizing from the Inside Out* is your handbook for getting there.

ORGANIZING FROM THE OUTSIDE IN

My years as a professional organizer and my own background of disorganization have taught me that most of us approach organizing from the wrong direction. When we are ready to get organized, it is usually because we have reached the breaking point; the clutter is driving us crazy and we want instant relief. Due to the accumulated stress of being disorganized, our knee-jerk reaction is to attack first, ask questions later—to just dive in and do whatever we can to gain control quickly.

We don't spend any time analyzing the situation, and typically we do very little planning—basically putting the cart before the horse. We search madly *outside* ourselves for the answers to our predicament and grasp wildly at anything we think will "save" us from it. See if any of the following behaviors strike you as familiar:

• You go shopping for containers to get your clutter problem under control without having measured, counted, or examined what and how much you have to store.

• You go on impulsive purging sprees, ruthlessly getting rid of as much as you can to create a spare existence, then discover too late that you tossed out something that was important to you.

• You "adopt" organizing tips from friends, magazines, and books with no thought as to whether they mesh with your personality or fit your situation and needs.

• You tackle the bits and pieces of your organizing problem without ever looking at the big picture.

• You grab on to mantras like "reduce your possessions 50 percent," or "touch every piece of paper only once," or "if you haven't used it in two years, get rid of it," in the hope that they will change your life forever.

This leap-before-you-look approach is what I call *organizing from the outside in*. It fails to look at the big picture before seeking quick solutions, grabbing at all kinds of random tips and techniques. Don't get me wrong: using the clever tips, smart techniques, and snazzy containers on the market is a critical part of the organizing process, but there are several steps you need to go through first in order to know which ones are right for you.

At best, this piecemeal approach creates an incomplete patchwork organizing system, leaving you with lots of holes. After buying a new container or implementing a new tip, you are excited by the novelty and experience a moment of hope, but this feeling soon wears off when the reality sinks in that information and objects are still falling through the cracks.

At worst, organizing from the outside in leads to selecting all the wrong systems, ones that just won't work for you. You try to force yourself to use them, but the effort is too great; after a few weeks you give up, watch the mess return, and consider yourself organizationally hopeless.

Organizing from the outside in fails time after time because it doesn't take into account how you think, relate to the world, pace yourself, like to operate, or your sense of visuals—*the total picture* of yourself that your organizing system should ultimately reflect.

ORGANIZING FROM THE INSIDE OUT

Organizing from the inside out means creating a system based on your specific personality, needs, and goals. It focuses on defining who you are and what is important to you as a person so that your system can be designed to reflect that.

Successful organizing forces you to look at the big picture, not one small section of the frame, so that the system you design will be complete. It is a nurturing process that helps you focus on discovering what is important to you and making it more accessible, rather than haranguing you to throw out as much as you can and organizing what's left over.

Organizing from the inside out means taking a good look at the obstacles that are holding you back from being organized so you can identify and remove them once and for all.

It means mastering strategies to speed up and simplify the organizing process, so you are sure to reach the finish line, not quit halfway there.

And it means organizing *before* buying any fancy new storage units or snazzy containers, so that your purchases will have meaning and be a perfect match for your particular needs.

Organizing from the inside out feels counterintuitive. It's not natural to stop and reflect when disorganization is at its peak. The impulse is to just dive in and attack. But if you invest a little time doing some thinking and analysis first, you will be able to zero in on just the right solution for you.

I once had a client named Carol. At first glance, she was an amazingly accomplished woman. She headed a high-profile arts organization and managed a staff of seven. She'd circulate at cocktail parties attended by important donors and celebrities, winning over one after another with perfect poise and confidence. She was dynamic, charming, and articulate. In the spotlight, she was brilliant, but behind the scenes her professional life was out of control.

Buried under an avalanche of letters, faxes, and e-mail from all those she had charmed, Carol was surrounded by a mountain of unanswered correspondence. With her very hectic and public schedule, she rarely made time to go through the mail, and often it went unopened for months. Grants were lost and opportunities to work with important artists went to other institutions.

Carol tried endless solutions to get and keep herself on track. All of them seemed quite logical: having her secretary open all the mail for her and type a summary sheet of the day's correspondence; sorting the mail into folders marked Extremely Urgent, Very Important, Important—Can Wait, and Less Important—FYI; holding calls for a half hour every morning to go through the mail. Unfortunately, none of these "solutions" worked because the problem was being approached *from the outside in*.

When Carol called me, I began by talking to her about how she felt about her mail, and why she thought she wasn't taking care of it the way she should. I mentioned that she seemed to be at her best face-to-face. She agreed, telling me that she thrived on human interaction, ideas, and problem solving. She found dealing with written communication painfully boring and isolating. Carol clearly needed a new system for dealing with correspondence—one that appealed to her personality, style, and need for human contact.

I began by encouraging Carol to make a mental shift: to begin viewing those mountains of letters, faxes, and e-mail messages not as paper but as real people who had come into her office with problems they needed her to solve.

I then suggested that she change the name of the time she spent dealing with correspondence from "the mail hour" to "the decision hour." This simple name change had an immediate impact on her because it sparked her love of ideas and action.

Finally, to counteract her feeling of isolation, I suggested her secretary stay with her as she worked through the day's correspondence. Carol could dictate replies, bounce ideas off her secretary, and have the kind of give-and-take that made her excited to be working.

Carol's relationship to correspondence changed completely. What had been a chore became energizing and gratifying, all because she had become *organized from the inside out*.

Easy as 1-2-3

Organizing from the inside out is a method that accommodates your personality, needs, situation, and goals rather than forces you to change. By following these three straightforward but very important steps you will be able to meet any of life's organizing challenges and achieve lasting success:

Analyze: Step back to take stock of your current situation by defining where you are, where you are going, what's holding you back, and why it's important to get there.

Strategize: Create a plan of action for the physical transformation of your space, including a realistic schedule for making it happen.

Attack: Methodically dive in to the clutter, sorting and arranging items to reflect the way you think, making sure you see visible, dramatic results as you work.

Equipped with your new view of organizing, you are about to embark on a great adventure that will lead you to enjoying the freedom of organized living forever. Throughout, I will be your guide, coach, and sounding board, providing you with ideas and examples of other people's systems to help stimulate your own thinking.

Now let's get to it.

What's Holding You Back?

"You can't fix it till you know what's broken."

Whoever first said that neatly summed up one of the most fundamental principles of organizing from the inside out: understanding the cause before seeking a remedy. It's actually a pretty logical step. After all, isn't that how we approach all of life's problems?

If you aren't feeling well, you go to your doctor and describe your symptoms. Let's say you've been suffering frequent headaches and an upset stomach. Your doctor doesn't just automatically prescribe pain relievers and antacid. She knows your symptoms may be caused by a variety of conditions and illnesses, from stress to food poisoning to something even more serious. Your doctor asks you more questions, examines you, and runs diagnostic tests to determine your illness. Only after this exploratory exam will treatment be prescribed; otherwise the medicine might only mask your illness—a dangerous situation that could lead to an escalation of your condition. The same is true of organizing. You need to identify the cause before seeking a solution.

One of the most enlightening results of my work as a professional organizer has been discovering that while many messes may look alike, their root causes are rarely the same. There are a lot of reasons for disorganization, and most people have no idea what the actual cause of their specific problem is. As a result, they spend a great deal of time, energy, and money addressing the wrong issue.

Most people assume they are disorganized because they don't have enough storage space, or because they are inherently sloppy, lazy, or incompetent. But in a decade of organizing, I have found that with 90 percent of my clients the actual cause of their disorganization was *not* a lack of storage space. For example, one recent client was referred to me by a concerned friend after announcing that she was going to buy the apartment next door just because she was out of closet space. All she really needed was a bit of purging, and learning how to make better use of the storage space she had. We accomplished the task in about five days, and saved her hundreds of thousands of dollars in the process.

As for the second belief: I haven't found one case in all my years as a professional organizer where the clutter was caused by sloppiness, laziness, or incompetence. Thinking this way inaccurately puts the blame on you, and is clearly not the best mind-set for achieving organizing success. After all, how can you expect to be enthusiastic about getting organized if you see your environment as a sharp criticism of your very nature? No wonder you avoid the dreaded task!

A THREE-LEVEL DIAGNOSTIC

The actual causes of clutter occur on three levels:

- **LEVEL 1: Technical Errors.** Simple, mechanical mistakes in your organizing system that can be easily fixed. Solving them is the equivalent of tightening a screw, changing a belt, or aligning the steering on a car. This is the first category of causes to review because all messes can be attributed to at least one technical error.
- **LEVEL 2: External Realities.** Environmental realities beyond your control that limit how organized you can be. Recognizing them will save you from having unrealistic expectations of yourself.
- **LEVEL 3: Psychological Obstacles.** Hidden, internal forces that make you gravitate toward disorganization, no matter how much you crave control. Unless you are aware of them, they can lead you to sabotage any system you set up. Through awareness, you can find a way to work around these issues and achieve organizing success.

Keep in mind that it is not uncommon to have several causes of clutter operating at once. Everyone struggling with disorganization suffers from at least one Level 1 cause, but may also be suffering from some Level 2 and 3 causes as well.

As you read through the following sections, be honest with yourself, not judgmental. There is no good or bad here. The point is that self-awareness is your most powerful tool in getting and staying organized. Only you can pinpoint what's holding you back. Remember, almost every issue is fixable.

LEVEL 1: TECHNICAL ERRORS

Start your cause analysis here because once you've solved these simple mechanical mistakes, you will be able to live in organizational bliss—unless there are some internal or external obstacles at play also. If so, fixing these errors will expose them.

Look back at these descriptions of the six most common technical errors whenever you feel your space is getting out of control—because, without a doubt, your cluttered space is prey to one of them.

Error #1: Items Have No Home

Simply put, things can't get put away if there is no place to put them. If items are piled all over the place, it is likely that you have never designated a particular spot for them. Life and interests change all the time and you may have accumulated items for which you haven't yet found a proper place. You'd *like* to put things away, but you just don't know *where.* You're wary of shoving them into drawers and cabinets that are already full for fear of losing them. So, you just leave items out and about, always in a different place, and you can never find what you need.

The solution here is to take the time to evaluate what you have and assign each item a single, consistent home. This way, you'll always know where to put each item away, and still be able to find it easily when needed. Chapter 4 will provide you with an effective model for deciding where each item in your office or home should be stored. Throughout Part 3 of the book, you will find suggestions for assigning homes and finding storage space for your items on a room-by-room basis.

Error #2: Inconvenient Storage

In this situation, you don't put things away because cleanup is too much of an ordeal. It could be that you're storing items too far away from where you actually use them—across the hall, in another room, or at the opposite end of the house, requiring a big trip to put things away. For example, if your books are stacked on the floor next to your favorite reading chair, that's probably because the bookcase isn't nearby. Perhaps access to your storage units is hampered in some way; maybe the drawers stick, the cabinets are broken, the closets are blocked by boxes and furniture, your storage bins are stacked too deep, or your shelves are too high to reach.

The bottom line is, if it's too hard to put something away, you simply won't do it—not because you're lazy, but because you have more important things to do with your time. In Chapter 4, you will the learn the basics for designing your space based on convenience, storing items at their point of use. Part 3 is filled with specific suggestions on storing things within arm's reach of where you use them in your office or any room in your home.

Error #3: More Stuff than Storage Space

If all your drawers, cabinets, and closets are packed full and you have additional stuff piled on the floor, countertops, tables, and windowsills, it's a safe bet that you have more possessions than places to put them. One solution is to reduce the number of your possessions by getting rid of any excess items. Another is to add storage units to accommodate your volume of belongings. And a third is to stretch storage by making better use of all that unused space between shelves, in extra deep drawers and cabinets, under hanging garments, and the vertical area on walls that's currently being wasted. In Part 3, you'll learn how to sort through your items and decide what to keep, as well as how to stretch space and find storage where "none exists" in each area of your office and home.

Error #4: Complex, Confusing System

It is quite common for people to set up impossibly complicated systems, over-categorizing items and ending up with too many places to look for things—for example, creating a hundred folders with two sheets of paper in each rather than twenty files with ten sheets in each. Your system may have seemed sensible to you when you first set it up, but weeks or months later, you've forgotten the logic behind it. When you go to find something in your drawers or cabinets, you feel baffled and frustrated. You know you put things in a safe, sensible place, but you can't remember where.

In this situation, you have created a system you don't *trust,* and before long you stop putting things away because you're afraid you'll never find them again. Chapter 4 will provide you with the basics for designing a simple, logical system that offers visual cues for quick and easy retrieval of any item. And Parts 3 and 4 will provide many specific suggestions on how to use location, containers, and labels to build trust into your system.

Error #5: "Out of Sight, Out of Mind"

Many people leave things out as visual reminders of what they have to do—e.g., a book that has to go back to the library, bills to be paid, or a coat that needs repair. This would be okay if there were only a few items strewn about, but once the volume builds, everything begins to blend into your environment, becoming a sort of visual "Muzak" that renders all your visual reminders invisible, defeating their purpose. Chapter 4 will show you how to create a less obtrusive system for reminding you what things are important, and where they're stored.

Error #6: Organizing Is Boring

In this situation, you don't put things away because, quite frankly, cleanup is too dull a chore. You can think of a million more interesting, enjoyable, and profitable ways to spend your time, like taking computer lessons, visiting friends, or calling upon customers. The problem is, very few people put much thought into the aesthetics of their organizing system. They view storage as purely utilitarian, and buy any old container whether it appeals to them or not, saying, "Gee, no one will see this stuff but me, who cares what it looks like?" As a result, their organizing system is boring, uninspiring, and ugly to use.

Organizing and putting things away is a repetitive task, but you can make it much more appealing and fun by adding a sense of personal style and flair. Don't underestimate the power of pizzazz; it can make a big difference in whether or not you maintain your organizing system. In each chapter of Parts 3 and 4, you will be given guidelines for selecting and labeling containers that will appeal to you aesthetically and call to your sense of fun so that you will feel inspired and excited to use them.

LEVEL 2: EXTERNAL REALITIES

We live in a complex, fast-changing world, one that presents challenges to all of us in our efforts to become organized. For the most part, we can usually overcome them and, at the very least, achieve a satisfying level of control. But there are times when no matter what we do, we can only get so far. Some external obstacle is putting a limit on how organized we can hope to be—unless we can find a way around it.

To recognize if you have hit some external ceiling that's holding you back, answer "True" or "False" to the following questions:

1. When your company "downsized," you inherited the workload of some of the employees who were let go.
2. Your company recently underwent a merger, or major procedure change.
3. You recently started your own business.
4. Your business is currently undergoing a major growth spurt.
5. You are a full-time working mom or dad taking care of an aging parent.
6. You receive over a hundred e-mails, voice-mails, faxes, and memos per day.
7. You feel pressure to respond instantly to faxes and e-mail.
8. You cannot keep up with the upgrades and changes in your computer system.
9. You suffer from constant interruptions at work.
10. You work in a deadline-driven business.
11. You work in a paper-intensive business.
12. You work in a global business operating twenty-four hours a day.
13. Your company just switched you from a private office to a shared workstation.
14. You are in the midst of a transition, such as changing careers, switching the focus of your business, getting married, divorcing, moving, or having a family.

15. Someone recently moved in to share your home or office.
16. You have a highly disorganized boss who constantly interferes with your workday.
17. Your spouse, child, or roommate is a clutter-bug who could care less about the mess.
18. Your employee organizes things completely differently than you, and always disregards your system.
19. You live in a tiny home with little or no storage space.
20. You work in a cramped office with little or no storage space.

SCORING

Use the chart below to determine whether you may be struggling against a roadblock to organizing success that's not of your own making, and what options you may have for managing them.

If you answered:	See:
True to questions #1–5	External Reality #1 and #3
True to questions #6–12	External Reality #2
True to questions #13–15	External Reality #3
True to questions #16–18	External Reality #4
True to questions #19–20	External Reality #5

External Reality #1: Unrealistic Workload
I once gave a talk on time management skills to the employees of a real estate management firm. In the middle of my talk, I sensed a resistance that was almost palpable, so I stopped and confronted them about it. They told me their firm had recently cut staff severely; as a result, workloads were now impossible to handle. Appointment schedules had doubled, projects quadrupled, and the number of people they had to oversee had multiplied exponentially. What they needed was not more organizing tips, but a miracle cure to a tough situation that was clearly not of their own making.

The result of "downsizing" and "rightsizing," dual-income families, and the boom in home-based businesses—work overload—is a very real phenomenon these days. If you're trying to squeeze eighty hours of work into a sixty-hour week, you may be suffering from an unrealistic workload.

To get an accurate picture of how realistic or unrealistic it may be, track how you spend your time for a week or two. Take a page in a notebook and divide it into two columns. List each task as you do it and how long it takes to complete in the left column. In the right column, note all the tasks you needed to do, but couldn't get to (along with your best guess as to how much time they would have required). When you're finished, your log may reveal instances where you didn't make the best use of your time, as well as show you, in black and white, just how many hours of work are actually being expected of you.

What to do about it depends on the situation. If you are a corporate employee, you may want to share your findings with your boss so that she or he can see the reality of your situation and brainstorm solutions with you. If you are a business owner, perhaps you can control growth, or hire additional staff to help you. If you are working *and* caring full-time for your children, aging parents, or someone else, take a hard look at all those home chores to see if any are superfluous (do you really have to scrub the floors *every* day?). Maybe you can find ways of delegating responsibility for certain chores to other family members, or hire an outside service to do them.

External Reality #2: Speed of Life/Technology

Because life today demands that we work smarter, move faster, and know more, surrounding us with so many opportunities, it's hard not to get caught up in the go-go-go frenzy of it all. The best response to this is to apply the brakes from time to time, to think before you jump and be willing to say "no" occasionally.

Not possible? Think about it.

Just because you *can* work twenty-four hours a day doesn't mean you should. Just because you are able to put your calendar on the computer doesn't mean you have to. Just because you received that fax or e-mail a second ago doesn't mean you have to respond to it instantly. And just because there are 15,000 periodicals and 50,000 books published every year doesn't mean you're obligated to read even a fraction of them. Subscribe to the two or three periodicals that are the most valuable to you and let the rest go. Aim to read one or two books per month, on carefully selected topics of interest.

Perpetual motion, whether at work or at play, will eventually burn you out. Sure, information is available to you at every turn, but be realistic about how much you can actually process. Remember that technology is a tool. Each new tool costs you time and money to learn and to maintain. Think about that investment before buying every flashy new piece of software or electronic gizmo that comes out. Let the need drive the purchase, not the other way around. (For more tips on taming technology, see Chapter 19.)

External Reality #3: In Transition

A businessman called me to reorganize his operation, which had grown from two to six employees in the space of a few months. He wanted to rearrange the space to accommodate the new staff. Trouble was, he was unsure what his new role was. This was revealed by his indecision over where to locate his own desk. Should it be at the center of things to maximize contact with his staff, or in a separate place to provide privacy? He wasn't really sure yet what the distribution of tasks would be. Eventually, we decided we had to wait a few months to see how the new roles and relationships emerged. Only then could we create a system that made sense and would last.

His story is not uncommon. Every time we go through a major change, we experience a breakdown in our organizational systems. It's inevitable, because we are dealing with a new set of realities, and it takes time to process the information and see clearly what we have to organize. Here are some common transitions:

- Moving
- Marriage
- New baby
- Starting school
- Graduating from school
- Retirement
- Illness or death of a loved one
- Job search
- Business merger
- Business growth spurt
- Career change

When you're going through a transition, it may be best to wait until you have a clearer picture of your new priorities and needs before starting to organize, if you can tolerate the chaos a little longer. Or set up a temporary system with the understanding that it may change as you learn more about your new situation. For example, for one client who was in the middle of a job search and doing some consulting on the side, I suggested setting up a temporary filing system for his various prospects with some manila folders and a couple of banker's boxes. This kept him organized and in control of his papers while he was juggling various possibilities in his life. Until he got a new job, it was premature to know what kind of filing cabinets or permanent system he'd need.

External Reality #4: Uncooperative Partners
There is nothing more frustrating than living or working with someone whose disorganized habits keep thwarting your own organizing efforts. It can happen with a boss, an employee, a roommate, or a family member.

My advice is to confront the situation directly and try to motivate the person into cooperating with you—by appealing to his/her own priorities, not yours.

For example, if your disorganized boss is trying to achieve a certain sales level or an award for outstanding customer service, point out that by constantly interrupting you to help out with her/his latest crisis, those goals may never be met. Then offer to design a system that will alleviate the crises and be easy for your boss to maintain. (Parts 3 and 4 of this book are full of ideas on designing easy ways to maintain systems for all kinds of offices.)

In the case of an employee who refuses to follow your system, could it be that you're expecting the person to adhere to a system you haven't adequately explained? Take the time to show exactly how you want things done, and explain the importance of adhering to your system—that it's how you're able to make the big bucks to keep him/her employed!

Finally, if the source of your frustration is a roommate or family member, be sure your system is easy to understand and simple to maintain. (Again, this book will offer many solid How-to's.) Get them to identify the costs of the clutter to themselves. Ask if they ever feel frustrated when they misplace important items, waste money, run late, argue with you. Explore why it's important to *both* of you that things go back where they belong. And consider differentiating between shared spaces and private ones, then get agreement from the person to at least keep the spaces you share orderly.

External Reality #5: Limited Space

Sandra asked me to organize her small apartment, which, as she put it, was "bursting at the seams." A quick survey of the place revealed that she had done a remarkable job of maximizing her available space in a clever and aesthetically appealing way. There was no sense of clutter at all.

First, I gave her the good news—that she had done such an extraordinary job making the best use of the space that I was ready to hire her for my team of professional organizers. Then I gave her the bad news: she had reached the storage limits of her environment. She had obviously pared her belongings down to just what she used and loved, and her only options now were to put things into off-site storage, or move to a bigger apartment.

It's important to recognize the difference between this external obstacle and Technical Error #1 ("More Stuff Than Storage Space") because *sometimes there really isn't any more room.* How do you know that you have reached the absolute limits of your space? Here are the usual signs:

• You have *no* excess items in your home or office—you actually use everything you own.
• You are very organized; everything has a home, and you know where to find each and every item.
• You have made the most of every inch of your space by going vertical with bookshelves and cabinets, using furniture that stores, and using space-savers and dividers to make the most of closets and drawers.

If you fit the above criteria and have run out of room, you have probably hit the limits of your space. Trying to store more things than it is physically possible to contain will only lead to frustration.

LEVEL 3: PSYCHOLOGICAL OBSTACLES

For many people, gravitating toward and holding on to chaos may serve a hidden purpose; as much as you crave freedom from it, there's a strong impulse inside telling you that you need it. You keep making efforts to get organized, but never let yourself quite finish the job. Or worse, you do finish it, then notice yourself subtly sabotaging your own accomplishments and unraveling your system.

To find out if you have some hidden investment in staying disorganized, answer "Yes" or "No" to the following questions:

1. Does the idea of a spare, clutter-free environment make you feel anxious or uncomfortable?
2. Are you a highly visual person?
3. Do you habitually buy things in large quantities?
4. Does the prospect of getting rid of anything disturb you?
5. Do you love displaying everything you collect so you can look at it?
6. Are you constantly buying more and more cubbies, containers, and baskets to hold everything?
7. Do you harass yourself all day long with the mantra, "I've *got* to get organized, I've *got* to get organized?"
8. Do you spend more time organizing and reorganizing than working or having fun?
9. Do you frequently turn down social activities to stay home and get organized?
10. Are you constantly rearranging your stuff, never satisfied with the system you set up?
11. Are you afraid getting organized might squelch your creativity?
12. Does the prospect of being truly organized fill you with simultaneous feelings of excitement and an accompanying dread?
13. Do you think disorganization has always been your primary obstacle to reaching your full potential?
14. Were you more organized at an earlier time in your life?
15. Does your disorganization keep you from delegating work to others?
16. Does the cluttered state of your home or office keep you from letting people visit?
17. Did you grow up in an extremely chaotic household?
18. Did you grow up in an extremely orderly household?

19. Did you have a traumatic childhood?

20. Does your accumulated clutter go back fifteen years or more?

21. Are you a high achiever who must do everything perfectly?

SCORING

If you answered "Yes" to three or more questions, a psychological obstacle is likely working against you. It's important to identify it and learn how to work around it. Keep reading to see which barrier hits closest to home, and what you can do about it.

Psychological Obstacle #1: Need for Abundance

People who struggle with clutter sometimes have a deep-rooted need for volume in their lives. If this is you, you like to surround yourself with lots of stuff. You are among the collectors of the world. You buy items in bulk, cook in bulk, save treasures in bulk. Nothing you do is small or stark. You may enjoy visiting people who live in spare environments, but the idea of living like that starts your stomach turning. You keep *a lot* of everything, and the idea of getting rid of anything fills you with anxiety and dread. You may associate volume with a sense of fullness, comfort, security, and identity. Your need for abundance can evolve from a childhood of deprivation or emptiness where you never had enough food, clothing, toys, or, most important, love and companionship.

Interestingly, even if you didn't grow up suffering from scarcity yourself, you may have "inherited" a need for abundance from someone who did. Perhaps your parents or grandparents lived through the Great Depression and World War II when shortages were commonplace. Perhaps they're immigrants from a less developed country or survivors of some traumatic life-and-death experience such as the Holocaust. If so, you may have picked up some of their habits developed from their experiences—e.g., always being prepared for shortages, and "pack-ratting" against future privation.

No matter where this need for abundance comes from, the key is to work with and build around it, rather than fight against it. There is nothing wrong with living your life surrounded by volume, as long as you possess sufficient organizing skills to keep everything accessible and orderly. Otherwise, you will wind up drowning in clutter, surrounded by stuff that you have no access to, and feeling badly about yourself.

Carrie was a perfect example. A stay-at-home mom with two kids, she was passionate about crafts. Her kitchen and dining rooms were filled with supplies scattered everywhere—in bags and baskets, in corners, on counters and in cupboards mixed in with papers and other household belongings. She had enough pom-poms, Styrofoam, fabric, paints, clay, sequins, and yarn to open her own nursery school, far more than she and her kids could possibly use up. But the thought of parting with anything connected to her passion filled her with anguish.

Carrie had grown up in a large household where money was always scarce, and attention even scarcer. Her parents both worked and, with seven other kids to care for, seldom gave her much one-on-one attention. She grew up feeling lonely and neglected; one of the ways she used to occupy her thoughts and entertain herself was doing arts and crafts.

As an adult, she was committed to spending more time with her own kids than her parents had with her. The centerpiece activity of the time she spent with her children was arts and crafts, and the massive collection of materials represented a volume of comfort and companionship she never experienced as a child.

Recognizing her need for abundance, I surprised her by suggesting that for now we focus on consolidating and organizing what she owned, not reducing the quantity. She was quite relieved.

We devoted an entire closet to her supplies, lining the shelves with attractively labeled containers that gave her access to everything she had collected over the years.

Creating this "Arts & Crafts Center" was a way of celebrating Carrie's need for abundance, rather than criticizing it. For the first time, she felt good about the volume she had amassed instead of ashamed of it. And with everything now accessible, she and her kids were able to make use of most of it. Ironically, once everything was consolidated, it became much easier for Carrie to part with those items that went unused.

If you have a need for abundance, it is often better to organize what you have rather than try to force yourself to throw stuff out. Once things are organized, it may be easier for you to see what is excessive, and part with it bit by bit. Just don't expect yourself to become a minimalist overnight.

Psychological Obstacle #2: Conquistador of Chaos
Some people keep their lives or spaces disorganized because they love the thrill of coming to the rescue and creating order out of chaos. If this is you, you thrive on the challenge of solving complex problems and seeing your way through almost impossible situations. You are actually capable of setting up wonderful organizing systems, but are always dismantling them to go off in search of something new and "better."

You may have grown up in difficult, challenging circumstances that led you to develop incredible survival skills. More than anyone, you know how to handle a crisis. You may have been the peacemaker in a violent household, or coped with tremendous losses as a child or a constantly disrupted home life.

Whatever the specifics that made you this way, conquistadors of chaos feel at their best when responding to crises—because they are so darn good at it. You may display the following behaviors:

- Keep setting up systems and not sticking with them.
- Feel your organizational systems are always in process, never complete.
- Thrive on solving challenging problems, but get bored with maintaining the solutions.
- Constantly operate in a crisis mode, a virtual whirlwind of activity.
- Get more done in a day if you have twenty items on your to-do list than if you have just three.
- Perform better under pressure.

Paul, a lawyer, was always in search of the perfect fix, constantly buying new planners (paper, electronic, computer) to organize his time, rearranging his filing system, and shifting from one system to another in the belief that the next one "would finally do the trick." As a result, his office was in a perpetually unfinished state, and he always felt disorganized. He was never able to get organized because his need for chaos kept him rooted to square one.

If you feel you may be a conquistador of chaos, consider redirecting your talent for fixing things. Instead of constantly rebuilding your organizing system, why not complete it and use your free time to focus on bigger, more meaningful tasks? Since you thrive on a busy schedule, don't expect to use the extra time organization gives you for unstructured leisure. Instead, fill your days with activities that make the most of your incredible problem-solving skills. Take on the challenge of becoming a better parent, learning a new language, or tackling a difficult social issue no one has been able to solve. Conquer your fear of heights, or start a dynamic new business. Your talents are far too great to waste on constantly rescuing yourself from disorganization.

Psychological Obstacle #3: Unclear Goals and Priorities

Given that organizing is about defining what is important to you and setting up a system to reflect that, it is logical that if your goals and priorities aren't clear, it will be very hard to set up a workable system.

Taking on too much and feeling scattered in a million directions are typical symptoms of having unclear goals and priorities. Almost everyone goes through a lack of clarity or focus at some point in their lives. Often, we may secretly know what we want, but we are shy or anxious about having it, because we get distracted by what we think we "should" want. The program in this book succeeds only when you give yourself permission to be who you are, and set up systems according to the way you think and relate to your work and life.

My friend Gordon, one of the most organized people I know, places extremely high value on adding to his knowledge about the world. He thirsts to absorb as much new information as he can about a variety of subjects. But, rather than try to accomplish this all at once, he selects one topic per year to focus his energies and studies on, then moves on to another topic the next year. Working this way, he never feels scattered in a million directions at once and is able to satisfy his quest. He's not only got his goals and priorities straight, but knows how to achieve them.

If you feel you have so many goals and priorities it's hard to focus, consider following Gordon's example and spreading what you want to achieve out over time, focusing on accomplishing a few goals now and postponing others for later in the year or some point in the future. The satisfaction of meeting a few goals well far beats the disappointment of having many goals left incomplete.

Psychological Obstacle #4: Fear of Success/Fear of Failure

If being organized allows you to accomplish anything that you want, and you have a deep-seated fear either of success or of failure, then you may be using disorganization as a convenient way of holding yourself back.

Stanley was a wonderful dentist whose practice wasn't flourishing as well as it might have because, in his own words, he was such a disorganized administrator. He'd been in business fifteen years and had never found a competent secretary; bills always went out late, and he could never get it together long enough to advertise or do any of the other things necessary to grow his business. He was frustrated that he wasn't making as much money as he knew he could. And yet for every practical suggestion I came up with, he found one way or another to refute it.

A self-reflective fellow, he suddenly realized, as I did, that he was just making excuses. He knew getting organized would make him more successful, and that my suggestions would make a real difference. Eventually, he realized that deep down, he was afraid of doing better than his father, who had never quite "made it," at least in Stanley's eyes. Once he acknowledged that his fear of success was holding him back, we proceeded to organize him bit by bit, so he could adjust to the idea of his own success more slowly, and keep from subconsciously sabotaging himself.

There are a host of reasons why we can be afraid of success, and as many books written on the subject. If you feel your fear of success is driving you to sabotage all your organizing efforts, I suggest that, like Stanley, you work slowly to overhaul your system, and stay away from any instant changes in your current structure. In the meantime, read a book or two on the topic of realizing your dreams, such as *Wishcraft* by Barbara Sher or *Say Yes to Your Dreams* by Harold Taylor, and try to become more comfortable with the idea of your own success.

Psychological Obstacle #5: Need to Retreat

Some people use clutter as a protective shield, a barrier between themselves and the "outside world" in the same way that many overweight people use their extra pounds as a "cushion" for keeping others at a safe distance. When your disorganization gets so extreme that you won't let anyone into your home or office, or turn down social invitations to spend all your time "organizing" and "reorganizing" your stuff, consider whether clutter has become your secret accomplice in keeping you hidden.

Dan had been living in extreme chaos for as long as he could remember. Every square inch of his two-bedroom apartment was filled with furniture, objects he'd collected over the years, six to eight months' worth of newspapers he kept planning to read, clothing in a variety of sizes due to several weight changes, and scores of organizing products he'd bought in the hope they would offer him control over the mess. There was barely a place to sit. He was so embarrassed by it that he never invited people in, and didn't date because getting organized consumed all his free time. He worked at home, and was having problems getting anything done. Insightfully, he called the apartment his "isolation tank." Now forty-five years old, he was feeling lonely, frustrated, and ready to change the way he was living.

Dan had a traumatic childhood in which he experienced many losses. The pain he suffered fostered in him a need to retreat, to insulate himself from the world and further hurt. Sensitive to this, I realized that even though Dan was ready for change, we had to move slowly. Any sudden overhaul of his environment would only leave him feeling unprotected and unprepared, and impede our progress. We organized his apartment gradually over the course of a year, focusing on one small section at a time and letting him get used to it before moving on to the next. It took great courage and determination on Dan's part to succeed, and even though he backslid a few times along the way, he eventually succeeded. I have a lot of respect for him.

Your situation may not be as extreme as Dan's, but if you are using clutter in a similar way and are ready to come out of hiding, go slowly. Give yourself a chance to get used to the changes you're making and deal with the emotions that may accompany them. Allow sufficient time to adjust and recenter yourself as your environment changes. Start by creating one clutter-free room in which you keep nothing but items you use and love. If the experience feels good, create another room like that after a while, then another. Keep sweeping back all that excess clutter, the "barrier," until it is confined to a single room. Then, perhaps, you will have the courage to get rid of it for good. But if you're still fearful of letting it go, try putting it in off-site storage as an experiment; see what it's like living apart from these items while still knowing you have them. Maybe, in time, you'll be able to part with them permanently without trauma because you've come to realize your life is just as complete without them. Remember, an organized work or living space can be a nicer "retreat" than a cluttered one.

Psychological Obstacle #6: Fear of Losing Creativity
Many creative or "right-brained" people who have always worked in chaos both crave and are frightened of getting organized. On one hand, you crave it because you feel the disorganization has kept you from achieving your full potential. On the other hand, you are afraid a more structured system might squelch your creativity, as you've usually produced high-quality work in spite of the chaos.

Jennifer was a freelance writer who was making a living at her craft, although she felt severely held back by her chaotic work methods. Her home office was a wreck. She spent an inordinate amount of time searching for misplaced research materials and other documents. She had millions of ideas for articles—even a book—but could never take action on them because she either didn't have the time or couldn't locate her notes. Her out-of-control workspace was making her increasingly inclined to procrastinate. She truly believed that if she were more organized, she'd be able to turn out more work, on time, and be more prosperous. But since the quality of work she did manage to produce was of such high caliber, she confessed a genuine fear that changing her environment might destroy her career at the same time.

Working together, we devised a system that both reflected and encouraged her creative process. We designed a color-coded filing system that allowed her to visually distinguish between works-in-progress, completed projects, and future ideas. As her creative juices were stimulated by working on several projects at the same time, we designed a "project box" (similar to a mailroom slot) that allowed her to keep eight or ten projects on her desk at a time and alternate between them without getting them mixed up.

Because she was such a visually oriented person, we also created two wall charts for her office. One allowed her to track the progress of her various writing projects, and deadlines for them, on a monthly basis. Another enabled her to "storyboard" that book she'd been dreaming of writing for years. Jennifer was both relieved and ecstatic. Everything was now in its place, her mind was clear, and she could be so much more productive. Instead of dreading to go into her office, she spent more time there than ever because it had finally become the visual "silent partner" she'd yearned for to energize her creative batteries.

Being organized releases rather than restricts creativity. It gives you immediate access to all the materials you need to do your work more effectively. The key is to design your system to be simple, fun, and visually appealing so that it reflects your creative personality, and feeds it.

Psychological Obstacle #7: Need for Distraction

Disorganization can serve as a convenient preoccupation to help you avoid issues or tasks you don't want to deal with or face. To put it another way, as long as you have a closet to clean or a stack of papers to sort, your mind remains distracted, leaving no room for weightier concerns you find uncomfortable or difficult to think about.

Kevin was a sales executive for a publishing house. He'd earned the reputation for having the messiest office in his department. Coworkers wouldn't send him important documents without making backup copies because they were sure he would lose them. He spent so much time searching for lost or misplaced papers and doing work over that he had to spend many nights and weekends digging himself out. He was in a constant state of anxiety about what he might be forgetting, or what might be lost in the piles in his office.

Kevin and I gave his office the total overhaul it needed. We rearranged furniture, color-coded files, and outfitted his desktop with clearly labeled trays to handle the paper flow. And yet, as his office bloomed, Kevin grew uneasy. He began canceling our appointments, ceased doing any filing, disregarded his desktop labeling system, and was soon on his way to re-creating the chaos he'd been stuck with for so long.

Finally, Kevin called me back for help. As we talked, he revealed that he hadn't been prepared for all the free mental space an organized office would give him. Suddenly his mind had flooded with more distressing issues in his life: job security, a troubled marriage, his aging parents. All these years his worries about being disorganized had conveniently distracted him from things he didn't want to think about. And yet, the disorganization had also become a real liability to him personally and professionally, adding to his anxiety. By understanding this, he was now free to search for a more direct way of coping with the major stress in his life, so he could tolerate and maintain his organized office.

Using disorganization as a distraction can be a pattern of behavior you adopt in adulthood when life gets complicated, or developed in childhood as a way of mentally escaping a difficult environment or traumatic experience. Whatever its roots, if you want to get organized and see your system last, you need to substitute a more head-on approach for dealing with the larger, more perplexing problems you're evading. Then you won't need to create chaos to keep you distracted.

Psychological Obstacle #8: Dislike the Space

In this situation, you find your room, home, or office so loud or so quiet, so dreary or lonely that you dislike being there. You haven't bothered "settling in" because you long to be somewhere else. It hardly seems worth it to set your space up nicely since you have such ambivalent feelings about being there. And so, you leave things out and about, piled on surfaces or inside boxes with no rhyme or reason to them, because you simply aren't inspired to "root" down.

Obviously, if you really hate your space, the first thing you should consider is moving to another room, home, or office more to your liking. But if this isn't an option, brighten your space by decorating it and giving it some of your personality. Add some artwork to the walls, put up some photos, buy some beautiful, hardy plants. If you feel good about your space, you're more likely to want to spend time there, and to maintain any organizing system you set up.

Psychological Obstacle #9: Sentimental Attachment

Often, it's hard for people to let go of things they aren't using anymore because they infuse them with a tremendous amount of meaning. These objects come to represent another time, person, or part of themselves that they feel will be lost forever if let go.

Sometimes, we project personality and emotions on our things based on where we got them, who owned them before, or where they've been. We hear ourselves saying things like, "That jacket has been all over the world with me" or "I think I'll put this vase over here, it looks so lonely on that shelf."

Objects can come to define who we are. But by projecting so much identity onto our possessions, we can wind up living in an enormous amount of clutter, surrounded by items we never use.

Periodically, I have encountered clients whose hesitation to let go of the past has created a striking "layered" phenomenon in their homes and offices. On the surface, their place looks incredibly cluttered and disorganized, almost to the point of uninhabitability. But beneath that surface layer of disorder, there is often a picture-perfect system of organization. The catch is, it's a system from an earlier time in their life that they're afraid to let go.

One of the most moving examples of this was Suzanne. She lived in a fancy high-rise building on the Upper West Side of Manhattan, overlooking the river. Her apartment was so filled with clutter that she had to move out and stay in a nearby hotel. Boxes of papers, books, and magazines covered every conceivable surface, including the sofa and chairs, the bathtub and stove. Garment racks filled with her clothing took up all the available floor space, leaving no room to walk or sit. The fascinating thing was that when I moved the boxes out of the way to look inside her drawers and closets, I found them so perfectly organized they could've come out of the pages of an organizing catalog.

As we spoke, I found out that her husband had passed away eight years before: she had never had the heart to disassemble the life they had shared together. As a result, she built her new life on top of the old one, storing newly acquired possessions on any available surface she could find, creating two layers of reality in one home.

Hers was an extreme situation, but you may see yourself doing some version of the same thing. If you have stuff piled all over the exterior surfaces of your home or office, see if what's filling your drawers and closets may stem from an earlier, no longer active part of your life—papers from college, a former career, clothing in different sizes from different stages of your life.

Remember, your identity comes from inside, not outside. Objects can remind us who we are, or who we want to be, but the real truth is inside us and doesn't go away. My biggest challenge ever was tossing all the old papers from the theater career I left to start this business ten years ago. I felt those papers were my only link to that part of my past, and I was afraid that if I got rid of them I'd be getting rid of that part of me, as well. But they were taking up a lot of storage space I couldn't afford. I was finally able to let them go when I realized that the person who had left that career is still inside me; I didn't need the papers to remember who that person was. I'm happy to report I haven't missed them at all.

Free up storage space by letting go of the old. You can still own all the memories of your past life without holding on to every physical reminder of it. But if you're not emotionally prepared to let go completely, just move some of the old to a less accessible location—an attic, a basement, or an off-site storage facility. This interim step will allow you to regain control of your space until you're ready to let go for good.

Psychological Obstacle #10: Need for Perfection
Often, clutter accumulates because people refuse to deal with it until they have the time to do the job perfectly. Consequently, they never get around to doing it at all.

Sharon is the CEO of a large pharmaceutical company with a huge staff. Always an overachiever, she was on the board of directors of several major institutions and maintained a busy speaking schedule in addition to writing many articles and several books about her field. As a result of this active workstyle, many papers, periodicals, mail, and other materials that came across her desk and that she didn't have time for just piled up and up and up.

When she finally called me in, there were thirty boxes of papers and files stacked in her office. Many of these boxes held unopened mail that was more than five years old. But she was not content to just "let it go." She felt like she was a failure if she did not open and go through every piece of paper in those boxes, which, of course, she never had the time to do because she was always too busy working. Her drive for perfection put constant pressure on her to complete every task perfectly, completely interfering with her ability to get organized at all, and making her feel terrible about herself every day those boxes went untouched.

Sharon was unable to get organized simply because her drive for perfection kept her from making any progress at all. Doing *something*, however imperfect, with all that unsorted mail would have helped her avoid some of the accumulation. But she needed to give herself permission to be "imperfect," to move forward and get out from under.

If you are constantly searching for the perfect organizing solution, be assured that none exists. There are a hundred ways to organize a filing system; the one you choose is less important than sticking to it. If you're having trouble deciding, commit at least six months to the one you like best. Then evaluate if it's working. If it is, stay with it, even if a new version does come on the market. Don't get so caught up in the process that you never see the result.

.   .   .

Identifying the actual causes of your cluttered condition so you can find an effective, lasting solution could be one of the most liberating experiences you have reading this book. It will free you from the self-criticism that saps your energy before you even start organizing—and allow you to enter the process with hope. Just remember that every technical error, external reality, and psychological obstacle must be handled in order to sustain *any* organizing system.

OK, with a new way of looking at organizing and some insight into the actual causes of clutter, you are now ready to learn your new skill—the remarkable, reliable process of organizing from the inside out. . . .

PART 2

Secrets of a Professional Organizer

3

Analyze: Taking Stock

"If you don't know where you are going,
how will you know when you get there?"

In order to reach any goal, you have to begin by defining it. People often skip this step because they don't realize how important a part of the process it is. Since each person's situation is so unique, it is critical to get a clear picture of where you are and where you are headed before taking one step forward.

This requires doing a personal needs assessment so you'll have all the pertinent information available for charting a solid path to improvement.

List your responses on a sheet of paper. Seeing them in black and white will help clarify your thinking. Be honest with yourself, and specific. These lists will become tools you'll use and refer to throughout the organizing process.

There are five basic needs-assessment questions:

1. What's working?
2. What's not working?
3. What items are most essential to you?
4. Why do you want to get organized?
5. What's causing the problems?

In order to be successful you must answer them of *each* organizing project you take on—whether it's your entire office, a room in your home, or just a sock drawer.

1. What's Working?
One of the best ways to custom-design an organizing system is to start by identifying what works.

"What works?!" you ask. "Nothing! My life is completely out of control. That's why I'm reading this book!"

Look more closely. No matter what state of disorder your space may be in, I guarantee that buried beneath the rubble are some systems that are working just fine for you.

For example, you may have a drawer where you *always* keep your banking supplies, or an old-fashioned address book you know you can rely on. There may be one room in your house that is in perfect order while all the others are in chaos. Or your office may be organized, but not your home.

Identifying and preserving what's working offers you many advantages. First, it saves you an enormous amount of time and energy. Too often, when people go on an organizing spree, they completely redo everything, including systems that are working pretty well, wasting precious effort in the wrong area. As the saying goes, "Don't fix it if it ain't broke." There is no need to dismantle something that is already effective. Doing so causes more harm than good.

Second, by recognizing that you've done something right, and giving yourself credit where credit is due, your self-confidence gets a big boost. If you can organize one thing, you can organize anything.

Finally, and most important, by studying what's working—what you like about those systems and why they're so easy for you to maintain—you learn what appeals to you as an individual and what you will want to replicate. Your answers become the organizing criteria for each new system you create.

For example, one client, Janet, had a clothes closet that was, in her words, a "calamity." She threw her clothes, shoes, and handbags inside haphazardly on a daily basis, making finding things and getting dressed each morning a nightmare of frantic activity. She was ashamed of treating her expensive clothing this way, and of her own embarrassing lack of discipline.

Interestingly, I noticed that standing alone amid the chaos of her closet was a solitary oasis of order: one perfectly organized belt rack. She wore belts every day and consistently returned them to that rack in their special places, arranged and separated by color and style. We talked about why this one system worked so well for her, and, lo and behold, we found several very logical reasons. First, the rack was the perfect size for the number of belts she owned, so she could fit them all evenly without crowding. Second, she loved the modern design of the piece, a rich polished wood with rounded pegs that appealed to her sense of aesthetics and gave her joy every time she used it. And third, since the rack was mounted on the inside of her closet door, which swung out into the room when opened, it happened to be the only part of the closet that received enough light.

Understanding this, our goal thus became making the rest of her closet work as well as that belt rack, which we did by carefully counting and measuring items to be sure we bought containers that were just the right size, selecting containers that appealed to her sense of design, and installing a closet light so she could see everything inside.

Another part of assessing what's working includes pinpointing those areas that are *partly* working, then seeing what you can do to refine them. By working with your habits rather than starting from scratch and trying to retrain yourself to do something that feels unnatural, you're more likely to sustain your system.

Let me give you some examples.

One client loved to dump her coat, briefcase, and purse as soon as she walked in the door of her house. Problem was, these items wound up piled on the floor because the coat closet was twenty feet away. Rather than retraining her to "be disciplined" and walk those twenty feet, open the closet door, pull out the hanger, etc., we worked *with* her habit by mounting a rack with hooks and a small shelf on the wall by the door so that she had a place to put her things as she walked in.

Another example: Cathy, a working mom with three kids, piled all her shoes on the floor next to her bed because that was where she liked putting them on and kicking them off. The closet was in another room, and she didn't want to be bothered carrying them back and forth. Instead of forcing her to learn a new habit, we bought a shoe rack and put it next to her bed so she could continue doing what was comfortable to her without creating a mess.

Mark, a businessman, always captured notes to himself on legal pads. He wrote every thought that came to him, including things to do, calls to make, ideas for his business, and notes from phone conversations. Writing things down helped him clarify his thinking. But each page had so much information scribbled on it, he couldn't keep track of it all; as a result, action items and critical data were frequently overlooked. He probably had twenty legal pads floating around his desk, and he was constantly shuffling through each one searching for important nuggets of information. Rather than ask Mark to change his behavior completely, I suggested he simply adapt his existing system by limiting himself to one topic per page. This way, he could continue his natural habit of writing everything down, but all the information would be separated, so he could easily act on, toss, or file each page by subject.

Study your environment for your natural habits and tendencies; see if you can work with rather than fight against them. A system built in this way will be infinitely easier for you to maintain.

2. What's Not Working?
Your answers here will identify everything that needs fixing. This is one of those rare moments in life when you get the opportunity to whine, kvetch, and complain as freely as you like. Let it loose. List absolutely everything that's frustrating you. Be precise and thorough; don't edit yourself.

The importance of capturing the whole picture at this point is to be sure you solve *all* the problems, not just some. If only some are fixed, the areas that remain disorganized will soon begin to spill over into your newly ordered areas, causing the whole system to erode before long.

Complete the following statements. If you come up with more than one response to each (and you probably will), write them all down.

- I can never find _____.
- I have no place to put _____.
- There's no room for _____.
- I am tired of _____.
- I can't _____ because of the clutter.
- I'm losing a lot of money on _____.
- The disorganization makes me feel _____.
- When people visit, I _____.

Here are some common responses to these statements:

- I can never find my address book, wallet, keys, contracts, research materials, to-do lists, calculator, winter gloves.
- I have no place to put mail, magazines and newspapers, active projects, shoes, belts, gift wrap, luggage, toys.
- There's no room for eating at the kitchen table, my off-season clothes, files, books, the vacuum, winter coats, the car in the garage.
- I am tired of always searching for things, forgetting appointments, spending so much money on stuff I can't find, feeling anxious, losing opportunities, fights with my boss, spouse, and/or kids.
- I can't concentrate, be efficient, achieve my goals, relax, invite people over, clean thoroughly, have meetings in my office, find anything because of the clutter.
- I'm losing a lot of money on duplicate purchases, items that end up lost or broken, lost opportunities, late fees and finance charges.
- The disorganization makes me feel nervous, incompetent, embarrassed, oppressed, cramped, held back, out of control.
- When people visit, I make excuses for how the place looks, feel embarrassed, cringe, throw everything into bags and closets, pretend I'm not home by not answering the door.

You now have a complete list of all the problems you want to solve, as well as an inherent sense of what they're costing you and what success in overcoming them will mean.

Post this list where you can easily see it on the wall of the room you will be working on. Cross issues off as you solve them. This will keep you focused throughout the organizing process and give you a wonderful tool by which to measure your success.

INSIDER'S TIP

"The Complete Picture"

To come up with a thorough list of problems, try brainstorming in the space you plan to organize. Responses will come to you more easily because you'll see reminders of your problems staring you in the face.

Alternately, you can keep a "problems log" for a week. Specify a particular notepad to record every frustration you experience in your space. After seven days, your list of what needs fixing will be complete.

---

3. What Items Are Most Essential to You?

I promised earlier that organizing from the inside out focuses not on *getting rid of things* but on *identifying what is important to you* and finding homes for those items. This is a much more gentle, practical approach

By taking a moment to step back and define which items are most essential to your job or life, you will give invaluable direction to the sorting and purging process later on. Decisions will come easier, and you won't be prone to distraction or confused by the many tempting "finds" you come across during your archeological dig.

Identifying what is most essential to you is easiest if you think in terms of your goals. The purpose of articulating them during the analyze phase is to be sure that by the end of the project you will have created a place for each of these critical items so you'll always be able to get your hands on them quickly and accomplish everything you deem important.

Here are some examples of identifying what is most essential to you:

• "I need to travel frequently to all kinds of climates for business, so I need both my summer and winter clothes easily accessible all year long."

• "I want to show my clients that I'm thinking of them all the time, so I need a place for the clippings and articles I save to send out to them."

• "I want to preserve my family's rich history so I need a safe, yet accessible place for family pictures, videos, letters, and memorabilia."

• "I enjoy playing music after a long day at work. I need places for my guitar, picks, sheet music, CDs and tapes."

It's not always easy to identify what's most important to you. We live in complicated times where there are so many options and opportunities, many of us feel pulled in a million directions at once and experience difficulty setting priorities.

To determine which items are most essential to you, define what I call your "Big Picture Goals." These are what you are actually trying to accomplish in your life or work as a whole, or in the space you're trying to organize in particular. In other words, when all is said and done, what really matters to you, makes life worth living, brings you the most joy, the greatest feeling of satisfaction, and the biggest sense of accomplishment?

Once you define this, it will be infinitely easier to identify which items you should keep in order to accomplish those goals. You will have a clearer sense of purpose and focus as you go through the mounds of objects piled all over the place, picking each item up and asking yourself, "Will this help me further my goals?" If the answer is yes, keep it. If no, it goes.

Sometimes it's hard for us to articulate what is most important. We may secretly know the answer, but feel shy or insecure about our desires. We aren't sure if it's OK to want these things. It may be different from what our friends, neighbors, or colleagues want. We may get distracted by what we think we "should" want. The program in this book is predicated upon giving yourself permission to be who you are, and setting up systems based on the way you think and relate to your work and life. If you are conflicted, if you are fighting your own impulses, your space will reflect that indecision, and no organizing technique in this book or any other will be effective.

The organizing process puts you in touch with what is most important to you, and gives you the permission, perhaps for the first time in your life, to go after it. One client described the experience as "incredibly cleansing." Another called it "liberating," and another said "it made me feel a hundred percent better about myself."

If you have a hard time zeroing in on what is essential to you, try these exercises:

• Use the 80-20 rule, which states that we only use about 20 percent of what we own. The other 80 percent is stuff we once used, feel we "should" use, or think we might use "someday." Pinpoint what that 20 percent is that you use all the time. Imagine that there were a fire in your home or office and you only had thirty minutes to save your most important possessions and papers. Which would they be? Your answers will tell you what really matters most to you.

• If you still have trouble identifying which items fall into that 20 percent, buy a package of small red adhesive dot labels. For about a month, stick a red dot on every object you handle, every file that you refer to, and every piece of art or knickknack that makes you feel good when you look at it. In addition, keep a log of every item you look for during the month, but cannot find. By the end of the month, you will know exactly which items really count, and purging will be a breeze.

4. Why Do You Want to Get Organized?

Now it's time to fortify your motivation for getting organized. No matter how you slice it, organizing takes time, effort, and lots of concentration. As motivated as you may feel right now, somewhere in the middle of the organizing process you're bound to get tired of making decisions, or feel the tug of other activities pulling at you. Before you know it, you will walk away and leave your organizing project unfinished. You know what I'm talking about. It's happened to you many times before.

By taking the time to articulate what's driving you to get organized *before* you start, when you're at the peak of your motivation, you create your own coaching tool to turn to for inspiration when the going gets tough.

Keep in mind that you must be driven by your own compelling reasons for getting organized. If you're going through this process just because your "neat" spouse, boss, or kids have asked you to, you're unlikely to make it to the finish line.

For example, a magazine publisher called on me to organize the employees' cubicles in the art department, which he considered embarrassingly messy. Each workstation was piled floor to ceiling with magazines, clippings, papers, and product samples. Yet the employees felt quite organized and productive; they knew where everything was, and were able to produce very high quality work in that environment without ever missing a deadline—something the boss confirmed. I recommended that instead of hiring me, money be invested in purchasing screens to conceal the "mess" from public view for the simple reason that people who feel no driving need to get organized (and rightly so in this case) will not be able to maintain any new system.

Identify what you expect to achieve by eliminating the clutter from your life once and for all. Here's a list gleaned from responses my clients have given to this question. They reflect common goals many people have for getting organized.

Why Do I Want to Get Organized?

- "Stop spending so much time looking for things."
- "Set a good example for my kids."
- "Reduce the feeling of being overwhelmed."
- "Achieve more in less time."
- "Make better use of my talents and skills."
- "Increase my self-confidence."
- "Gain a sense of control."
- "Project a better image to my clients, colleagues, and friends."
- "Make more money."
- "Spend less money."

- "Have more time to spend on what's really important to me."
- "Improve my relationship with my family."
- "Gain energy and calm from my space."
- "Reduce my stress, frustration, and anxiety level."
- "Clear my head of all the clutter."

When you're done, post this "Motivation Sheet" on the wall in the area you are going to organize. Halfway through the organizing process, when you're feeling overwhelmed and forget why you wanted to get organized in the first place, a quick glance will remind you, and inspire you to keep going.

5. What's Causing the Problems?
Using the diagnostic tools in Chapter 2, identify what issues are at the heart of your organizing challenge. Specify which technical errors, external realities, and/or psychological obstacles are at play so that you are sure to be addressing the right problem. Remember that the issues will vary from room to room, so you need to ask this question of each space you tackle.

WHERE DO YOU GO FROM HERE?

Although going through the Analyze process takes a little extra time compared to just diving in, it is the most important investment you can make toward achieving your ultimate goal: becoming truly organized at last.

If you skip any one of the Analyze questions, cheat on another, or don't honestly examine your situation, you might as well put this book away. Your efforts to get organized will likely be in vain. Your answers to the five Analyze questions will lead you to the strategies that will help you successfully attack your organizing problem, regardless of how insurmountable it may seem.

On the other hand, if you're ready to make that commitment, read on.

4

Strategize: Creating a Plan of Action

OK, with your analysis in hand, you've got a handle on your organizing problems and what's causing them. You've zeroed in on what is essential to you, and you know more about your personal style. You've articulated what your disorganization is costing you in time, money, and happiness, and what you will gain from winning the war against clutter. You're ready to dive in and get to it, right?

But wait . . .

As you scan the endless piles of clutter and "monumental" chaos before you, an old, familiar anxiety rises within you, and your mind begins to reel with all-too-familiar questions:

"Where do I start?"

"How long will it take?"

"How in the world can I make my efforts last?"

During the Analyze stage, you identified *where you are*. Now it's time to visualize *where you're going*, and, more specifically, *how you will get there*. This requires a plan of action.

Creating a plan of action takes very little time (about an hour), but if you skip it you are setting yourself up for disaster. See if the following scene sounds familiar.

As you remember from Chapter 2, I grew up as an exceedingly disorganized kid. My room was so messy, one friend recently told me she used to be afraid to visit me, because every time she did, she'd end up losing something in the chaos.

As a theater person and dancer, I collected *everything*, from costumes, props, and vintage cooking utensils to old class notes, souvenir restaurant menus, and Playbills. These were my treasures.

But I could never find anything.

There wasn't a day that you could see even a square inch of the floor. It was a nice floor, too—Congoleum, a jazzy turquoise and blue design I had begged my parents for and that they bought me in the hope it would inspire me to keep my room neat and navigable.

No such luck. Within a day of being installed, the Congoleum was covered in rubble, rarely to be seen again.

Every six months or so, my parents would "hit the roof," and banish me to my fourth-floor "jungle" for the weekend with direct orders not to come out until it was cleaned up.

Truth is, I wanted to be organized. I really did—because it was almost as frustrating to me to have my room in such turmoil as it was for them to see it that way. My junkyard of debris was actually a collection of wonderful memories, projects, and ideas. Yet, when I wanted to take action on any of them, I had no idea where to look.

So, my Friday nights always started with the best of intentions. But as I surveyed the actual mess, I would freeze in my tracks, paralyzed with confusion as to what action to take.

I'd say to myself that success meant eliminating the clutter. So, I'd get in gear by aiming to place the stuff that was strewn all over the floor, desk, bed, and dresser put away neatly in my drawers, shelves, and closets. Oops . . . not possible. Each of my storage units was already packed to the brim.

So, figuring I had to make space, I'd begin by dumping out all the drawers and emptying all the closets in an effort to decide what "junk" I could get rid of.

In the course of sorting through this stuff, I would rediscover lost treasures I hadn't set eyes on since the last time I'd attempted to get my room in shape.

"Wow, this reminds me of that trip I took" or "Gee, I could really use this someday" became constant refrains, slowing the cleanup process to a crawl—followed by "Oh no, I forgot to send this letter!" or "Oops, I never finished making this scarf," which would bring the process to a grinding halt as I tried to complete each unfinished chore that second.

Surrounded by my newly unearthed treasures, and unable to part with any of them, I would revise my goal to at least sort everything into categories, creating piles with some kind of logic. But before long, there were piles on top of piles, and I lost track of what I had sorted, what I hadn't, or where I was. I was at sea again.

The clock was ticking. Sunday night was fast approaching. Soon there would be a knock on the door. My parents, ready for the grand unveiling! I would look around my room and realize that it actually looked *worse* than when I had started. In a panic, I'd quickly gather stuff from every direction and shove it into drawers, closets, and under the bed, with no rhyme or reason.

The knock arrived; my parents came in, saw the Congoleum, and applauded me for my efforts. The room was perfect.

But I knew better.

Sure enough, by the next day, the Congoleum would start to disappear again as the piles returned.

I'd have spent sixteen hours of determined activity with no visible payoff for my efforts whatsoever: another marathon organizing session down the tubes! In six months I would be at it again.

There is no doubt that as a teenager I *had the desire, time, and determination to get organized.*

So what was missing?

I had no *strategy*, that's what. I had no plan, no focus, no idea of how to approach getting organized at all. I was working without a model of success to guide me, and with no sense of direction or timing by which to pace my efforts. As a result, I just dove in blindly, went in circles for hours, and ended up exactly where I started. Sound familiar?

Working without a strategy is like trying to drive across country with no map, no idea of what your destination looks like, and no sense of how long the trip will take. Your chances of getting lost and confused along the way are better than 1,000 percent!

This chapter will teach you how to navigate the path from chaos to order by showing you where to start, how to map out the journey, and how long it will take you to get there.

In order to successfully strategize, I offer you my two "secret weapons"— techniques you can rely on to quickly map out a plan of action for every organizing job, no matter how large or how small.

JULIE'S SECRET WEAPON #1:
THE KINDERGARTEN MODEL OF ORGANIZATION

Begin by developing a clear picture of where you are headed. This requires visualizing what you want your space to look like when it's finally organized.

As I've written, organizing is not just about getting rid of clutter and making the space look "neat." It goes much deeper than that. Organizing is about designing your space so that it reflects who you are and what's important to you and arranging things logically and efficiently so that staying organized will be easy for you.

So how should your space look?

From the day I started my business, I have designed every home, every office, and every schedule for every client I've ever worked with on the model of a kindergarten classroom. It's my secret weapon for attacking any space because it is simple and effective, it works every time, and it represents the *essence* of being organized from the inside out.

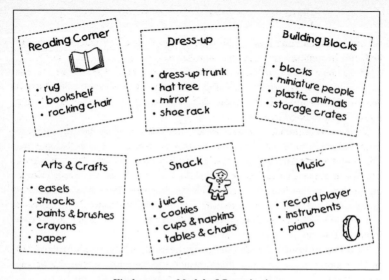

Reading Corner

- rug
- bookshelf
- rocking chair

Dress-up

- dress-up trunk
- hat tree
- mirror
- shoe rack

Building Blocks

- blocks
- miniature people
- plastic animals
- storage crates

Arts & Crafts

- easels
- smocks
- paints & brushes
- crayons
- paper

Snack

- juice
- cookies
- cups & napkins
- tables & chairs

Music

- record player
- instruments
- piano

Kindergarten Model of Organization
What Makes It Work: 1. Room is divided into activity zones.
2. It's easy to focus on one activity at a time.
3. Items are stored at their point of use.
4. It's fun to put things away—everything has a home.
5. Visual menu of everything that's important.

Walk into any kindergarten classroom in the world, and you will behold the perfect model of organization. Think about what makes it work.

First, the room is divided into activity zones: the Reading Zone, the Dress-up Zone, the Arts & Crafts Zone, the Music Zone, the Snack Zone.

Second, it's easy for the child to focus on one activity at a time. Each zone is well defined and fully self-contained, so that the child can concentrate 100 percent on a given task; nothing else competes for his or her attention.

Third, everything needed for each activity is right there at the child's fingertips because items are stored at their point of use. For example, if the child is doing arts and crafts, all the paper, crayons, markers, paints, brushes, and smocks needed for a creative session are gathered in one convenient location.

Fourth, in a kindergarten classroom it is almost as much fun putting things away as it is playing with them. Every item has a clear, well-labeled home in a container that is the perfect size to hold it. There are sliding trays for the puzzles. Wooden blocks with holes in them for scissors (points down, handles up). Cubbies and hooks have the child's name on them, maybe even the child's picture. As a result, you seldom see a kindergartner trying to figure out where to return something or struggling to shove fifty paintbrushes into a twenty-five-brush container. Cleanup is fast and easy. The teacher rings the bell, and in a matter of moments, the room is in tiptop shape once again.

Fifth, and most importantly, it offers a visual menu of everything that is important to the people who inhabit that space. A child can walk into that classroom, look around, and *decide* what to do and where to do it based on a set of clearly defined cues.

The beauty of the kindergarten model is that it can be applied to anything: from a whole home or office to just one room or a single drawer. By following this model, you will design your space for easy access and retrieval of any item. The space will be inviting and enjoyable to use and allow you to concentrate on one activity at a time. Your surroundings will give you visual cues as to what there is to do, and when life gets busy and priorities get confused, a glance at your very environment will help keep you focused on who you are and what is important to you.

Let's look at how the kindergarten model would work in a kitchen, one of the key rooms in the house, and one which you may have already intuitively set up this way.

The typical activity zones of a kitchen are Food Preparation, Cooking, Dishwashing and Dish Storage, Food Storage, Utility, and Household Paperwork. As you identify each zone, think about what supplies are required to perform that activity and what storage units you might use to house those supplies.

As food preparation is where you do all the cutting, chopping, mixing, and seasoning of food before it is cooked, the best location is on the longest available counter somewhere between the sink and the stove or the sink and the refrigerator. Cabinets above and below this countertop should be used to store necessary food preparation supplies such as cutting boards, knives, mixing bowls, measuring cups, spoons, appliances, seasonings, and plastic wraps.

Naturally, the Cooking Zone is best located around the stove and cooktop. It is here where you would store all your pots and pans, pot holders, bakeware, and cooking utensils to make cooking a simple and convenient task.

For the Dishwashing and Dish Storage Zone, store everyday dishes, glassware, flatware, dish towels, and detergent as close to the sink and dishwasher as possible. This makes it easy to reach up and put away items from the dishwasher or dish drainer, without requiring long trips across your kitchen to some remote and inconvenient location.

The Utility Zone—for heavy-duty cleaning and maintenance of the kitchen—can be located under the sink or in a nearby closet to conveniently hold your full supply of sponges, cleaners, mops, brooms, garbage bags, and possibly even pet supplies.

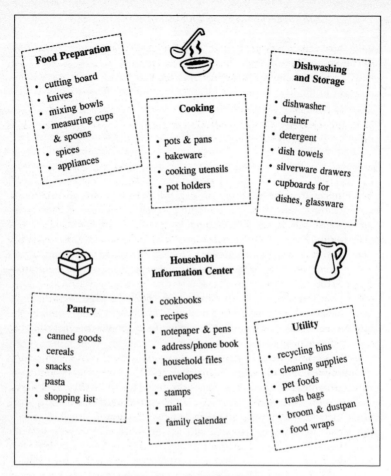

Food Preparation

- cutting board
- knives
- mixing bowls
- measuring cups
  & spoons
- spices
- appliances

Cooking

- pots & pans
- bakeware
- cooking utensils
- pot holders

**Dishwashing
and Storage**

- dishwasher
- drainer
- detergent
- dish towels
- silverware drawers
- cupboards for
  dishes, glassware

Pantry

- canned goods
- cereals
- snacks
- pasta
- shopping list

**Household
Information Center**

- cookbooks
- recipes
- notepaper & pens
- address/phone book
- household files
- envelopes
- stamps
- mail
- family calendar

Utility

- recycling bins
- cleaning supplies
- pet foods
- trash bags
- broom & dustpan
- food wraps

Kindergarten Model of a Kitchen

The Food Storage Zone is where food is kept, and it is composed of the refrigerator, and, if you are lucky, a separate pantry. In kitchens where there is no pantry, consider storing food in cabinets near the refrigerator to keep all food together and make it easy to gather ingredients for a meal.

The household information center is that area in your kitchen where the mail is dumped, phone calls are made, coupons are kept, and sometimes even bills are paid. Not everyone keeps this paperwork in the kitchen. Wherever you choose to keep your household papers, this particular zone is so involved, I have devoted a whole chapter to it. See Chapter 10, Household Information Centers.

So, how do you take your current state of chaos and transform it into my Kindergarten Model of Organization? The answer is as easy as A-B-C. You need a couple of sheets of paper for this exercise.

A. Define Your Zones
To design the zones you will need, take out a sheet of paper and divide it into three columns, labeled as follows:

Activity	Supplies	Storage Unit

In the first column, write all the major activities that go on in the space you are organizing. Down the center column, list all the supplies needed to perform each activity. In the third column, list the storage units you have or may need to store the supplies in each zone. We already looked at the zones you would find in a kitchen. Let's look at a few other examples.

In a living room, your activities may be entertaining friends, watching television, listening to music, reading, and playing board games and cards. In an office, your activities may be working on the computer, making phone calls, doing paperwork, and assembling mailings. Your core activities comprise the zones of the room. Keep in mind that the average room can accommodate three to five activities.

In the second column, list the supplies you need to perform each activity. As an example, for watching TV, you need the *TV Guide,* remote control(s), and videotapes. For listening to music, you need compact discs, audiotapes, cleaning cloths, and headphones. For reading, you need books, magazines, newspapers, and perhaps your reading glasses and a pen.

For the third column, look at all the storage units you have in your space and assign which units might make sense for each activity zone. Inventory every drawer, closet, cabinet, and shelf available to you in the space. For example, in the living room, you may have a couple of bookshelves, an entertainment unit, and two end tables with drawers. In your office, list each of the filing cabinets, desk drawers, bookcases, and supply closets that you have. If you are zoning the dining room, include each of your china cabinets, hutches, sideboards, and linen cabinets.

As you fill out this column, you may feel you have no appropriate storage units—or not a sufficient number of them—for some of the items that must be stored. Even if that's the case, *don't go on a shopping spree now.* You will probably just waste money. Make a note of your anticipated needs by zone, but don't worry about the solution until the Attack stage, where you may find that you already have what you need after all.

Remember, you can get creative by using storage units in untraditional ways. For example, if you do your paperwork in the dining room, consider storing papers in a sideboard rather than a traditional filing cabinet.

Here's an example of a filled-in Zone Planning sheet for a living room:

Activity	Supplies	Storage Unit
TV	Remote *TV Guide* Videotapes	Armoire with drawers below
Music	CDs Audiotapes Cleaning cloths Headphones	Stereo cabinet *(may need more storage)*
Reading	Books Newspaper Magazines	2 Bookcases Cedar chest
Family fun	Board games Knitting supplies Photo albums	*May need storage unit*

B. Map Out the Space

Now that you have figured out what zones you need, it's time to determine where in the room each zone should be located.

On a second piece of paper, draw a map of the space and sketch out some ideas for rearranging the room to create each activity zone, including what storage units will go in what zones. It doesn't have to be precisely to scale, but you may want to use a ruler to help draw straight lines. A tape measure will also be helpful in determining whether something will fit in a particular zone.

As you plan the space, don't feel constrained by the location of outlets and phone jacks. This is what extension cords are for. Later, if necessary, you can always have an electrician or telephone specialist come in to install new outlets and jacks. Your comfort, convenience, and logic are your prime considerations in locating zones. Let the wiring accommodate you.

In determining where each zone should be located, there are several points to consider.

First, try to build them around your *natural habits and preferences*. Eyeball where the piles of clutter seem to accumulate; this will give you a clue as to where certain zones should be. For example, if books and magazines are piled on the floor next to the sofa, obviously that's where you like to read. Make it easy it to grab and return reading materials with minimum effort in that spot by moving a bookcase and magazine basket next to the sofa—*voilà*, you've got an instant Reading Zone that you will find easy to maintain.

A client of mine who worked from home always had papers and files piled high on her dining room table. Fed up with having no place to eat at mealtimes, she called me in to help her design a built-in office in her living room. Yet I noticed that the dining room table was located in her favorite spot in the house, next to a big picture window overlooking some beautiful trees—whereas the area of her living room where she was planning to build her office was far removed from the natural light and scenery she loved so much. I persuaded her to build the office cabinetry on the wall adjacent to the dining room table (where most people place their china cabinet) so she could continue working where she loved to be, yet could still clear the table easily for meals.

Second, think about the *relationship of one activity to another* in determining where your zones should be. For example, in a living room you may want to locate the TV Zone at one end of the room and the Reading Zone at the opposite end so that different members of the family can enjoy the space simultaneously. On the other hand, you may wish certain zones to be located near each other because they are naturally related. For example, in an office, it is convenient to locate the Computer Zone near your main Paperwork Zone because the materials from one are often used in conjunction with the other.

The *architectural configurations and restrictions* of the room are the third element to consider, as sometimes they provide a starting point for designing the space. For example, in zoning a bedroom, you would do well to create a compact Dressing Zone by moving all chests of drawers nearer to the closet. This arrangement will make it easy to get dressed in the morning without having to run back and forth across the room. Built-in cabinets and wall units can also influence where to set up zones. But if you discover that you're consistently performing an activity far away from the built-in unit where your supplies for this activity are stored, it may be time to seriously consider finding a new, different use for that built-in to work with, not against, your habits.

C. Rearrange Furniture

If the clutter is too expansive, rearranging furniture may not be feasible until after you've done some sorting and purging. But if you can, start moving furniture and storage units around now to make your zones come alive. It will offer some wonderful benefits. First, you'll actually see what will fit where, and how you like it there, so you can make any necessary adjustments to your design choices. Second, and most important, it will give you a rewarding feeling: having plunged into the organizing process head-on and seen a dramatic, visible change in your environment right away. This instant transformation is very motivating and will boost your enthusiasm for following the project through to the end.

To make it easier to move things around, you might need to temporarily box up some of the piles of stuff cluttering the floor and surfaces. This is sometimes a bonus because once things are in boxes, it is often less intimidating to sort through them. The room seems instantly cleaner and more spacious, and you can tackle one box at a time until the job is done.

If your space is too chaotic to move furniture at this point, don't panic; just hold off until later in the Attack stage, by which time you'll have much more freedom of movement.

JULIE'S SECRET WEAPON #2: ESTIMATE THE TIME

One of the biggest mistakes people make when it comes to getting organized is not being realistic about how long the job will take. Most people either dramatically overestimate or drastically underestimate the time required.

If you overestimate how long a project will take, you're likely to procrastinate forever and never get started. Let's say it's actually a three-day project but you've estimated three months. The job will seem hopelessly large, and you'll say, "Forget it! It's not even worth starting, I'll never get through it all!"

On the other hand, saying, "I'll tackle this Saturday morning before I go to the beach," absurdly underestimates the amount of time almost any organizing project will take. You'll put in the time, but then, seeing little or no result for all your effort, you'll walk away well short of the finish line, grumbling, "This isn't worth it. It can't be done."

The truth is, most rooms in the home take an average of one to one and one-half days to complete. The average one-person office takes two to three days. Some spaces like bathrooms and small closets may take only a few hours, while others such as extremely packed garages or offices may take an extra day or two, but every organizing project is manageable. The key is, once you know how long the job will actually take, you can set aside enough time in your schedule to ensure that you'll get it done.

In Part 3 of this book, I will provide an average time required to attack each area of the home and office. These guidelines will help you estimate how long your project will take so you can create an effective work schedule.

Establishing a work schedule means deciding when you will work and literally blocking out the time on your calendar. In determining your work schedule, take into account your available time, your sense of urgency, and how quickly you want to see changes. Based on your analysis of what's holding you back (Chapter 1), you may decide you need time to adapt to the transformation of your space, and so you will choose to work slowly, a few hours a week over a month or two. On the other hand, you may want to see results instantaneously and decide to dive in and finish the job in a matter of days.

The biggest mistake many people make is to skip establishing a schedule at all. "I'll just fit it into my spare time," they say. This approach practically *guarantees* failure because there is no such thing as "spare time." Even if you were able to find some, would organizing really be your automatic first choice of how to spend it? I don't think so.

INSIDER'S TIP:

Is It Worth the Time?

As you ponder whether the required investment of one to three days per room is worth your time, let's look at what the disorder is costing you.

- Americans waste nine million hours per day searching for misplaced items, according to the American Demographics Society.
- The *Wall Street Journal* reported that the average U.S. executive wastes six weeks per year searching for missing information in messy desks and files. (That translates to just one hour per day!)
- Cleaning professionals say that getting rid of excess clutter would eliminate 40 percent of the housework in an average home (National Soap and Detergent Association).
- "Crisis" purchases related to disorganization could cost as much as 15 to 20 percent of your annual budget—buying duplicates of misplaced or broken items, last-minute shopping at premium prices, and unnecessary interest, rush, and finance charges on late payments.
- Realtors regard "first impression" improvements such as decluttering closets to be one of the smartest ways to speed the sale of a home and fetch a better price, according to the New York State Association of Realtors.

Show your commitment to getting organized by scheduling appointments with yourself to do the job, and write them on your calendar in indelible ink. Then honor that commitment.

Here's an example of an effective work schedule for a twelve-hour living room job:

HOW LONG WILL IT TAKE?

Attack

1. Sort	Saturday	5 hours
2. Purge	Saturday	2 hours
3. Assign a home	Sunday	1 hour
4. Containerize	Sunday	4 hours
5. Equalize	Daily	3–5 min.

"Hmmmmm. *Sort, Purge, Assign, Containerize, Equalize* . . . What's all that?" you ask. Those are the steps you will follow as you move into the next phase of the organizing process—Attack! Analysis and strategy in hand, you are actually ready to plow through the piles and get organized. Now, turn the page, and let's dive in. . . .

Attack:
Getting the Job Done

Congratulations! You've analyzed and strategized, and now you're ready to put on some comfortable clothes, roll up your sleeves, and begin the rewarding experience of transforming your space.

Of course, even this stage requires a methodical approach. To remember the steps of the attack phase, think of the word "SPACE."

It breaks down as follows:

1. **S**ort
2. **P**urge
3. **A**ssign a home
4. **C**ontainerize
5. **E**qualize

The key to succeeding with the SPACE formula is to do *every one* of the steps, and most importantly, do them *in order*. Many of the actions may be familiar to you, but my guess is in the past you only did some of them, and you may have done them out of sequence. For example, when you felt ready to get organized in the past, you probably started either by *purging* ("I'm going to get rid of as much of this junk as I can") or by *containerizing* ("I'm going shopping for containers and bins to get myself organized"). Done out of sequence, these actions are highly ineffective, because you do not yet have enough information gathered to make the right decisions.

Now, let's look at each critical step, and how it works.

1. SORT

If your space is disorganized, you undoubtedly have many related items scattered in multiple locations. Not only does this make it hard to find them, it makes it almost impossible to quantify what you really have. So, here is where you go through each possession and create a sense of order.

It is crucial that you handle everything. Pick up every item of clothing, piece of paper, or collectible and evaluate it individually, asking yourself these questions: "Do I use this? Do I love this? Does this make or cost me money? What category does this belong in?"

Don't put off or ignore those large piles of stuff in corners or scattered pockets of clutter that seem too intimidating. Skipping them or postponing them to "some other time" will prevent you from seeing the big picture *before* you set up your system, and result in an unsatisfying feeling of incompletion, which will inevitably cause your system to unravel.

As you sort, focus on the following:

Identify what is important to you—focus on those items you currently use, love, and/or that make money, not those that *used* to be important to you, or *might be* important to you someday. This task will be much easier as a result of the questions you answered in the Analyze phase.

Group similar items. As you identify the important items you want to keep, place them on the floor or another surface in related categories that reflect *your* associations, not someone else's. They only have to make sense to you. This is one of the keys of organizing from the inside out: to design a system that is intuitive and natural to you so that you can find things and put them away again without too much thought. Using seasonings as an example, some people might group allspice and basil together because they think alphabetically. Others might group by flavor (basil with oregano, marjoram, and thyme; allspice with cinnamon, cloves, nutmeg, and vanilla). Just keep categories as broad as possible so they'll be easy to remember and you'll have the least number of places to look when you start assigning items a home. For example, if you think according to flavor, try grouping your seasonings into just two categories: sweet and savory. Unless you're a master chef and have huge numbers of flavored seasonings, breaking your savory seasonings down into subcategories—leafy herbs, powdered herbs, Italian, Chinese, and Spanish flavors, etc.—would be overkill, making it both confusing and too time-consuming to put things back in their proper place.

JULIE'S LAW OF VISIBLE, DRAMATIC RESULTS

There is nothing more frustrating or disheartening about sorting than investing hours and hours of effort but seeing absolutely no improvement in your space. This kind of discouraging experience is really the result of poor organizing techniques, which are easily fixable. Use the following sorting secrets of a professional organizer to make sure you see visible, dramatic results each time you work. The visual display of your progress will keep you inspired and driven, determined to make it to the finish line.

• **Attack what's visible first.** Remember those marathon weekends I spent as a teenager? A classic mistake I made was deciding to attack the "invisible" clutter—the stuff inside drawers, cabinets, and closets—before tackling the stuff I could see. It's a natural impulse, because you think you must immediately make room for all the stuff that's been left out in the open. But working that way is a mistake because instead of shrinking, the clutter grows instantly, and you're discouraged by the feeling that you're not making much headway—which, in fact, you aren't. Furthermore, it's quite likely that the "invisible" stuff is old, even archaic, while the "visible" stuff is more active and relevant to you.

Use your initial burst of enthusiasm and energy to organize the stuff that has the most meaning and impact on your life; leave the "invisible" clutter till later.

• **Quick-sort for quick results.** "Quick-sort" is a tactic designed to get and keep you moving through your stuff swiftly because you don't belabor your decisions about what to keep and what to toss, which just slows the process down and makes it grueling. You can't allow yourself to get sidetracked. Your focus should be on *identifying* items and *categorizing* them. If a decision to toss something comes to you easily (and many will), great! If not, move on. (I'll give you some tips on making decisions quickly and easily later on.)

As for those incomplete projects, unanswered phone messages, and unread articles you discover, now is *not* the time to do them. Place all unfinished to-do's in a separate box or file folder labeled "Action," and schedule a separate appointment with yourself to deal with them. Remember, this is a *sorting* session, not a *catch-up* session. If you stay focused on your sorting task, you will see results before you know it.

• **Avoid "zigzag organizing."** Most people make the mistake of scattering their organizing efforts, working back and forth between several rooms at once. This is what I call "zigzag organizing," a method that is guaranteed to provide the minimum results in the maximum time. You start with a drawer, find a book inside that belongs elsewhere, go to the bookcase, and discover the shelves are so messy there is no place for the book. So you abandon the drawer and start organizing the bookcase. Then you find some stray papers on the bookshelves that really belong in your filing system. But of course, the filing system is a wreck, so you abandon the drawer *and* the bookshelves and start organizing the filing system. Before you know it, you've started five, six, seven different areas, finished none, and quit in despair.

The opposite of zigzag organizing is to work one section at a time. That means completing one room before moving on to the next, and within each room, tackling the space one section at a time. Decide up-front which corner of the room you want to serve as the launchpad for your organizing efforts, and complete that section before moving on to the next. If you find something that belongs elsewhere, just put it in the doorway for now, and take care of it at the end of your organizing session. Working one section at a time allows you to see progress; it also gives you logical places to take breaks to recoup your energy and determination. If you need a rest, you can say, "Okay, I'll finish this corner and then go get a cup of coffee." When you come back to the room, the first thing you'll see is that beautifully organized section, which will encourage you to move on to the next section, and the next. . . .

2. PURGE

Here is where you decide what stuff to get rid of, and how. You will always have several choices: toss, give away, sell, put elsewhere, store. Have appropriately labeled boxes on hand throughout the Attack process to sort your discards into.

If you're the type of person who is traumatized or threatened by the thought of having to get rid of anything, remember that you don't have to purge anything right now. Just organize everything you've got so that it's finally accessible; once you've lived with that satisfying experience for a while, you can decide later on if you want to "lighten the load."

Even those of you who are ready to start getting rid of stuff may find it a difficult process. Here are some tips to make it easier:

Some items to toss—those I call "no-brainers"—will be obvious. These are items that are in such bad shape, and so irrelevant to your life right now, that you couldn't or wouldn't use them if you wanted to—e.g., rusty nails, dried-up nail polish, six-month-old newspapers. Each chapter in Part 3 will include a "no-brainer toss list" to get you started.

Other items may pose tougher choices. For example, once you've consolidated them in the sorting process, you may find you have too much stuff in a single category, e.g., sixteen pairs of running shoes, even though you only use three. In the interest of saving storage space, and simplifying the retrieval process, pick only your favorites and give the rest the boot.

You may also discover it difficult to part with certain items because you (or someone) spent good money on them, even though they're never used. It could be an impulsively purchased piece of clothing, an expensive piece of art you don't like anymore, a fancy organizing gadget that never worked, or a gift someone gave you that you already have or just don't want. How do you motivate yourself to part with these things? Think about what you'll gain in return:

- Space—for the things you really use and love.
- Time—saved searching through all the unused clutter to get at what's really important to you.

• Money—it's costing you to house and maintain these items. Giving them away, or selling them, could yield a tax deduction or put some extra dollars in your pocket.

• Satisfaction—share the items you no longer use; surely there are people in the world who could use them.

To decide what to do with those discards not consigned to the trash, consider the following options:

• **Adopt-a-charity.** Pick an organization that is meaningful to you and will pick up the stuff if you don't have the time or transportation to get it there yourself.

• **Adopt-a-friend.** You may feel better knowing your cast-offs will be going to someone familiar—a close pal, acquaintance, neighbor, housekeeper—who would love to have them.

• **Have a tag sale or sell through a consignment shop.**

• **Put it into storage.** Getting unused things out of your home or office into off-site storage will allow you to experience clutter-free living without the trauma of parting with them permanently. Rates are not high, and some companies (like Public Storage) offer pickup and delivery service; they bring a container to your door, you fill it, and they whisk it away. Couldn't be more convenient! Once it is off-site, you may even find it easier to decide what to keep long-term.

3. ASSIGN A HOME

Now it's time to take all the items you're keeping and decide precisely where, within each zone, you're going to store them—which shelf, which drawer, which side of the bed.

If you weren't able to do so before, now is the time to move the furniture around to see how your zone design looks and if your available storage units will accommodate everything you want to put in them.

Avoid being vague and indecisive about where to put items by applying the "Select One Rule" of giving each item a single, consistent home. This is key to "trusting" your system.

Use the following guidelines in assigning homes:

• **Appropriate sizing.** Match the size and number of the items to the size of the storage unit to avoid wasting or taking up too much space. For example, use a shallow drawer for belts, a deep one for sweaters.

• **Single-function storage.** Don't mix categories within a storage unit; it makes retrieval too complicated. For example, when possible, put T-shirts in one drawer and jeans in another, rather than putting both in the same drawer.

• **Logical sequencing.** Position similar groups of items near each other. Again, follow your own associations. In your dresser, for example, you might place workout clothes and swimsuits in drawers next to each other because they are both related to fitness.

• **Accessibility.** Make it easy to retrieve and put back frequently used items by not jamming too many things in drawers or stacking them on shelves too high to reach.

• **Safety.** Don't store anything that is heavy or fragile too high in a storage unit; injury or breakage could occur as you attempt to retrieve or put it back. For the same reason, don't jam fragile items too close to each other on a shelf or in a drawer. If you have children in the house, be sure to place items that could harm them out of reach, or behind locked doors.

As you put items away in their assigned homes, you may discover you don't have enough storage space for everything. Your options are either to reevaluate and purge some more (get rid of or relocate all those "maybes") or increase storage room. There are often hidden pockets of storage space that can be found, and ways to make the most of every square inch inside those closets and cabinets. Each chapter in Part 3 will provide numerous tips for stretching space.

4. CONTAINERIZE

Containers make it easy to keep your categories of items grouped and separated within their assigned homes so that retrieval, cleanup, and maintenance are a breeze.

Imagine a linen closet, for example. You've spent hours sorting and purging the contents, and now have piles of items grouped by category: dental stuff, soaps, hair care, first aid, extra paper goods. As you loosely place these groups of items on your shelves, it will be hard to tell where one category leaves off and the next begins. But if you put each group into a plastic basket, and label your baskets on the shelves, retrieval and return will be a snap. As will cleaning the shelves: just remove the baskets, wipe the shelves off, then return the baskets. Try doing that as easily with eighty loose bottles, jars, and boxes!

Another big benefit of containerizing is that it helps limit how much you accumulate in any given category; you can only save as much as the container will hold.

Finally, and most important, containerizing is where you can really get creative and have fun infusing your system with your personal style.

KEEPING YOURSELF MOTIVATED

Somewhere along the way, you're bound to get tired of making decisions, distracted, or feel the tug of other activities pulling you away. It's happened to all of us. Give yourself tools to see you through these tough spots. Select one or more of the following options:

- **Post your goals.** Tack your answers to the fourth Analyze question ("Why do I want to get organized?") on the wall of the room you're working in; when you feel yourself starting to become overwhelmed by what you've gotten yourself into, reread your answers to get the impetus to press on.
- **Use before and after photos.** Take a snapshot of the space you're going to organize and tack it to the wall next to your goals. It will spur you on. Then take another snapshot of the same space when you're finished and tack it up next to the "before" photo. Allow yourself to wallow in the satisfaction of having completed a job well.
- **Reward yourself along the way.** Think about activities that you enjoy the most, and plan to dole these out as rewards when you complete various milestones along the way. Then, as you are working, you can say to yourself, "When I finish this corner, I'll make reservations to see a show"; or "As soon as I finish this desktop, I'll take a walk for some fresh air." But be careful not to snatch your reward away when it's due by saying, "Ah, I'm on a roll. I'll just keep working." Honor the bargain you've made by actually giving yourself what you've promised.
- **Make it fun.** If music will give you energy to keep working, select some tapes or CDs ahead of time, or decide which radio station you want to listen to. Play games with yourself to stay motivated. Say, "Okay, by the time this song is over, I will have finished this bookshelf." Do one shelf per song or one section of the room per CD. And don't get down on yourself if you *haven't* finished that shelf by the end of the song. Just finish it by the end of the *next* song.
- **Work with a buddy.** Sure, misery loves company . . . but who, you ask, would want to join you in your misery? Make arrangements to team with a colleague or a friend who is also struggling with a disorganization problem. Working together will actually make the job go smoother and faster, and make it be more enjoyable. You'll have somebody to bounce ideas off who can offer an objective viewpoint and keep you focused on the job at hand when you start falling prey to self-criticism *("How could I let things get so out of hand!")*. Arrange to trade weekends and help each other out. You'll be amazed at how much you can accomplish working together, and how rewarding the whole experience will be.

Select Appropriate Containers

What to look for:

- **Aesthetics.** Choose containers that you love. They should be delightful to use and blend attractively with the decor you've chosen for your space, whether it's shabby-chic, country-cozy, or high-tech steel.
- **Sturdiness.** Don't be tempted to economize. Your containers must be tough enough to withstand repeated use. If they fall apart, break, or feel flimsy, you'll stop using them.
- **Manageability.** Containers should be easy to handle. If you'll be storing a lot of items in them, consider their weight when full.
- **Size.** Make sure they are a proper fit for the number of items you will be storing, without overcrowding. Consider leaving a little room for growth—but not much.

Prepare Your Shopping List

To avoid having to make fifty trips to the store, be sure to plan ahead. Start by making a complete shopping list of all the containers you'll need. I like to organize my shopping list by zone right onto my original zone planning sheet, so that when I'm at the store (or rummaging in the attic), I can see exactly how I plan to use each container, in case I need to find a substitute.

To ensure you buy the right size containers, measure, measure, measure *before* you go shopping. There is nothing more aggravating, not to mention costly and time-consuming, than discovering the drawer dividers you bought are a quarter of an inch taller than the drawers they're supposed to go in.

- Measure the height, width, and depth (and count the number) of items to be stored to know what size container you'll need.
- Measure the height, width, and depth of each space a container will go in to know what will fit. For example, measure the shelf or drawer your basket must fit into.
- Measure the actual containers in the store itself to be sure they'll fit by taking along a tape measure for added insurance. And don't forget your shopping list!

Labeling

Once you've got all your containers installed, it's time to label them. Labeling is not just for kids. It ensures that things get put back where they belong, making cleanup a quick, painless, and mindless activity. Labeling is especially important if others will be sharing your space to make sure things are consistently put back where they belong.

Depending on what you're labeling, you can choose to label in a highly visible or more subtle manner. For example, if the container will go inside a

SAMPLE CONTAINER LIST

Zone	Supplies	Storage Unit	Container Needed
Reading	Books: 200		Bookshelves (30″ × 70″)
TV/Music	Videos: 65 CDs: 200	Wall unit	Drawer dividers CD tower (12″ × *4″)
Napping	Quilt Pillows		Storage ottoman (27″ × 21″)

medicine chest, file cabinet, or storage closet, labeling the container itself is desirable. But if the container will be exposed to view—stored on an open shelf, for example—you might prefer to label the edge of the shelf or the surface the container will sit on rather than the container itself.

Whichever method you choose, it is critical that your labels are legible, neat, and attractive and that they adhere; no one, not even you, will respect your labels if they look like chicken scratch or a doctor's prescription, or if they fall off. White labels with bold, black lettering work best. You can write them by hand, but for best, easy-to-read results, use a label maker or a word processor. Each chapter in Parts 3 & 4 will give special labeling hints keyed to the area it discusses.

Voilà! You're done! Well, almost . . .

5. EQUALIZE

As you drive off in your car, you don't just set your steering wheel in one position and "lock" it in place until you get to your destination. One curve in the road could send you into a crash. Rather, you constantly, naturally monitor and make tiny adjustments to the steering wheel to equalize things so you're always heading straight.

So it is with organizing.

About two weeks after you've finished, make an appointment with yourself to evaluate how well your system has been working. Is everything as easy as you'd like it to be? Are you following your system? Do the zones and categories you set up work well for you? Are there any rough spots that a quick review of your needs assessment in Chapter 3 might help to iron out? Reevaluate again every couple of weeks thereafter until you're completely happy with your system.

Once you've got a system that works totally, you need to integrate a daily and periodic maintenance program into your lifestyle so that it becomes a matter of routine. Keep it simple. If your maintenance program is too time-consuming and complex, you won't follow it.

Clean up and put things back at the end of each day. Regardless of how messy your space gets in the course of the day, this will only take a few minutes because everything now has a logical, accessible, and identifiable home. Never put off daily cleanup, or the clutter will build up and become formidable in no time.

Some ongoing maintenance is also required to keep your system running smoothly. This involves applying small but highly effective maintenance tricks and techniques that can be fit into your daily routine without requiring much extra time. Parts 3 and 4 are full of such tips.

Last but not least, periodic "tune-ups" are essential so your system will always keep up with any changes in your needs, goals, possessions, and priorities. Schedule appointments with yourself on the calendar at regular intervals to evaluate how your system is working, make adjustments for any new items you've acquired, purge old stuff that's no longer relevant, and even buy yourself a spiffy organizing gizmo you've been looking at to keep your system fun and engaging. These occasional face-lifts will prevent you from getting tired of your system and abandoning it out of boredom. Each chapter in Parts 3 and 4 includes a recommended schedule for maintenance.

SKILLS FOR A LIFETIME

Like anything else worth doing, organizing takes time to master. You're bound to make mistakes and stumble along the way. Try not to panic or get angry with yourself. Just relax, work out the bugs, and simply get yourself back on track.

Once you've mastered these skills, they'll last you forever because they're skills *for life*. That's their greatest value. You can apply them over and over again to almost any task.

They will give you a lasting sense of security, personal identity, pride, and peace—a necessity in the increasingly complex, fast-paced, and rapidly changing world of today.

Now that you've learned the process for getting organized from the inside out, let's start building on it by putting what you've learned into practice.

PART 3

Applying
What You've Learned

How to Use This Section

Each of the following chapters in Parts 3 and 4 shows you how to apply my foolproof Analyze-Strategize-Attack formula to specific areas of your office, home, and life.

Resist the temptation to dive into these chapters without having read and absorbed the material in Parts 1 and 2, which provide you with the full context of the many tips provided in these practical chapters. Parts 1 and 2 are designed to change your entire approach to the organizing process so that you will finally meet with success when you tackle the spaces of most concern to you.

Each chapter follows the structure of my Organizing from the Inside Out formula, starting with Analyze and moving through Strategize and Attack. Rather than explain again what each step means, I will provide sample responses from my clients to spur your own thinking, and specific tips related to the particular area you are working on. The examples are neither definitive nor meant to be followed to the letter. Their sole purpose is to give you ideas so that you can custom-design and maintain an organizing system that conforms to your unique way of thinking, your own habits, and what's important to you.

GATHER YOUR SUPPLIES

Before getting started on any organizing project, it is extremely helpful to gather all the supplies you'll need to accomplish it. This will keep you focused on the work because you won't be distracted looking for cleaning materials, making sure you have enough garbage bags, or setting up that CD player to help you keep your nose to the grindstone.

Banker's box—very handy for housing temporary files and archiving papers and more *(courtesy of Fellowes Manufacturing)*

Here are the supplies I recommend:

- **Large, durable trash bags.** Clutter can be heavy and bulky; cheap bags will tear, adding frustration.
- **Empty boxes** for sorting your items, labeled as follows:

  Give away—Use a separate box for each destination if you will be giving things to several sources.

  Belongs elsewhere—Save orphaned items in this box to relocate to their proper room at the conclusion of your organizing session.

  Needs repair—Use this box to assemble items you want to keep that need fixing. Write a deadline for repairing them on the box; for example, one month. If you haven't repaired the items by then, it's time to let them go.

- **Dust buster, dust cloth and spray, broom and dustpan** for cleaning temporarily emptied shelves, drawers and floor space behind furniture, a prime opportunity not to be missed.
- **Box of plain manila folders** for sorting papers.
- **Post-it Notes** for temporarily labeling piles of stuff and groups of items as you sort.
- **Pencil and notepad** for writing instructions to yourself about action items, such as future to-do's, that may come up as you work.
- **Corrugated banker's boxes** for keeping file folders with sorted papers neat, tidy, and upright as you design your new system, and for archiving papers designated for storage.
- **Beverages and snacks** for preventing dehydration and maintaining your energy; also prevent having to disrupt your session with a quick trip to the store.

OK, turn the page and let's get organizing!

6

Traditional Offices and Filing Systems

The term "traditional offices" refers to private offices with a door, in any size company outside the home. However, this chapter also contains the most detailed information on designing a user-friendly filing system, so those with any type of office would benefit from reading it as well.

ANALYZE

1. What's Working?
Examples:

> "One thing that works is my invoicing and bookkeeping system. The rest of the papers are up for grabs, but I watch my cash flow closely."
> —*Owner, Retail Store*

> "I have one drawer where I keep copies of all the speeches I give by date and place. It's easy to refer back to anything I need."
> —*Chairman of the Board*

2. What's Not Working?
Examples:

> "Every morning, I race in to answer the phone, drop my briefcase on the desk, knock a pile of papers to the floor, and cringe as the person on the other end asks to review something I sent. I know it's here somewhere, but where? I have to bluff my way out, then hunt for it. The daily pressure, stress, and embarrassment are taking their toll."
> —*Human Resource Administrator*

"I am so disorganized I can't make the most of my support staff. Critical projects get held up on my desk all the time. My assistant can't even file for me because neither one of us understands my filing system."

—Vice President, Sales and Marketing

"I work until 8 or 9 p.m. every night. I know it's because I spend so much time every day sifting through my piles of stuff to see what needs to be done. This is today's pile. That's yesterday's. Last week's are on the floor. Last month's are on the credenza. I am completely reliant on my memory to find what I need—and it doesn't always work!"

—Corporate Chief Financial Officer

"I have a terrible reputation in the department for losing things. No one ever gives me anything without keeping a copy for themselves. Unfortunately, I'm sure they are also holding back giving me additional responsibility. My notorious ways are stifling my career."

—Advertising Account Manager

3. What Items Are Most Essential to You?
Examples:

• **Charlotte M.,** an international trade lawyer at a busy firm, needed places for her current work (cases), research materials (weekly legislation, updated newsletters, law books, sample cases), files borrowed from the central filing room (so she wouldn't get them mixed up with her own files and forget to return them), time-keeping logs, articles and presentations she has written for her own professional development.

• **Joel K.,** president of an office-supply dealership, needed places for his price-list binder, monthly promotions, and order book (for negotiating deals); business cards and leads for sales; three categories of files ("Product Sources," "Business Planning," "Personal Finance"); separate locations for paperwork he routed to his bookkeeper and administrative assistant.

• **Janice Z.,** development director for a nonprofit, needed places for current event files; past event files; a planning calendar; publicity, mailing materials and props for various fund-raising events; contributors' information; checks to deposit.

4. Why Do You Want to Get Organized?
Examples:

• "Speed information retrieval office-wide."

- "Clear the clutter to make a better impression on customers, supervisors, and support staff."
- "Reduce stress related to lost information."
- "Manage multiple activities and deadlines more easily."

5. What's Causing the Problems?
These are common causes of clutter in these spaces:

- **Inconvenient storage.** In 90 percent of the offices I see, the credenza is placed directly behind the desk, while the filing cabinet is across the room, making filing and retrieval a huge hassle. By simply switching these two pieces of furniture, you will place the maximum number of files within arm's reach of your desk chair, and boost your chances of keeping your desktop clear by about 500 percent!
- **Items have no home.** If papers are piled up on your desk, it is likely you have never assigned a particular home for them. It could be because new categories of papers keep coming into your office and you never stop to create new files. So they pile up on the desk. Another common situation is that the file drawers are filled with your predecessor's files—which you never had a chance to clean out to make room for your own system. In any case, without a home, there's no place for them to go but into stacks.
- **Speed of life/technology.** Often, in the fast pace of today's work world, people cannot find or make the time to stop and get themselves organized. Consider this common complaint from one workshop attendee: "No matter how much I yearn for an organized office, finding the time to make it happen without interfering with my daily workload seems impossible—even dangerous; I might miss a deadline, fall behind, lose business."
- **Organizing is boring.** A large part of office organizing usually involves filing, one of life's most detestable tasks. It would never occur to most people to spice up their system with a little style and flair. So they use manila folders, dull labels—the whole thing is boring, boring, boring. Yet the information in our filing system is the lifeblood of our work—and easy access to it is often critically tied to our success. Later in this chapter you will find ways to add pizzazz and dignity to your filing system to make dealing with it on a daily basis a lot more fun and engaging.

STRATEGIZE

Plan Your Zones
Here are some typical activity zones, accompanying supplies, and storage units for a traditional office.

Activities	Supplies	Storage Units
Paperwork & phone calls	Files Phone directories Business card file Paper, pens, pencils Stationery Paper clips Stapler	2 file cabinets Desk drawers
Computer	Diskettes & CDs Backup cartridges Computer manuals Printer paper	Desk return & shelves
Reference	Books Magazines Newsletters Newspapers Video- & audiotapes Reference binders	Bookshelves
Interoffice communication	In/Out boxes for assistants, colleagues, supervisors	Desktop
Meetings	Notepads Pencils Plants & artwork Certificates Trophies Coffee, tea, sugar, mugs	Credenza

Tips on Rearranging Furniture

• **Use "L" or "U" shapes.** Create your own mission control center by arranging the furniture in your main paperwork/phone zone into an "L" or a "U." This will give you the maximum amount of work surface and storage capacity in the smallest amount of space.

• **Position desk.** You spend a lot of time there, so what makes you the most comfortable will make you the most productive. Do you prefer to face a window, the door, the center of the room, a wall? If you work with others and cannot close the door to your office, would you prefer to face them so that you're always open and aware of what's going on around you, or have your back to them to reduce the number of interruptions? Be creative. There are more possibilities than you think.

• **Keep most files within arm's reach.** The most common mistake I see in most offices is locating the file cabinet too far away from the desk. That's why papers pile up on the desktop. If it's inconvenient to file, you won't. By having most files within easy reach, you can work out of your file drawers all day, retrieving and putting them back with no effort at all. But if you have files you want an assistant to be able to access without interrupting you, keep those closer to the door of your office.

Ideas for Stretching Space

• See if you can get your company to replace your two-drawer lateral file with a five-drawer lateral file. You'll more than double your filing capacity without taking up more floor space.

• Float your desk in the center of the room, or place it perpendicular to the wall. This will free up space for an additional file cabinet or computer table behind or at a right angle to your desk.

• Add a small filing cabinet or bookshelf near the door of your office for materials you share with an assistant. She or he can come in and out of your office without disturbing you.

• Place your computer monitor on a riser on corner of your desk to free up work surface.

• Mount hook(s) on the back of your office door for coat, bags, change of clothes.

• Mount wall pockets near your desk to store hot files, sorted mail, or literature you need to keep handy.

• In lateral files, use cross rails to turn files to face from front to back rather than side to side. This can increase your filing capacity in the same drawer by 15 percent, giving you another foot of file storage in the same space.

Lateral file drawer showing front-to-back versus side-to-side filing *(courtesy of Meridian, Inc.)*

Planning the Zones of Your Files

Instead of a straight A–Z file, which, ironically, can sometimes be confusing, files can be sorted into zones as well. In an A–Z system, related files often end up scattered, with "Accountant" under "A" and "Taxes" under "T." Filing by category enables you to group similar files, and create "activity" zones within your filing drawers. Consider sorting your papers by category, to reflect your main categories of responsibility in your work. Here are some examples of ways clients have sorted their files into zones for a visual snapshot of their work activities and responsibilities.

Career Counselor

Clients—Corporate
    —Individual
Testing Materials
Clippings & Articles of Interest
Presentations

Publicist for Publishing House

He first sorted papers by:

Author (manuscript, galleys, appearance schedule, publicity materials, and photo)

Then he grouped projects by:

Season (Feb.–May; June–Sept.; Oct.–Jan.)

Note that often, though it is good to plan your categories on paper first (Strategize), it is also advisable to sort through all your papers before making a definitive decision about your final categories. Ultimately, it's best to aim for between three and five broad categories. Any more than that is hard to remember. However, if your papers do break down into more categories, see how a smart CFO solved the problem. He broke his files into two main categories, each of which was broken down into three related subcategories.

CFO for a Retail Chain

External Issues
    Building Landlords
    Manufacturers
    Professional Consultants

Internal Issues
Human Resources
Finance
Strategic Planning

Estimate the Time

Here are some average times required for organizing a traditional office.

HOW LONG WILL IT TAKE?

Attack
1. Sort   16 hours
2. Purge   1 hour
3. Assign a home   1 hour
4. Containerize   6 hours
5. Equalize   10 minutes daily

ATTACK

1. Sort

"I dreaded sorting because I knew I'd be facing all my mess-ups—the deadlines I missed, the opportunities I lost, the contacts I blew. And it requires such intense concentration and mental effort. Making all those decisions is excruciating. Yet once we got into it, I found the process of getting rid of those reminders of my past failures to be incredibly liberating. As we went through those stacks, I kept getting clearer and clearer about what's really important to me *now*, and where I want to focus my energies in the future. I was able to start all over, this time with an organized system that reflects what really matters to me."

—*Janet R., Marketing Director*

Here are some suggestions for how you might sort the contents of your office into categories.

Ways to Sort Office Supplies

Writing (stationery, notecards, business cards, express envelopes, postage, postal scale)
Computer (manuals, diskettes, CD-ROMs, cartridges, printer paper, laptop accessories)
Banking (deposit slips, check register, checks to deposit)
Telephone (Rolodex, address book, telephone directories, headsets)

Office tools (pens, pencils, stapler, scissors, paper clips, rubber bands)
Office equipment (label maker, camera, overhead projector, tape recorder)

Ways to Sort Books and Magazines

By subject:

> Finance
> Leadership
> Marketing
> Office Procedure Manuals
> Presentation skills

Ways to Sort Papers

Unless your filing system is 75 percent effective as is, I recommend starting from scratch. This is a much cleaner and faster way to work and you'll have a clean slate when you're finished.

In order to do this, you will need a box of one hundred manila file folders, a pencil, empty banker's box(es), and your piles of papers. Go through every stack in your office, picking up each piece of paper, and asking yourself "what is this?", "why am I holding on to it?", and "under what circumstances would I look for it again?" Write the first word that pops into your head onto a manila folder, slip the paper inside, and move on to the next piece of paper.

Place completed folders on the floor or in your empty banker's boxes to create the beginning of your brand-new filing system. If you find a piece of paper in one of the piles for which a file already exists in one of your drawers, pull the folder out, file the paper inside, and integrate that old file directly into the new system you're creating. The old file has just justified its existence. By working this way, you will discover which files from your old system are useful, and which no longer have value—they'll be the ones left over in the drawers at the end of the sorting process.

NAMING FILES

How do you select a title now that will still make sense to you later on? Here are a few tips:

• **Keep titles simple and categories broad.** The secret of quick retrieval is to have the fewest places to look for a given document. There are products on the market that will allow you to subdivide and organize the contents of your folders, called self-adhesive file dividers which we'll discuss under Containerize.

• **Title files based on retrieval, not storage.** In other words, select file names based on where you would *look* for something if you needed it again.

Often, that is the subject, not the source. For example, if you come across a *Wall Street Journal* article on college investment funds, it might be easier to file it under "Financial Planning," rather than *"Wall Street Journal"* or "Clippings." If you're saving a computer seminar brochure, decide whether you're holding on to it to give to someone, or planning to take the seminar yourself, or intending to use it as a model for designing your own seminar brochure. Then file accordingly.

• **Use titles to group similar files.** For example, you can have a "Sales" section containing separate files, such as "Sales—Domestic," "Sales—International," "Sales—Projections," or "Sales—New Accounts."

• **Use titles that incite you to action.** Instead of using passive titles such as "Invoices to Write," "Bills Due," and "Letters to Answer," try more action-oriented titles that will be hard to ignore, such as "Create Invoice," "Pay Bills," and "Write Thank-You."

• **Use titles that speak to your soul.** Language evokes many responses; it can be a gateway or a barrier to the information you keep. See if these substitutions would change your perspective on your files and how often you use them.

Passive Title	Active Title
Business Growth	Rainmaking
Financial Planning	Wealth
Articles of Interest	Fascinating People

REEVALUATE
When you're finished, review the files you've created and make any refinements necessary to keep your system simple. Here are the three basic things to reevaluate:

• **File titles.** Do they make sense to you? Are they active? Do they invite you to look inside? Do you have files with duplicate names? If so, consolidate, pick one title, and stick with it. For example, one of my clients wound up with one file folder titled "Phone Numbers," another called "For Rolodex," and another for "Potential Contacts." These were all the same subject.

• **Thickness of folders.** For example, if you created a folder called "Trade Associations" that by the end of the sorting process is hugely fat, you may want to break it down into separate folders for each trade association. On the other hand, if you have several folders with just one or two pieces of paper in them, consolidate and group them. The fewer folders you have to look through to locate a piece of paper, the better.

• **Categories.** If you've got too many piles of file folders, chances are you've got too many categories. See if you can group them into much broader categories—three to five, tops. More than that number will be too hard to remember, and it usually means your system is too complex. Keep it simple. Here are some categories my clients came up with:

Vendors
Personnel
Strategic Planning & Confidential
Outside Projects
—Corporate Chief Financial Officer

Stories
Sources
Administrative Forms
—Investigative Reporter

Clients
Administrative
Marketing
Financial Data
Financial
—Business Owner

Board Reports & Agendas
Travel Planning
Forms
Correspondence
—Administrative Assistant

2. Purge

Our offices are deluged with paper daily, and 80 percent of what gets filed is never referred to again. Think about the cost of the filing cabinets used to house all that paper, the price per square foot of space those filing cabinets occupy, and you see how expensive unnecessary saving can be.

Here are some tips for controlling the volume of paper you keep.

1. Check with your accountant, lawyer, or office manager for retention guidelines on tax and legal papers. If you must keep certain papers for legal reasons, place them in storage.

2. Keep only "core information," those materials you actually use. To decide what is and is not core information, ask yourself these questions of each piece of paper. A "Yes" means you should save it, a "No" means deep-six it.

• Does this paper tie in with the core activities of my business?
• Will this help me complete a project I am working on right now?

- Does this paper represent a viable business opportunity?
- Do I refer to this paper on a regular basis?
- Will this paper help me make money?
- Do I have time to do anything with this paper?
- Are there tax or legal reasons to save this?
- Would my life/work change if I didn't have this piece of paper?

3. If you have file drawers filled with papers you haven't looked at in over a year, make room for your new system by boxing them up and storing them elsewhere, marking a date about three months hence on your calendar to pull them out and sort through them. By then you'll have lived with your new system for a while, and the process will go much more quickly.

Julie's No-Brainer Toss List

- **Product solicitations.** Ads and mailings for software, catalog items, etc. If you aren't ready to buy right now, toss them. Mailing lists are a form of immortality; you never get off them. Any new solicitations most surely will be mailed to you, and when you're ready to buy, you'll buy from the most current mailing.
- **Old magazines, books, and articles.** If you haven't referred to them in the last twelve months, commit them to the circular file because the information is probably stale by now. Besides, new or updated information on practically everything becomes available faster than I can write this sentence. Letting go of this stuff can be cathartic; you will also instantly recover a huge amount of storage and breathing space.
- **Old research materials and literature.** These items are bulky; they take up a lot of space, and most of us never refer to them again. To save space, repeat this: "Keep the source, toss the paper." Maintain a list of sources (actual and potential) by topic in your Rolodex or contact manager. If you ever need the material again, you can contact your source and get the most updated version.
- **Duplicates of documents.** Generally speaking, there is no reason to keep more than two copies of any given document. Keep the original in a plastic sleeve to prevent loss, and, if you must, keep one copy on hand for easy circulation.
- **Previous drafts of letters and proposals.** Retain only your final version. Out with the others; after all, they mostly contain material you decided not to use!
- **Supplies.** Get rid of bulky, space-taking supplies you don't use. Keep your supply drawers and cabinets lean and organized so you can easily see if you're running out of important items *before* a crisis hits. Post a list of basic supplies on the inside of the drawer or cabinet door to remind you of what you do need.

THE LAW OF VISIBLE, DRAMATIC RESULTS

Avoid these common pitfalls:

Reading everything. Ah, what to do with all those articles you saved, and publications you haven't gotten around to reading? How can you decide whether to keep or toss them unless you know what they're about? As you glance through them to make your decision, their contents recapture your interest; you kick back and start reading. Before long, hours have passed, and you're disheartened because you've accomplished nothing. Stay focused on identifying the general content of the articles, then put them into a folder by topic. If you have a bunch of unread newsletters or magazines you aren't willing to toss until you've read them, place them in a separate reading basket or pile, and schedule a specific time in the future to read them. Or keep a stack of them on a shelf by the door of your office. On your way to lunch or to go home, grab one or two to read while you're eating or commuting. Your job right now is to just keep sorting.

Dealing with "Maybes." If you come across an outdated cruise brochure that you're hesitant to toss because travel is a big interest of yours, create a "Travel File" and slip the brochure inside. In the end, if your filing system enables you to find your papers quickly and easily, it's less important whether some of the papers in the folder are extraneous. At least all the travel stuff is now together, and you can always purge the contents of that folder in the future.

---

3. Assign a Home

• If you have enough file drawers within arm's reach of your desk chair, decisions regarding category placement should be pretty easy. In this case, assign each category of files to a different drawer, even if the category doesn't fill the whole drawer. This makes retrieval easiest. For example, put financial files in the top drawer, personnel files in the middle, and administrative files in the bottom.

• If drawer space is limited, you can put two or three small categories in a single drawer, separating them within the drawer by location (e.g., front, middle, back).

• If you have file drawers that are actually part of your desk, consider using them for confidential files, daily files, or personal files.

• If you have files you want your assistant to have access to without interrupting you, consider placing them closer to the door.

• Send files you do not use on a regular basis but need on hand for occasional reference to your assistant's filing area or the central files.

• Give your office supplies specific homes, too. Assign one drawer to banking supplies; another to stationery and notepads; another to pens, paper clips, and scissors.

• Assign the utility drawer in your desk closest to the phone to telephone directories, company phone lists, and phone books.

Create a File Index

Once you've decided your file categories and titles, create a simple one-page file index to remind you what goes where and why. This is an invaluable tool if you've been historically inconsistent about how you categorize and name files. It makes you adhere to your categories and names, speeding retrieval. When you're unsure of where to find or file a piece of paper, a glance at your index is more precise than rifling through an entire drawer.

Sample File Index

Administration (Blue)

Associations—*alpha by name*
Books/Tapes
Business Plan
Business Documents
Classes
Clippings
Consultants—*alpha by name*
Contracts
Forms
Logo
New Business Ideas
Stationery Masters

Sales/Marketing (Gold)

Advertisements
Articles Written
Copy Ideas
Gift Certificates
Leads—*alpha by industry*
Mailing List
Networking
Newsletter
Publicity Ideas
Press Clippings
Research and Statistics
Speeches

Financial (Green)

Bank Accounts—*alpha by name*
Budget
Credit Cards—*alpha by name*
Health Insurance
Investment Information
Tax Returns—Current Year
Tax Returns—Past Years

Paid Bills and Receipts—filed by
  month in a separate file drawer

Personnel (Lavender)

Applications—New
Applications—Rejected
Employees—*alpha by name*
Job Descriptions
Time Sheets
Training Materials

For safekeeping as well as easy access, put a copy of your index in a plastic sleeve at the front of your file drawers. And if others will be using your file system, give a copy to them as well.

INSIDER'S TIP

Keep a copy of your index in a folder labeled "File" in your briefcase, along with a small pack of Post-it notes. As you accumulate papers or articles on the road, you can scan your index and stick a Post-it on the paper indicating where it should be filed. When you return to your office, filing those newly acquired papers will be a quick and mindless chore for you or any assistant.

---

4. Containerize

Here is where you get to add some style, flair, and pizzazz to your filing system. But take heed: the purpose of the following containerizing techniques is not just to add a sense of fun to an otherwise boring activity (although that will certainly happen). These suggestions for filing will add enormous visual clarity to your system, which will boost the speed with which you file and retrieve information. Use the following containerizing techniques to create a filing system you enjoy and trust.

• **Color code.** Instead of plain manila folders, invest in some attractive colored folders and assign each category of your filing system a different hue, reflecting its contents. For example, financial files might be green (for money); personnel files might be lavender (the color of the heart); marketing files might be red (to indicate flashiness and get attention). Note: I prefer colored folders with white labels, rather than manila folders with colored labels. Colored folders are more fun, engaging, and easy to identify from afar.

• **Use quality folders.** Invest in two-ply top folders for just a few pennies more per folder. They have a reinforced edge, which makes them much more durable than single-ply folders. In addition, they don't dog-ear or sag in the file drawer, they have substance and weight, and they feel good—lending appropriate dignity to the information you are storing in them.

• **Label clearly.** For some reason, a label produced on a labelmaker, word processor, or typewriter speaks with far more authority than a quickly scribbled handwritten label in pencil. As a result, you tend to honor the titles more when they are labeled this way. Take the time to create beautiful labels, either mechanically or by handwriting in very neat, block letters with a medium width marker, and you will see the difference it makes. Always use bold, black lettering on white labels for clearest reading.

Box-bottom files accommodate bulky papers *(courtesy of EsseltePendaflex Corporation)*.

• **Place colored folders in standard green hanging files.** The dark background makes the colored folders stand out, and when you remove a file to work with it, the hanging folder stays in the drawer, conveniently marking its place. When you open the drawer, it's easy to see what files are missing and exactly where you should return files.

• **Use "box-bottom" hanging files to group related folders.** Box-bottom files have a wider bottom than standard "V" hanging files, and can accommodate extra-bulky groups of papers without having them jam up at the top of the drawer. For example, I keep five related folders (NAPO, NSA, Toastmasters, SBA, and NAFE) grouped in a two-inch box-bottom folder called "Associations." At a glance, I can see all the groups I am involved with and see if I am giving each one equal attention.

• **Use straight-line filing.** Most of us were taught to alternate file tab positions left, center, right, left, center, right. There are two problems with this approach: (1) the minute you add or delete a file, you break the pattern, and consequently you begin to worry about what folders might be hiding behind others; (2) scanning back and forth between the titles makes many people anxious—a sort of horizontal vertigo effect. Straight-line filing (with all tabs in the same position lined up one behind the other) is much more peaceful and easy on the eye. You can add or delete files at any time, and always feel confident that your sense of order is being maintained.

• **Use tab coding.** Once you have established a pattern of straight-line filing, you can alter tab position to communicate important information to yourself. For example, I keep active clients and prospects in the same drawer, arranged alphabetically by last name. Clients are in folders with a left tab, prospects are in folders with a right tab. This gives me a visual inventory of my work status and enables me to prospect right out of that drawer. When a prospect converts to client status, I simply turn the folder inside out so now it has a right tab position. You could apply this same principle to actual vs.

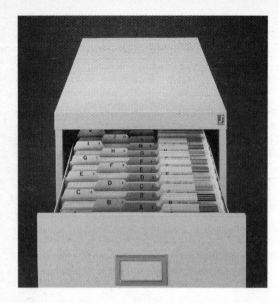

Straight-line filing is easier on the eye and mind *(courtesy of Smead Manufacturing)*.

potential investments, story ideas vs. completed articles, or reference materials vs. active projects.

My Favorite Office File Containers

- Stackable lateral files and modular cabinets allow you to increase file storage as your needs grow.
- Two-ply, ⅕-cut file folders (letter- and legal-sized) can be used within standard green "V" hanging files; they're sturdy and come letter- or legal-sized. I prefer styles that are the same color inside and out so you can invert them easily and double the number of left or right tab files.
- Standard "V" hanging folders are good for storing file folders; they come reinforced and recycled. Get some with pockets for computer diskettes.
- Box bottom files are good for accommodating bulky folders or grouping related folders (e.g., my "Associations" file); they come in one-inch, two-inch, and three-inch thicknesses.
- A metal file frame fits easily and snugly into your file drawer to hold hanging "V" files if the unit doesn't have a built-in one.
- "Out" guides or Post-it Notes are perfect for flagging the place where documents or files have been temporarily removed; they make refiling much easier.
- Plastic file folders are safe and durable for organizing and transporting files in your briefcase when traveling.
- Pocket files are ideal for financial records, small receipts, and designers' swatches.

• The self-adhesive file divider (with and without pocket) is a clever device for subdividing and organizing papers within a file (available from Smead).

• A step rack on the desk can be used for "hot" or transient papers (e.g., bank deposits, invitations to RSVP, Thank-you notes to write, items to enter into the computer). Flex-sort and Fellowes have interesting styles.

• Classification folders, placed in a step rack, are great for hot project or client files on your desktop. They come with a divider to easily subcategorize papers within the folder.

• Mesh baskets/stationery trays are perfect for In/Out baskets or separating communications for various coworkers. They're also great for grouping stacks of newsletter and reading material on bookshelves.

• Bookends are great for saving space, keeping bookshelves neat, and categories separated.

• Magazine holders are perfect for grouping publications by category or title neatly on bookshelves.

5. Equalize

Congratulations! Your office is beautiful, and completely organized—from the inside out. Here's how to maintain it.

• **Daily.** Sort mail over the trash can. Be brutal about what you keep. Set aside fifteen minutes at the end of each day to put everything away. This will give your day closure and enable you to return to a clean office in the morning with a clear mind.

• **Ongoing.** Purge your Rolodex while on the phone. Take a moment to scan through and clean out files as you use them. Keep a supply of colored file folders on hand; as you add a new file, write a label in pencil and add the file to your system. Periodically, make professional-looking labels for all new file folders that have been added, or have that helper with the better handwriting do it for you.

• **Yearly tune-up.** The value of maintenance is high in the workplace, where jobs, responsibilities, and projects change frequently. Expect change. Try the "pencil dot test." Every time you use a file, put a pencil dot in the upper right corner of the folder. At the end of a year, take everything that doesn't have a pencil dot and either toss it or, if it has tax or legal implications, archive it. Take a full day to update your system to keep step with the times. Reassess your categories. Purge what is no longer relevant, and store old files. Update your file index to reflect this. Make new labels if the old ones are worn. Rearrange file drawers if necessary. And periodically buy yourself a neat new organizing gadget to keep your system fun and interesting—but always think about where you will store it first!

7

Home-Based Businesses

ANALYZE

1. What's Working?
Examples:

> "I keep a supply of promotional packets assembled and ready to go. When I get an inquiry, I can add a quick cover note, slap on an address label and stamp, and send it right out."   —*Consultant*

> "My vendor catalogs all live on this shelf by my phone, and I toss out the old one as soon as the new one comes in. It's nice to know I can get my hands on the most up-to-date issue in a second."   —*Interior Designer*

2. What's Not Working?
Examples:

> "My office started out in a four-foot by four-foot corner of my bedroom. As my business grew, so did the office—first up to the ceiling, then out in every direction imaginable. I end most days with papers all over my bed and spend many nights sleeping on the couch. Help! I want my bedroom back."   —*Professional Speaker*

> "I am constantly losing things in my office. Last week I lost a major proposal the day before my presentation to a major client. I was up all night hunting for, then reassembling it. Somehow, I always manage to pull things off at the last minute, but my stress level is always unbearably high."   —*Photographer-Writer-Teacher*

"I sometimes don't send invoices to my clients because I can't find the documentation, and I have no way of tracking receipts for reimbursement. I'm losing money!" —*Architect*

3. What Items Are Most Essential to You?
Examples:

• David T., a financial advisor, needed places for his active client files, prospect files, inactive client files, daily and weekly financial publications, and information on various investment products and companies to watch.

• Mary B., a motivational speaker and model, needed places for her promotional materials, speeches, and outlines; presentation equipment and proposals; archives of video- and audiotapes, reference books, and articles; and invoicing information and receipts for reimbursement.

• Marlene G., an actress and singer, needed places for her acting picture and résumé, her singing picture and résumé, demo tapes, two Rolodexes (one for each career); her personal financial papers, sheet music, monologues and scripts, and office supplies.

4. Why Do You Want to Get Organized?
Examples:

• "We'll be able to use the living room again because my work area will be separated from it."

• "Uninterrupted peace and quiet during work hours."

• "I'll have more room to work in and get more done."

• "Better access to project notes, files, and idea starters so I can grow my business as I want to."

• "I won't be anxious all the time that I'm forgetting something."

• "Feel good when I walk in to work!"

5. What's Causing the Problems?
These are common causes of home office clutter:

• **Unclear goals and priorities.** Often people do not create a well-defined area for their office space based on specific priorities. So it ends up a part of one room or another, which makes it hard for the person and his or her family to separate work from home. This chapter offers many suggestions for better defining the boundaries of the office, both in the physical layout and in work habits and goals.

• **Inconvenient storage.** Often, people set up their home offices without enough storage units—or with the wrong type altogether, selecting pieces either because they like them or because that is what they have available. One client was working with an antique lawyer's desk; it was a beautiful piece of furniture, but drawers barely opened and were of a shape that couldn't accommodate contemporary hanging files.

• **Dislike the space.** People often select a location for their home office based on where they think it will fit—without giving any thought to whether they will be happy in that spot. When the space turns out to be too close or too far from the activity of the house, or to have too much or too little light, or simply to be uncomfortable, the office ends up more a repository for piles of unfiled paper than an actual working office. This chapter will help you decide the best location for your home office so you will enjoy spending time in it.

• **Complex, confusing system.** Entrepreneurs tend to have a tremendous range of interests that are always evolving. It can be hard to keep things simple and broad; many items they save have significance for many other areas of their work. They often set up overly complex systems with hundreds of file folders, many with overlapping titles, and find it impossible to keep it all straight.

STRATEGIZE

It's not uncommon to start your home-based office in one room, then move it after you discover more about your needs, family patterns, and personal preferences. Decide the best location for your office based on the following guidelines, adapted from Paul and Sarah Edwards, *Working from Home*.

• **Full- or part-time?** Home offices used full-time require more work and storage space, whereas part-time ones can usually afford to be smaller and tucked away (beneath a stairwell, perhaps).

• **Compact or spacious?** How much space you need also depends on the type of work you do and your preferred style of working. For example, a writer who does all his or her work by computer and phone requires less space than an artist or craftsperson who needs and wants to have much elbow room to spread things out.

• **Remote or central?** If noise and activity will disturb your concentration, select the quietest, most private location in the house—the basement or a guest room upstairs, perhaps. But if you can block out such distractions, or thrive on them because they make you feel stimulated and connected, select a more public location—a breakfast nook near the dining room, perhaps.

• **Visitors or no visitors?** If employees or clients will be coming to your office, you may want to locate it closer to the front door so the rest of your home remains private.

• **Multi-use?** If the space will be used for a dual purpose—e.g., home office by day; bedroom, kitchen, guest room, or family room by night—this will have an impact on tax-deductibility.

• **Partners or employees?** If more than one person will be working with you, you need space for each of you and your supplies.

• **Windows or windowless?** Some people find looking out a window to be distracting, while others need the natural light and scenery to avoid feeling cut off and claustrophobic.

Selecting Furniture

As many home offices are squeezed into small spaces, it's important, especially if you will be working there full-time, to choose furniture that is comfortable and ergonomically supportive.

• **Desk.** Be sure it is adequate to your needs. You may love that old rolltop, but is it practical? Be wary of computer desks, which often leave no room to spread out and do paperwork. A minimum size of 59 inches wide, 33 inches deep will ensure sufficient work surface.

• **Chair.** Invest in a good chair because you'll be sitting in it a lot. Buy used to save money and get the best on the market. Allow 39 inches of space between the desk and any furniture behind the chair so you can get in and out easily.

• **Filing cabinets.** Buy the best quality you can afford; insist on full-extension drawer glides to avoid scraping knuckles when reaching for files in the rear of the drawer. Cheap cabinets bend and rust quickly, making opening drawers difficult and uncomfortable. Allow 36 to 39 inches of clearance in front so you can open drawers comfortably. (For more on filing cabinets and filing systems, see Chapter 6.)

• **Lighting.** Whether it's natural or electrical, be sure you have enough light to work in without causing eye strain. Halogen lamps are excellent for increasing brightness in the room with indirect light.

• **Wiring.** Have an electrician inspect your wiring to make sure it can safely handle your equipment needs. Adding outlets, surge protectors, and changing circuitry to prevent overloading can be a lifesaver.

Plan Your Zones

People who work at home generally juggle many roles: sales, marketing, proposal writing, customer service, and the like. Your space can be set up to reflect these various roles, as "prompts" to what activities you should be taking care of. Some typical activity zones, related supplies, and storage units for a home office are as follows:

Activities	Supplies	Storage Units
Main work zone	Files Business card file Message pad Paper, pens Office supplies	5-drawer cabinet Desktop Desk supply drawers
Design zone (for artists, designers, and architects)	Drawing supplies Craft materials Designs	Supply cabinet Floor bins Bulletin board
Library	Reference materials Books & tapes Writing guides	3 bookshelves
Mailings/literature	Promotional kits Envelopes, labels Stamps, postage meter Express envelopes, forms	Armoire
Planning/scheduling	Calendar and scheduling information	Wall
Computing	Computer & printer Manuals Diskettes, CDs Backup cartridges Printer paper	Computer cart
Storage	Bulk office supplies, archival files	Guest closet

Note that many entrepreneurs often juggle several careers out of their home offices. It is part of their creative nature. For example, one of my clients is both a lawyer and the leader and marketing director of a jazz band. Another client is a language teacher, novelist, and photographer. If you have multiple careers or businesses operating out of the same office, I suggest you divide your space into zones to reflect each separate venture. This will enable you to fully concentrate on one "career" at a time, even if you switch between them a couple of times a day. Self-contained zones for each business will increase your attendance to detail for each area of your life and reduce your chances of important activities slipping through the cracks.

INSIDER'S TIP

Keeping the Boundaries Clear

It is especially important to divide space into zones in dual-purpose rooms. Without boundaries, the office will sprawl across the rest of the room and render it unlivable, and this lack of demarcation will cause problems for yourself and your family. Here are some ways to define the boundaries between work and home:

- Put up screens.
- Use a bookcase, filing cabinet, or desk as a room divider.
- Build your office into a cabinet that can be closed at the end of the work-day.
- Establish work hours and post them for family members.
- Inform clients (and friends) of your availability.
- Get dressed for work every day.
- Earmark a storage closet in another room for supplies.
- Install a separate phone line for business calls.

Tips on Rearranging Furniture

• **Position desk.** Locate your desk facing the window or the door to the room, whichever spot makes you the most comfortable and that you will enjoy. Build the rest of the furniture layout around that.

• **Use "U," "L," "J," or triangular shapes to achieve maximum storage in minimum space.** Place desk, bookcase, filing cabinet, or computer cart perpendicular to the wall, or even "float them" in the room as space dividers. (For more tips on this, see Chapter 6.)

• **Use bookcases.** They can store supplies, even files—and serve as dividers in dual-purpose rooms.

• **Allow enough clearance** in front of supply cabinets to fully open doors and access contents.

Ideas for Stretching Space

• Mount your computer monitor on a swing arm and place the CPU under your desk to give you more work surface.

• Store supplies in an armoire or nearby closet to get them out of the work area.

• Add storage space over your desk by adding shelves.

• Go vertical by installing floor-to-ceiling shelves. (Allow a minimum 24 inches of space in front of shelves for easy access.)

Mesh desktop accessories provide attractive storage for paper flow
(courtesy of Reliable Home Office).

• Don't limit yourself by placing storage units against walls. For example, two bookcases set up back to back create extra storage on both sides, and even act as room dividers—one side for books for the office, the other for the home.

• If you have a door in your home office, use the back of it to mount shelves and/or hooks and wall pockets for additional storage.

• Do what I recommend for kitchens (Chapter 16): buy a rolling cart to store certain items. When needed, just wheel the cart to your desk for convenient access; when finished, wheel it out of the way again.

Estimate the Time
Here are some average times required for organizing a home-based business office:

HOW LONG WILL IT TAKE?

Attack
1. Sort   16–18 hours
2. Purge   3 hours
3. Assign a home   1 hour
4. Containerize   6–8 hours
5. Equalize   15 minutes daily

> ### AVOIDING COMMON PITFALLS
>
> --
>
> ***Shortcutting sort and purge.*** People who work at home, especially entrepreneurs, feel that if they aren't spending their time working, they're not making money. So they start the organizing process but get antsy and quit before they are through. This incomplete approach is sure to lead to a breakdown of any system you set up. Don't give your organizing project short shrift. Set aside all the time you need right now, and you will benefit immensely—and almost immediately—in time, money, and opportunities.

ATTACK

1. Sort

Entrepreneurs tend to accumulate lots of potentially valuable information, but they are not sure how to categorize it, so it ends up lost and forgotten in miscellaneous piles or folders. Consider sorting your papers into the following categories and setting up an easy retrieval system for them.

• **Client files.** Naturally each client gets her or his own file. If your work requires you to keep a lot of paper on each client (especially true for financial advisors, lawyers, and designers), consider sorting each client file into regular subcategories; e.g., "Contracts," "Invoices," "Work Product," "Background Information," and "Correspondence." Use color or tab position to indicate the difference between the main client file and the subfiles. (For more on filing techniques, read Chapter 6.)

• **Prospect files.** I keep clients and prospects together; in my mind they both fall under the same customer service category, needing equal attention and care. Clients are distinguished from prospects by tab position: clients have a left tab position, prospects a right tab position. When a prospect becomes a client, I invert the folder and reattach the label, and that prospect has joined the ranks of my clients.

• **Subject files.** These are for articles, clippings, notes, and observations that keep you current in your area of expertise and that you might include in an article, speech, or proposal, or want to share with clients, colleagues, or family members.

• **"Spark" files.** Sample brochures, mailing and marketing pieces, and forms from others in business, collected to stimulate your own creative juices and business ideas, go into these files.

• **Cash receipts.** My friend Anthony, a florist, has designed the easiest method I know for tracking deductible cash expenses. Keep an envelope for each week of the year, into which all receipts for the week are placed. At the end of each week, categorize and total the receipts on the outside of the envelope, and write a check to cash for the total. That sum will serve as the petty cash for the next week. If you will be submitting cash receipts for reimbursement, sort those in envelopes by project, trip, or date.

• **Notes from seminars and courses.** These can be kept, if you put them in a useful form. Try summarizing the top ideas from each course attended on no more than one page, and place these pages into a three-ring "Golden Nuggets" binder, which you keep handy on a shelf or near your telephone for daily review.

• **Financial papers.** Sort paid bills into pocket folders by month and place in banker's boxes by year for storage. (Keep up to six years at a time for tax purposes.)

• **Business ideas.** If you have the kind of mind that generates ideas for new businesses faster than you can act on them, create a section of your file called "New Business Ideas." Give each new business idea its own folder and keep them all grouped in a big box-bottom hanging file called "New Business Ideas." Periodically add notes to and review these ideas to see if you are ready to act on any of them.

• **Sort ideas for fun.** Put restaurant reviews, sporting activities, hobbies, and cultural events into a file section called "Lifestyle" or "City Directory." If you travel frequently, keep one for each city you regularly visit.

• **Sort files into zones by role or function.** Here are a couple of sample file indexes to give you some ideas.

Writer

Stories: Current
          Past
          Story ideas
Reference materials & sources
Finance: Invoices
          Paid bills
          Tax records

Consultant

Clients
Marketing
Financial
Administrative

2. Purge

This can be a big challenge, especially to entrepreneurs who tend to see value in holding on to everything that crosses their desk in the belief it might be useful in growing their business. But things that "might come in handy someday," or that used to be relevant, only become barriers, blocking access to the important information that makes you money. Space is at a premium, so keep it lean.

Julie's No-Brainer Toss List

- **Information you already know.** Articles that confirm your knowledge in an area are reassuring to read, but altogether unnecessary to keep. Save only new information that you can learn from.
- **Outdated vendor brochures**—unless you refer to them often and can't get updates. Remember the mantra "Keep the source (on your Rolodex), purge the paper."
- **Stationery you no longer use.** Keep only one or two sheets of each in a history file—toss the rest.
- **Old receipts, bank statements, auto records**—unless needed for tax purposes. Check with your accountant for retention guidelines (usually six years).
- **Early drafts of creative writing.** Some writers have a habit of referring to earlier drafts of a project they're working on until it's done—sometimes even afterward. Be honest with yourself. Save your earlier drafts only if you've ever gone back to them. If so, file earlier drafts chronologically behind the final version.

3. Assign a Home

- Use a deep cabinet or even a top bookshelf to store oversize binders, reference books, literature, and mailing envelopes.
- Place banking supplies in one drawer, telephone directories in another. Ideally, assign a different file drawer to each category of files, even if each category doesn't fully utilize the whole drawer. This will make retrieval easier and keep you focused on one topic at a time.
- Place items near each other based on your own associations. For example, I keep my client and marketing files side by side in the two top drawers of my filing cabinet because they are interconnected keys to my business. Stationery, envelopes, and paper supplies are best placed next to the printer (if you have one), or on your desk in trays.
- If you buy office supplies in bulk, keep an everyday supply in your main work area and store the excess in a closet or other location. If you tend to work for hours on end at your desk without a break, consider placing certain

items intentionally out of reach. Having to get up to get them will keep the muscles moving and blood flowing, and provide a nice change of pace. For example, consider how often you refer to your research library. If infrequently, store it elsewhere in the room, away from your desk, near a convenient chair and table. Several people I know deliberately place the fax machine on the other side of the room just to get themselves off their chairs once in a while.

• Keep floors clear to prevent tripping. Don't overload outlets. Keep computer and heavy equipment (paper cutters, craft machinery) out of reach of young children. Anchor shelves securely to the wall. One client spent a day organizing books and binders onto wall-mounted shelves only to wake up in the middle of the night to the sound of a huge crash when the shelves gave way under the weight. He spent the next three days cleaning up the wreckage.

4. Containerize

Home-based offices are the perfect place to get especially creative and expressive in your choice of containers. Without the restrictions of a corporate environment, you can use color, texture, and style to create a space you will love being in.

My Favorite Containers for Home Offices

• Plastic-coated, wire mesh, or pegboard wall grid—great for storing supplies and files; keeps them off your desk but still within easy reach.

• Rolling taboret—excellent for storing drafting or office supplies; wheels out of way or under desk when not in use (available from Reliable Home Office and Lillian Vernon).

• Portable file boxes—great for storing files on shelves to supplement or take the place of file cabinets; organize papers by category, giving each category a separately labeled box (e.g., "Insurance Claims," "Bill Paying," "Invoicing").

• Project boxes or literature sorters—attractive way to store papers on desktop by project; keeps them accessible, yet organized.

• Magazine racks—ideal for storing groups of files or periodicals neatly on shelves.

• Wire In/Out baskets—a must for organizing incoming and outgoing mail, as well as memos and daily reports.

• Desktop "pigeon-holer"—perfect for creating an elevated storage area above desktop to free work surface and keep supplies within easy reach.

• Fabric-enclosed shelving—great for storing supplies attractively (available from Hold Everything).

Project box or Literature Sorter. Great for creative people. Keeps projects accessible yet organized on desktop *(courtesy of Levenger Catalog)*.

• Stationery stacker—just the thing for organizing business stationery and literature on bookshelves or in a cabinet.

• Wall-mounted literature display—excellent for separating promotional clippings and literature to make assembling packets easy and know when supplies are running low.

• Galvanized boxes—attractive storage for CD-ROMS and diskettes.

5. Equalize

Nice job! You've created a custom-designed home office that expresses who you are and will be both comfortable and supportive in your work. Here's how to keep it that way:

• **Daily.** Set aside fifteen minutes at the end of each work day to put everything away, so your office will be tidy and ready for action when you come in the next morning. Doing it "when you have a free minute" is a recipe for never doing it at all.

• **Routine tune-ups.** Home businesses grow and change, especially those of entrepreneurs. Make sure your space stays current with the requirements of your operation by spending a half day to a day each year reevaluating your setup (especially your filing system), and updating it to reflect any shift in your goals and priorities. Add new files, delete irrelevant ones, and slim down travel and household files that have gotten too fat.

8

Cubicle Workstations

ANALYZE

1. What's Working?
Examples:

> "I stack oversized projects in the overhead bin. It keeps them off my desk until I'm ready to file them."
> —*Newspaper Reporter*

> "I have a different In box for each of my three bosses mounted on the wall. That makes it easier for me to assess what I really have to do, by person."
> —*Administrative Assistant*

2. What's Not Working?
Examples:

> "I have so much equipment on my desk, there is absolutely no room for paperwork. I end up doing work on my lap."
> —*Stockbroker*

> "With two bosses, I get deluged with a huge volume of mail, memos, letters to type, and assignments from each of them every day. It all gets mixed up, and I panic whenever I have to find anything."
> —*Administrative Assistant*

> "I can't get any quiet time to work or even put things away. People constantly interrupt me, just because there is no door. And they leave papers and memos for me everywhere—on my desk, my chair, my work in progress. Stuff gets lost here all the time."
> —*Insurance Department Manager*

3. What Items Are Most Essential to You?
Examples:

- **Alessandra A.,** a production assistant for two fashion magazine editors, needed places for sample beauty products, model agency books and portfolios, vendor files for photo shoots, forms and stationery, and separate In and Out boxes for her two bosses.
- **David R.,** an investigative reporter, needed places for his current stories (up to eight at a time), one year's worth of past scripts, files for sources and reference materials, and a hefty supply of steno pads, which he went through like wildfire.
- **Steve M.,** a stockbroker, needed places for his client activity log, client files, product files, two weeks' worth of financial reports, the daily newspapers, and his Rolodex.

4. Why Do You Want to Get Organized?
Examples:

- "Enjoy my job more."
- "Room to work!"
- "My boss's trust. The respect of my coworkers."
- "A clear head. The ability to concentrate on my work, instead of my piles of stuff."
- "Control over my information."
- "Handle the high-speed pace of the office better."
- "Less stress and worry about misplaced information."

5. What's Causing the Problems?
These are common causes of cubicle workstation clutter:

- **More stuff than storage space.** Let's face it, cubicles are compact workstations, leaving you very little room for excess. It's easy to accumulate more than will fit.
- **Inconvenient storage.** Cubicles are "one-size-fits-all," but your job may not fit the standard prototype. Most cubicles are designed primarily for computer usage with a limited amount of paper storage. If your job is paper-intensive and/or requires you to store a lot of equipment, supplies, or products (e.g., if you are in a computer support department), you will have trouble fitting your stuff to the space.
- **Uncooperative partners.** Working in a cubicle means you are working with and for other people. It is quite common to have disorganized bosses, coworkers, and even cubicle mates who keep ignoring or undoing your systems.

• **Speed of life/technology.** Working in a corporate, open environment usually goes hand in hand with short staffing, a fast pace, and constant interruptions that make it hard to find the time to get and stay organized.

STRATEGIZE

Plan Your Zones

The big plus of a cubicle workstation is that its "U" shape is already the ideal configuration for an efficient workspace, providing maximum work surface and storage within arm's reach. But you can still divide your workstation into zones, using various sections of the cubicle to reflect your various roles and responsibilities.

Some typical activity zones, supplies, and storage units for a cubicle might be as follows:

Activities	Supplies	Storage Units
Telephone	Card file	Desktop
	Message slips	
	Company directory	Desk drawer
	Telephone books	
Filing	Project files	Right file drawer
	Boss's files	Left file drawer
Supplies	Pens, pencils	Desk drawer
	Stapler, clips	
	Scissors	
	Calculator	
Reference	Policy manuals	Overhead bin
	Computer manuals	
	Dictionary	
	Thesaurus	
Personal items	Spare shoes	Under the desk
	Stuff to take home	
	Toothbrush & paste	Desk drawer
	Tea bags, sugar, mug	

Ideas for Stretching Space

• Use the area under your desk; most cubicles have enough room beneath for more than just your feet. Don't overlook and waste this invaluable, and versatile, option for expanding storage space. Large tubs will keep items organized.

INSIDER'S TIP

Sharing Cubicle Workspace

If another person will be using the cubicle, you might want to divide the workstation into two zones, one for each person, giving each his or her own drawers, shelves, and hooks. This will minimize confusion and potential loss of each other's files and supplies. If you share work, set up a Message Zone as well, with In/Out boxes for work-in-progress and memos to each other to simplify communication.

- Go vertical by adding shelves and trays to cubicle walls and area dividers.
- Use your desktop for storage; in fact, this is sometimes unavoidable. But if things are left out in the open on your desktop, employ products (see My Favorite Containers, below) that will preserve your desktop's neat and tidy appearance.

Estimate the Time

Here are some average times required for organizing a cubicle workstation:

HOW LONG WILL IT TAKE?

Attack
1. Sort   4 hours
2. Purge   1 hour
3. Assign a home   15 minutes
4. Containerize   2 hours
5. Equalize   10 minutes daily

ATTACK

1. Sort

The good news about a cubicle workstation is that you can't afford to be a packrat; its limited storage space virtually forces you to be selective about what you keep—a prime motivator in learning how to "work lean" and stay focused.

Be brutal in making your decisions. Space is at a premium; it simply doesn't allow holding on to anything that isn't essential and used.

Keep some personal items (photos of family and friends, artwork, poems, or stories from your kids; little inspirational quotes or treasures). Consolidate them in one area—a little "joy shelf" or corner—to personalize your cubicle.

Here's a list of possible ways of sorting to help you make your own associations.

Ways to Sort Papers

By function (human resources, finance, forms)
By action (projects vs. reference)
By supervisor or support staff

Ways to Sort Supplies

By category (paper, computer, phone)
By project
By work-related vs. personal

AVOIDING COMMON PITFALLS

Hoarding. Employees sometimes hoard files and documents in their cubicle just to be sure they have them when they need them. Being too lazy to go to the central filing room may be one explanation for this no-no behavior. But very often, especially in large companies, it's due to a lack of trust in how well the file room is organized and fear of losing these items. Look for ways to build your trust; keep a log of what you send there, and when, to make tracking and later retrieval easier.

Keeping duplicate supplies. Keep enough supplies in your cubicle to last two weeks, and mark your calendar when to reorder. Or check the central supply room weekly for stock status. This way, you'll never run short of anything at critical moments; you'll always be a week ahead in case stock has to be replenished.

---

2. Purge

To make room in your cubicle for the essential items, you need to get rid of what you don't need at your fingertips. Here are some ideas of what to do with the excess.

• Take older work home and store in a filing cabinet there. For example, an investigative reporter kept all his older manuscripts in his house in case he ever needed them again, reserving his cubicle for current work only.

• For papers such as memos, letters, and daily reports that you "may" refer to again "someday," log the title and source and keep them rather than the papers. Remember my Golden Rule: "Keep the source, toss the paper."

• Check your company's retention guidelines on what documents must be saved for tax or legal purposes and send "must-save" papers to central filing rather than holding on to them yourself.

Maximizing space with workflow rails
(courtesy of Details, a division of Steelcase)

Julie's "No-Brainer" Toss List

• **Dated reports**—especially if they are never referred to; request updates when needed.

• **Newspapers.** If more than a week old, they're ancient history. Make way for the latest editions and current news, which come in every day.

• **Magazines.** Toss if more than a year old; keep only a year's worth of any publication, unless it's part of a collection that you refer to often for business.

3. Assign a Home

• Everything in a cubicle is already within reach. But you can take further steps to enhance that. For example, if you have a printer in your cubicle, place stationery, envelopes, and related supplies right alongside it for added convenience.

• Use the overhead storage bin for bulky items such as binders, reference books, and audio- or videotapes.

• Place all active projects in the top drawer of your file cabinet and reference materials in the bottom one. (For more on filing, see Chapter 6.)

• Keep floors clear to prevent tripping. Don't overload electrical outlets.

4. Containerize

My Favorite Containers for Cubicles

• Workflow rails and slatboards—a handy way to add trays, shelves, and hooks to cubicle walls and area dividers for storage.

• Under-desk tubs—perfect for storing bulky projects, supplies, and personal items out of the way under a desk.

• Literature sorter—clever way to store papers from several projects neatly on the desktop for quick access (see illustration on page 101).

• Step files with classification folders—ideal for keeping current projects organized and at your fingertips.

• Self-standing file frame—great for adding a significant amount of file storage on your cubicle desktop.

• Hanging wall pockets—add storage without interfering with your work surface. Great for interoffice communication.

• In/Out mail boxes—a must for sorting incoming and outgoing mail, memos, and daily reports, especially if you have several bosses.

Labeling

This is especially important if you share the workspace with someone else so that *both* of you know where things go. The outside of many containers can be labeled without spoiling their looks or "busying up" the appearance of your cubicle. People expect to see a lot of external labeling in an office environment. Still, you may want to be more subtle with shelves by labeling surfaces rather than edges; with drawers, desk, and cabinets, label interior rather than exterior areas.

5. Equalize

Take a bow. Organized from the inside out, your cubicle work station is now a model of comfort, attractiveness, order, and efficiency. But keeping it that way requires constant vigilance, because it's easy to accumulate again more than this small space will hold. Follow this simple maintenance plan and your cubicle will always be a joy rather than a misery to work in. You'll never feel cramped and claustrophobic. You'll retain a certain amount of privacy, be more relaxed, and increase your productivity.

• **Daily.** Set aside ten minutes at the end of each day to put everything away so that you when you return in the morning, your space will be as ready for work as you are.

INSIDER'S TIP

Privacy and Cohabitation

Privacy is a paramount issue with cubicles, especially if they are shared. Here are some tricks that will help. Hang a DO NOT DISTURB sign on the entrance to your cubicle to prevent interruptions. If a project demands concentration, work on it in the quiet and solitude of the company library. Speak in a low voice when on the phone to cue coworkers to respect your need for quiet and to respect their need for the same thing. If the desk is shared, use an IN PROGRESS wall pocket or bin to communicate project status to each other. And select a desk chair that is easily adjustable, so you can each be comfortable.

• **Ongoing.** The people who are most successful at keeping their workstations consistently well organized develop a habit of purging brutally at the end of each week. Set aside thirty minutes or so on a Friday to toss out any reports and publications that will be old news by Monday; collect all pulled files you're done with and return them to central storage at this time.

• **Routine tune-ups.** Because their tight quarters leave no room for excess, and because roles and responsibilities change constantly in large organizations, cubicle workers need to monitor and adjust their systems more frequently than their counterparts in traditional or home-based offices. Every three months, take a couple of hours to reevaluate your use of the space and what you need places for. A temporary responsibility may have become permanent, the items associated with it now requiring a permanent home in your cubicle. Review what other new company developments may require a tune-up of your system. For example: Has there been a change in personnel? Do you have a new boss? Are you now sharing your workstation with someone else?

9

Mobile Offices

ANALYZE

1. What's Working?
Examples:

> "Whenever I have a trip coming up, I start a file into which I throw every-
> thing related to the trip—itinerary, airline tickets, meeting agendas,
> papers I will need. This prevents last-minute gathering and panic."
>
> —*Corporate Lawyer*

> "I keep all my names and addresses on a small electronic organizer.
> It's lightweight, portable, and helps me stay in touch with colleagues,
> clients, and friends—even if they forget to leave their return number on
> my voice-mail!"
>
> —*Salesman*

What's Not Working?
Examples:

> "I live in such mortal fear that I'll leave for a trip without some critical
> file or document that I start assembling papers three days beforehand in
> order not to overlook anything. My desk ends up a mess."
>
> —*Political Director*

> "I travel every week and am home just one or two days at a time. When
> I'm home, I'm always overwhelmed by the amount of mail I have to sort
> through and the list of chores I have to catch up on. I never have time
> for my family or social life."
>
> —*TV Producer*

> "The real challenge is figuring out how to work out of such small, tight
> spaces (car, airport terminals, airplanes, hotel rooms). With no desk or

filing cabinet, I'm always scrambling for a comfortable place for myself, trying to work as compactly as possible." —*Consultant*

3. What Items Are Most Essential to You?

• **Mike M.,** a national accounts manager for a major manufacturer, needed places for travel documents (itinerary and ticket, passport, travel ID, money, checks, credit cards, business cards, receipt envelopes, expense reports), phone calls and appointments (calling card, cell phone and beeper, important phone numbers, calendar), supplies (writing pads, stationery, note cards, envelopes, stamps, mailing labels, pens, pencils, paper clips, Post-it Notes, mini stapler).

• **Sarah T.,** an author and speaker, needed places for work papers (client or project files, reading materials, paper and literature collected on the road, other people's business cards), presentation materials (literature, samples, reference binders and books, flip chart, markers, overheads).

• **Susan L.,** a salesperson for a computer software firm, needed places for slide equipment, computer and cables, tape recorder, Walkman and tapes, alarm clock, clothing (business, evening, and casual attire and shoes; exercise wear and sneakers; sleepwear, underwear, socks, pantyhose, swimwear, toiletries, medicines), emergency supplies (flashlight and batteries, jumper cables, road flares, spare tire and jack, bottle of water, snack foods in case of getting stuck on the road, spare underwear, blouse, and pantyhose).

4. Why Do You Want to Get Organized?
Examples:

• "Reduce my stress and frustration level during business trips because I'll be more in control of what I'm bringing, and know it'll be with me when I get there."

• "Save time packing and unpacking, which currently takes too long."

• "Improve my posttrip follow-up, which is currently sloppy because I forget to unpack my bags and lose notes to myself regarding calls and letters to write."

• "Avoid the embarrassment of missed flights, appointments, and being late for meetings due to not knowing where to be, when, and how to get there."

5. What's Causing the Problems?
These are common causes of mobile office clutter:

• **More stuff than storage space.** Obviously, the most common cause of travel clutter is overpacking—bringing far more stuff than your suitcases will handle. Pockets and suitcases wind up overstuffed and jammed.

• **Items have no home.** People often pack in a haphazard fashion, placing the items they carry with them in a different place of their suitcase, or car, or briefcase each time. This approach makes it very hard to know at a glance if you have everything you need with you.

• **Inconvenient storage.** Often, mobile professionals purchase or use suitcases or briefcases without first thinking through what they have to store; as a result, they end up with a storage unit of inadequate size, configuration, and space for their items.

STRATEGIZE

Plan Your Zones

People who work out of a suitcase need to set up zones more compactly than others because they're always on the move. There's no going back to get something you need once you're in the air, on the train, or halfway to your destination in the car. Let's look at some typical zones, supplies, and storage units for a mobile office, and how they might be stored for air/train travel and car travel.

AIR-TRAIN TRAVEL

Activities	Supplies	Storage Units
Work	Client or project files Laptop computer Reading materials Literature collected Business cards collected	Briefcase
Phone	Cell phone Beeper Calling card Important phone numbers Calendar	Coat pocket
Presentation & selling	Sales literature Samples Reference binders Flip chart & markers Overheads Slides	Tote bag
Dressing	Clothing Toiletries Shoes Coats	Roll-on bag Toiletries bag

CAR TRAVEL

Activities	Supplies	Storage Units
Work	Client or project files	File bin on front seat
	Laptop computer	
	Reading materials	Briefcase
	Literature collected	
	Business cards collected	
Phone	Cell phone	Briefcase
	Beeper	
	Calling card	
	Important phone numbers	
	Calendar	
Presentation & selling	Sales literature	Trunk bin
	Samples	
	Reference binders	
	Flip chart & markers	
	Overheads	
	Slides	
Dressing	Clothing	Garment bag
	Toiletries	Toiletries bag
	Shoes	
	Coats	Back seat

Ideas for Stretching Space

The best way for mobile professionals to stretch space is to learn to travel light.

Tips for Traveling Light

• If you have a laptop computer, store as much important information on disk or hard drive as possible, limiting your hard copy needs to the essentials (contracts, sales literature).

• Ship heavy presentation materials directly to your hotel or meeting site, rather than carrying them with you.

• Carry preprinted labels and envelopes for shipping processed paperwork and mail back to your office. Use a tape recorder to dictate responses to letters, and mail the cassettes back to your assistant for completion.

• Limit your travel wardrobe to one or two basic colors (e.g., black and white). Everything will match, stretching your wardrobe for days and making packing a breeze. Periodically add a couple of colorful pieces or accessories for variety.

• Take along travel-size versions of your favorite toiletries and leave the large sizes home, unless you'll be away for an extended period.

• Before packing a blow dryer, iron, or steamer, call ahead to find out whether the hotel offers such amenities.

• Carry just the essentials in your wallet: driver's license, one credit card, telephone calling card, ATM card, an index card with all your frequent flyer numbers on it. This is safer, too!

• Develop a packing checklist. If you travel extensively, come up with a couple of versions for different types of trips (overnight vs. three to seven days; hot climate vs. cold climate, etc.).

Estimate the Time

Here are some average times required for organizing a mobile office:

HOW LONG WILL IT TAKE?

Attack

1.	Sort	3 hours
2.	Purge	1 hour
3.	Assign a home	1 hour
4.	Containerize	2 hours
5.	Equalize	30 minutes at end of each trip

ATTACK

1. Sort

Mobile offices force you to be more selective about how you sort through and group your items than almost any other organizing situation because you simply can't afford to be a traveling caravan on a plane or train, or in an automobile. Here's a list of possible ways of sorting to help you make your own associations.

Ways to Sort Paperwork

By client account
By chronology of events during trip
By territory or location

Or you can divide in the following ways:

Trip-related work
Non-trip-related work
Reading
Project vs. action files
Work to do on the plane
Work to do in meetings

Ways to Sort Literature

By product category
By size and bulkiness
Alphabetically
By client type

Ways to Sort Clothing

By event
By outfit
By casual vs. work vs. workout wear
By clean vs. dirty
By outer garments vs. undergarments vs. accessories
By hanging vs. folded items vs. loose items

Ways to Sort Toiletries

By category (dental; hair care; bathing and washing; cosmetics; perfumes)
By size and weight
By critical (in purse) vs. regular (in suitcase)
By fragile vs. durable

Ways to Sort Equipment

By category:

Computer
Communication
Presentation

Ways to Sort Travel Documents

By category:

Files
Tickets and itineraries
Credit cards
Passports
Money

Ways to Group Supplies

By category:

Writing supplies
Computer supplies

AVOIDING COMMON PITFALLS

Organize your home office. Part of the key to staying organized on the road involves having your home office organized too. Plan to attack your home office after completing your mobile office, so that one system supports the other.

Attack what's visible first. Many mobile professionals have an intimidating collection of bags and cases stuffed away full of items they never unpacked from previous trips. Plan to tackle each of these after you have cleaned out your main suitcases and car. It is important not to skip these, but it will be easier to sort through them once you have a sense of what your system will look like.

---

2. Purge

For mobile office professionals, this involves cleaning out excess items that are not being used and that have accumulated in your car, suitcases, and briefcases, as well as deciding what you will *not* bring on trips. You want to travel lightly and comfortably.

Julie's No-Brainer Toss List

- **Literature or sales books**—if they're dated, mangled, torn, or stained.
- **Supplies, samples, and presentation materials**—if they're never used.
- **Old reading material**—if it's gone unread for at least six months.
- **Files from previous meetings**—if you never unpacked or pulled them out after the meetings.

• **Toiletries**—if they've been hanging around for a while unused, you probably never will use them.

INSIDER'S TIP

Using Travel Time Productively

Mobile professionals often say they get their best work done while they are on the road, away from the constant interruptions from the telephone, clients, and colleagues. Select the best work for you to do on the road based on your own habits, workstyle, and response to the travel environment. Mike M. packs low-level work to do on planes because he finds the constant interruptions of flight attendants and plane announcements distracting. Sherri G. easily tunes those interruptions out and brings her most difficult work to do on planes; being away from telephone allows her to concentrate, and she uses the flight time as a built-in deadline to complete her work.

Other ideas for work to do while traveling:
• Clean out your briefcase (or purse) between departures while waiting in the terminal. One client of mine stations herself next to a big trash can between flights and tosses all her used notepads, crumpled napkins, broken pens, and read magazines and reports into it. When she reaches her destination and opens her briefcase, it's immaculately organized.
• Take along a reading file for catching up on the latest news and information about your business or industry.
• You can hone many a skill by listening to seminars and educational books on tape related to your field while driving. Keep a tape recorder handy for making verbal notes as you listen. Then send the cassette to your assistant for transcribing so you'll be able to take action when you get back to the office.
• Keep a folder or large manila envelope stocked with writing supplies (stationery, note cards, envelopes, stamps, greeting cards), and catch up on old correspondence and thank-you notes on the plane or train. Mail when you arrive.
• Use your calendar/planner to record all your "to-do's" and phone messages. Avoid having to rewrite or transfer information by using the same calendar/planner at home as on the road.

---

3. Assign a Home
For mobile professionals, the value of creating a regular, consistent home in your bags or car for each of your items cannot be underestimated. It will:

• Dramatically speed packing and unpacking.
• Allow you to do a quick visual check to see if you have everything with you, and instantly get your hands on anything you need at any time during your trip.

- Boost your sense of control and confidence when you travel.
- Increase your safety on the road. Fumbling and looking disorganized or distracted while traveling can set you up as a target for crime. For example, I have a narrow pocket in my briefcase in which I always store my ticket and itinerary, while I keep my identification conveniently stored in a small card case in my wallet. As I slide up to the gate, I can pull out the ticket and my identification quickly and easily, without any fuss or worry.

Use the following guidelines to plan which items you want to store where. Naturally, you need to make decisions based on your own habits, associations, physical needs, and comfort.

Plane/Train Travel

- Jacket pocket or purse—items you need to keep most accessible and secure (e.g., money, identification, business cards, keys, beeper, itinerary).
- Briefcase—work-related items you need at your fingertips throughout the trip (e.g., laptop, files, calendar, reading material, directions and maps, writing supplies).
- Secondary carry-on tote—work-related or personal items that are too bulky for your briefcase, and that you can't risk losing in transit if your check-in luggage gets mislaid (e.g., presentation materials or props, books, running shoes, water bottle, snacks, travel pillow, emergency supplies such as toothbrush, cologne, spare underwear, or hose). On his way to a sales call with a major prospect, one client stopped to fill his gas tank, and as he pulled the nozzle out, gasoline poured onto his pants and shoe. After a twenty-minute jog in the freezing cold trying to air himself out, he entered the client's building, praying the odor had finally dissipated. The receptionist sniffed at the air curiously and asked if he smelled lighter fluid. Would that he had had a spare set of clothes and shoes in his car!
- Main luggage (check-in or carry-on)—items you could function without, or easily replace, if they got lost (e.g., clothes, shoes, underwear, socks, workout clothes, toiletries, spare collapsible tote, laundry bag).
- Cosmetics and toiletry bags—small items for grooming (e.g., cologne, shaving gear, cosmetics, deodorant, shampoo, soaps, first aid). Assign a separate compartment of your toiletry or cosmetic bags to each category, rather than dumping them together. Keep bags prepacked to avoid rush assembly. Buy duplicates of regular toiletries and cosmetics and keep them with your luggage along with an inventory of contents, including "perishables" to be added at the last minute (e.g., prescription medicines, vitamins, current nail polish). If you travel extensively, keep two versions: one with travel-size toiletries for short trips; another with full-size toiletries for long trips.

Auto Travel

To transform your car into an efficient mobile office, George Phirripidus, president of the Mobile Outfitter, suggests you think of the interior as your desk and the trunk as your file and supply room.

• Front passenger seat—desktop work items requiring quick, frequent, easy access (e.g., laptop, tape recorder, calendar or planner, client files).
• Glove compartment—vehicle identification and maintenance documents/ items (e.g., registration, insurance card, maintenance records, disposable camera and accident report, flashlight).
• Door pocket—narrow, flat items you need handy (e.g., maps, receipt envelope, notepads and pens).
• Storage well—bulky work-related and personal items you need handy (e.g., music and educational tapes, cell phone, handiwipes or napkins). Don't place heavy items in the back seat if you'll need access to them while driving. Twisting to retrieve can cause back problems, as well as accidents.
• Back seat—fragile or delicate items that might get damaged in the car trunk (e.g., presentation materials, clothing on hangers).
• Trunk—items you don't need access to while driving (e.g., bulk files, samples and reference books, literature, promotional materials, props, clothing).

INSIDER'S TIP

As soon as you arrive at your hotel room, take fifteen minutes to unpack and assign homes to everything you've brought with you. In this way you'll keep your hotel room organized too. Here's how:

• Set up zones in your hotel room. Some suggestions: Dressing Zone, Grooming Zone, Work Zone, Supply Zone, Suitcase Zone, Eating Zone.
• Make it a habit to assign your room key the same section of your handbag or briefcase every time you go in or out; you'll always find it. For example, I usually keep it in the same pocket of my handbag where I store my house keys—the logical, natural place for me to look.

---

4. Containerize

My Favorite Containers for Mobile Professionals

• Expandable briefcase—just the thing if you expect to come home with more paperwork than you took with you.
• Portable CD and diskette holders—leather or plastic envelopes for organizing and protecting data on the road.

- Expandable file—perfect for organizing paperwork chronologically, by meeting, when traveling.
- Personal digital assistants (PDAs)—lightweight, slim alternative to bulky day planners, which can be impractical for traveling. Allows you to electronically manage appointments, "to-do's," phone numbers. PDAs like the Palm Pilot Professional allow for e-mail. You must be comfortable with digital interfaces to use these, however.
- Preprinted receipt envelope—easy way to track expenses as you go and be ready to submit your expense report as soon as you return home (Day Runners makes a great one).
- Portable file boxes—great for organizing files, samples, and product books in the trunk of your car. Use Velcro strips on the bottom of containers to keep them from sliding around as you drive.
- Auto-desk—transforms the front seat of your car into a convenient work surface for papers, laptop, and supplies (available from Newell).
- Trunk organizer—Clever way to store a variety of materials in the trunk of your car—especially good for traveling salespeople.
- Plastic file folders—ideal for preventing paperwork stored in briefcase from bending, tearing, or spilling; they're indestructible.
- Cellular phone mount—perfect for safer, hands-free operation while driving.
- Notebook computer clip-on light and computer privacy screen—discreetly illuminates keyboard on planes so you won't disturb passengers sleeping next to you.
- Leather sleeve and collapsible tote—a great supplement to your briefcase for use on location so you don't have to lug the entire briefcase to every meeting.
- Bumper clothing protector—a plastic sheet that attaches to the bumper of your car; great for keeping you clean while packing and taking things out of the trunk.
- Laptop backpack—a custom backpack for carrying your laptop; distributes weight evenly, prevents back strain.
- Multiple-pocket toiletries case—just hang it on the hook of the bathroom door in your hotel and eliminate the need to need to pack and unpack these items. Note: The Mobile Office Catalog specializes in products for mobile professionals.

Labeling

Attach labeled key tags to zippers to indicate contents. Or place a note in each pocket of your suitcase to identify what goes inside.

5. Equalize

Now that you've got your mobile office beautifully under control, here's how to keep it that way:

• **Daily.** As with any office, it's important to set aside fifteen minutes at the end of each day to straighten things up and get yourself ready for the next day. While on the road, this is doubly important because you'll likely be handling a huge volume of papers, phone messages, information requests, and e-mail accumulated during your trip. So set aside thirty minutes daily to sort and purge.

• **Ongoing.** Check voice-mail and respond to what you can from the road. Use e-mail to stay connected and keep projects moving forward while you're away. Make arrangements to have your assistant sort all your mail so that when you get back the stacks will be less intimidating to tackle. Be realistic about your need for "reentry time" and schedule one or two hours minimum to get caught up. But if you travel extensively, have your assistant send your mail and paperwork to you so you can stay on top of it. While on the road, if you discover you've either omitted an item from your packing list or included something unnecessary, revise your list then and there. Don't wait until you start packing for the next trip, when it will be almost impossible to remember the changes you want to make. Immediately upon your return home, unpack your briefcase and bags and replenish any supplies used up while you were away. This will enable you to continue working seamlessly, and shorten your prep time for the next trip.

• **Regular tune-ups.** Keep a tight control on clutter by cleaning out your briefcase and car (trunk as well as interior) on a monthly basis, purging any dated literature, materials, useless supplies, toiletries, and files.

INSIDER'S TIP

Staying in Control at Conventions

Do you always come home from conventions with tons of notes and ideas that never get unpacked or used? That's because conventions are magnets for unnecessary paper accumulation if you don't define up front your goals for going there. Stay focused by attending only those seminars and gatherings that will help you achieve your convention goals, whether you're there to network, meet people with a shared interest, or gain knowledge about specific topics. When people give you their business cards, write a memory jogger on the back to help you remember them (e.g., "tall redheaded guy with a funny laugh") plus any follow-up action you want to take (e.g., call, write thank-you, send literature), and give cards a special place in your briefcase for the return trip home. Use your flight time to summarize on a sheet of paper the hot ideas gleaned from the convention that you intend to implement when you get back, and place it in a "Golden Nuggets" file (see Chapter 7) as soon as you arrive.

10

Household Information Centers

ANALYZE

1. What's Working?
Examples:

> "I keep tickets to concerts and sporting events in the top drawer of my buffet because I know I'll always find them there." —*Bruce C.*

> "I store all my tax receipts in a pocket file because I don't have many and it's easy to store away. Plus the sides on the file folder keep the little receipts from falling out." —*Risa S.*

2. What's Not Working?
Examples:

> "What to do with all this paper! My kitchen counter is covered with stuff from my kid's school, invitations, mail, bills, you name it. When it's time to eat, I throw it all in bags to clear space and never look at it again." —*Alice L.*

> "I never pay bills on time. I don't even know where they are half the time. I am constantly paying late fees and finance charges." —*Libby C.*

> "It's so hard to know what to keep and what to throw out. So I save everything. Paper has taken over my house!" —*Sharon L.*

> "I save a lot of articles and recipes for future reference. But I can never find them when I need them." —*Martha G.*

3. What Items Are Most Essential to You?
Examples:

- **Joan K.,** mother of three, needed places for household bills and receipts; school records; financial records; important family documents; correspondence with friends; travel information; and topic files on parenting, entertaining, and self-improvement.
- **David P.,** retiree, needed places for bills and receipts; tax records; bank statements; investment statements; real estate documents; medical records; stationery, stamps, and envelopes; and travel ideas and literature.
- **Janice and John R.,** a married couple, needed places for banking and investment information, bills to pay and payment receipts, appliance records and warranties, art purchase records, telephone numbers, and take-out menus.

4. Why Do You Want to Get Organized?
Examples:

- "Pay bills on time. Stop wasting money on late fees and finance charges."
- "Regain the use of my dining room table!"
- "Reduce tension caused by all that hideous paper cluttering everything!"
- "Feel more in control instead of always anxious that I'm forgetting something!"
- "Save time and eliminate stress searching for misplaced papers and documents."

5. What's Causing the Problems?
These are common causes of household paper clutter:

- **Items have no home.** Because most people hate dealing with household papers, they seldom consider setting aside a specific location in their home to do so. As a result, important papers wind up scattered all over the house: piled on kitchen counters, dining room tables, or the floor beside the bed.
- **Dislike the space.** Equally common, and the result of similar resistance, is setting up a space for doing paperwork in a room or area of your home that is as off-putting as the job itself. For example, one of my clients created a study for doing her paperwork, but it was so dark and dreary that she always wound up sorting her mail and paying her bills in bed so that she could watch TV at the same time. As a result, her study turned into a catch-all, and her bedside table was littered with stacks of papers. The solution was to organize and redecorate her study so that it would be as pleasurable to use as her bedroom.

• **Out of sight, out of mind.** People who do not know how to set up a reliable filing system for handling household papers will tend to leave bills and other critical documents out in the open as "to-do" reminders. The impulse is honorable, but the result is usually failure because these visual cues eventually get stacked on top of one another, lost, or forgotten. The solution is to create a system you can trust with a place for everything.

STRATEGIZE

Whether you're married or single, live in an apartment or a house, work from home or elsewhere, every household requires its own little information hub, an actual spot for handling all the paper and information related to daily living, e.g., phone messages, shopping lists, flyers from school and community organizations, and household bills.

Pick a central location where you and everyone else in the household naturally gravitate, spend a lot of time, always dump the mail, make phone calls, etc. Wherever you choose—the kitchen, dining room, or a place near the front door—you'll need a work surface (for writing letters, paying bills, signing forms), file storage (a file drawer or portable file boxes on a shelf), and a supply drawer or basket (for stamps, stapler, scissors, paper clips, Scotch tape).

Plan Your Zones

Sometimes people like to do certain kinds of household paperwork in one area of the house and other kinds in a different area. For example, you may prefer doing all family record keeping and making phone calls from the kitchen, but like paying bills and doing tax-related work in your bedroom, where it is more private. This is fine, as long as you assign a specific paperwork activity to a specific room or area (workstation) in your home and stick to it. Scattering all kinds of paperwork all over the house without pattern, focus, or distinction will make it extremely difficult to know where any given piece of paper is at any given time.

Here are some typical activity zones, supplies, and storage units for a household information center located in a kitchen.

Activities	Supplies	Storage Unit
Mail & paper flow	Mail In box	Kitchen counter
	Mail Out box	(far end)
	Invitations	
	School papers to sign	
	Stationery & notecards	Kitchen drawer

Activities	Supplies	Storage Unit
Bill paying	Bills to pay	Kitchen cabinet
	Credit card & bank statements	
	Catalogs	
	Envelopes, labels, stamps	
	Calculator, pens, Post-its, stapler	
Insurance claims	Medical bills to submit	Kitchen cabinet
	Insurance claim forms	
	Claims pending	
	Claims completed	
Messages & calendar	Telephone	Kitchen wall
	Message pads or board	
	Shopping lists	
	Telephone directories	Kitchen drawer
	Family or personal calendar	Kitchen wall
	Cultural events/ brochures	
	School calendars	
	Tickets to events	
	Directions and maps	
Filing & record keeping	Financial records	Filing cabinet
	Tax records	
	Medical records	
	Vital documents	
	Travel information	
	Memorabilia	
	Hobbies & interests	
Meal planning	Cookbooks	Kitchen shelf
	Cooking magazines	
	Recipe file	Card box

Tips on Rearranging Furniture

• If your household information center is located in the kitchen, it is unlikely that there will be any furniture to move around. However, you may need to empty out a cabinet and a drawer or two for storing relevant supplies.

• Consider mounting a shelf on the wall for cookbooks or In/Out boxes for family mail.

• Use nearby shelves or countertops to store papers (see section on my favorite containers) if space won't permit a file cabinet.

• Hang family calendar and message board on the back of the kitchen door to save space.

• If you plan to do your paperwork in the bedroom, use a two-drawer filing cabinet covered by an attractive fabric cover for double-duty as a bedside table.

• If the location is the dining room, consider using the drawers and cabinet space of a breakfront or buffet for papers and supplies.

• Allow enough clearance in front of file cabinets to fully open drawers and access contents (36–39").

• If you have a spare room where you're setting up your home information center, make it as attractive as possible with lighting, plants, artwork, and pictures, so that it will be a space you'll enjoy using. Otherwise, those bills may never get paid!

Estimate the Time

Here are some average times required for setting up a household information center:

HOW LONG WILL IT TAKE?

Attack

1. Sort	4 hours
2. Purge	4 hours
3. Assign a home	2 hours
4. Containerize	6 hours
5. Equalize	15 minutes

ATTACK

1. Sort

AVOIDING COMMON PITFALLS

The likelihood is that you have papers piled in various locations around the house. Don't start by cleaning the papers out of those remote spaces or you'll burn yourself out quickly. Start with the space where you've decided to locate your home information center, and organize that; after one or two sessions, your center will be functional, and you'll be ready to transfer papers from those other rooms after sorting and purging.

Ways to Sort Papers

By category (financial, vital records, travel, etc.)
By person (medical records—John's, medical records—Mary's)
By storage location (home, archive, safe deposit box)

Ways to Sort Recipes

By category (appetizers, soups, low-fat, company, etc.)
By tried vs. may try

Ways to Sort Photos

By year
By event or trip
By person

Here's how one of my clients categorized her household paper files (and what she put in them). Stay away from "Miscellaneous" as a category. It will be too tempting to use, and make retrieval almost impossible because *no one* ever remembers what "Miscellaneous" refers to after the fact.

Financial	Vital Records	Lifestyle
Accountant	Adoption records	Address lists
Bank statements (by account)	Automobile records	Books & tapes
	Birth certificates	Church or synagogue
Bills to pay	Credit report	Classes
Credit card statements	Death certificates	Correspondence
Financial consultant & information	Divorce decrees	Decorating ideas
	Educational records (by person)	Directions & maps
Financial statements		Entertaining
Investment records	Résumé	Events calendars
Loan agreements & payment books	Employment information (by person)	Fitness
		Gift ideas
Pay stubs	Household inventory	Hobbies
Pension plan records	Insurance records (by type)	Humor
Property (by location)		Memorabilia (by person)
Receipts	Legal records	Past calendars
Appliances	Marriage certificate	Pets
Art & antiques	Medical records (by person)	Recipes
Collectibles		Restaurants
Clothing	Military records (by person)	Self-improvement
Furniture		Travel—day trips
Home improvements	Power of attorney	Weekends
Household repairs	Religious records	

Financial	Vital Records	Lifestyle
Social Security	Religious records	Vacations
Tax records & receipts	Safe deposit box	Frequent flyer
Returns	inventory	Volunteer work
Warranties & service	Storage inventory	
contracts	Vital documents map	
	(see Insider's Tip on	
	page 132)	
	Will	

2. Purge

The big question people always ask me is, "How long should I keep certain papers?" It is imperative that you check with your accountant and/or lawyer before throwing out any financial or legal papers, because they know most about your individual situation. That said, here's a general guide of what to keep and for how long, adapted from Barbara Hemphill's *Taming the Paper Tiger.*

• **Automobile records** (titles, registration, repairs)—for as long as you own the vehicle(s).

• **Appointment books (past)**—1–10 years, according to your comfort level and whether you use them for tax records, reference, or memorabilia.

• **ATM slips**—maximum six years if needed for tax purposes.

• **Bank statements**—maximum six years if needed for tax purposes.

• **Credit card statements**—maximum six years if tax-related purchases on statements; otherwise, until annual interest statement is issued by company.

• **Catalogs & magazines**—until the next issue.

• **Dividend payment records**—until annual statement is supplied by company, then just annual statements.

• **Household inventory & appraisal**—as long as current.

• **Insurance policies** (auto, homeowners, liability)—as long as statute of limitations in the event of late claims.

• **Insurance policies** (disability, medical, life, personal property, umbrella)— as long as you own.

• **Investments** (purchase records)—as long as you own.

• **Investments** (sales records)—maximum six years for tax purposes.

• **Mortgage or loan discharge**—as long as you own, or six years after discharge.

• **Property bill of purchase**—as long as you own the property.

- **Receipts:**

  Appliances—as long as you own item.

  Art, antiques, collectibles—as long as you own item.

  Clothing—for the length of the returns period, unless tracking household budget.

  Credit card slips—until statement comes and you can match purchases.

  Furniture—as long as you own item, in case repair is needed.

  Home improvements—as long as you own home, or six years after sale.

  Household repairs—for life of warranty, or longer to track reliability record of service people and their rates.

  Major purchases—life of item.

  Medical and tax-related—maximum six years.

  Rent—your canceled check is sufficient.

  Utility bills—current bill and one previous year's to check billing patterns.

  Warranties and instructions—life of warranty or item. Stick label with warranty expiration date and service repair number on bottom of appliance. If something breaks down, you've got an easy way to check if the item's still covered without even having to go to your file drawer.

- **Résumé**—as long as current.
- **Safe deposit box key & inventory**—as long as current.
- **Tax records** (bank statements and canceled checks, certificates of deposit, contracts, charitable contributions, credit statements, income tax returns, lease and loan agreements, loan payment books, pension plan records, pay stubs)—current year, plus six prior years.
- **Vital records** (adoption papers, birth & death certificates, citizenship papers, copyrights/patents, marriage certificate, divorce decree, letter of "last instructions" to executor or heirs, medical illness and vaccination records, passports, power of attorney, Social Security records, wills)—permanently.

Julie's No-Brainer Toss List

- **Junk mail.**
- **Expired coupons.**
- **Outdated schedules.**
- **Old greeting cards**—unless they contain a very special message.
- **Old grocery receipts.**
- **Invitations** to past events.

- **Expired warranties and service contracts.**
- **Instructions** for items you no longer own.
- **Expired insurance policies.**
- **Unread magazines**—if they're more than three months old.
- **Old catalogs**—keep only the current one.
- **Investment and banking brochures you never read.**
- **Canceled checks**—unless needed for tax purposes.
- **Checkbooks**—if they're more than six years old, or the account has been canceled.
- **Receipts for non-tax-deductible items.**
- **Business cards** from people whose names you don't recognize.
- **Old tourist brochures** from past vacations.
- **Road maps** you haven't referred to in ten years.
- **Solicitations** from charities you don't intend to give to.
- **Recipes** you haven't tried in five years.
- **Bad quality photos** or ones you simply don't like.
- **Articles or clippings** you haven't reread in more than five years.

INSIDER'S TIP

Feel guilty about tossing all those solicitations from charities you can't always afford to give to even though you wish you could? A student in one of my workshops had a wonderful method for handling this. She'd save up mailings from charities she was considering in a file called "Annual Giving." Then, once a year, on her birthday, she'd go through the file, pick three charities, and write checks to them as a guilt-assuaging gift to herself.

---

3. Assign a Home

- If you will be using a file cabinet, assign each group of papers a specific drawer or section of a drawer. Place the group you use most frequently (for example, "Financial Papers") in the top drawer for convenient access.
- No room to put a filing cabinet within easy reach in the space where you want to do paperwork? Give yourself the mobility to do your paperwork anywhere you like, make it easy to put papers away, and focus your energy on one task at a time by storing household papers in a set of portable files boxes (see section on my favorite containers) on a shelf. Assign one category of papers to each box.
- Use the tab positions of file folders to convey meaning, and track the status/flow of items. (For more on the use of tabs as visual cues, see Chapter 6.) For example:

Bill-Paying Box

- Bills due 1–15 of month (left tab)
- Bills due 16–31 of month
    - Credit card accounts (one for each) (center tab)
    - Bank accounts (one for each)
        - Receipts: (right tab)
        Appliances
        Auto
        Clothing
        Food
        Rent

Insurance Claims Box

- Blank claim forms (left tab)
- Bills to submit
    - Submitted, pending, primary carrier (center tab)
    - Submitted, pending, secondary carrier
        - Claims processed, balance owed to doctor (right tab)
        - Claims completed (eventually this folder should go into your tax records)

Vacation Planning Box

- Frequent flyer (by airline) (left tab)
- Travel coupons
    - Trip ideas: (center tab)
    - Day trips
    - Weekend trips
    - Adventure travel
    - Spa vacations
        - Trips taken: (right tab)
        France
        California

• If you use a safe deposit box, here's what to put in it. Except where noted, all documents should be originals; keep copies of each in your household information center files.

Adoption papers
Automobile title of ownership

Birth certificates
Citizenship papers
Copies of wills (keep the original with the county registrar of wills)
List of credit card accounts and numbers
Death certificates
Deeds & mortgage papers
Divorce decrees
Family historical information and negatives of important photos
Household inventory & appraisals (include negatives of pictures and/or
    videotapes)
Important contracts
Investment certificates
Leases
Life insurance policies
List of bank account numbers
List of insurance policy names and numbers
Marriage certificate
Military records
Passports
Patents and copyrights
Retirement plan information
Stock and bond certificates
Vital documents "map" (see following Insider's Tip)

INSIDER'S TIP

Create a Vital Documents "Map"

A vital documents "map" is an index of all your most important records so that you will be able to reconstruct them easily in the event of emergency—if you lose your wallet; your records are destroyed in a fire or natural disaster; something happens to you and your family needs to know where everything is kept. Photocopy each important piece of identification in your wallet and keep in your "Vital Documents Map" file. In addition, make a list of all your vital documents and financial records, where they're stored, plus contact names and numbers for replacing them in case of a disaster, and store in your safe deposit box. Keep another copy of this list in a plastic sleeve in your "Vital Documents Map" file at home, and send another copy to your attorney, a friend, or a distant family member since a fire, earthquake, or flood could destroy your records at home as well as at the bank where your safe deposit box is stored.

SECRETS OF A PROFESSIONAL ORGANIZER

Create a Rotating Six-Year Tax File

To conveniently archive all tax-related documents, outfit a banker's box with six box-bottom file folders labeled Years 1 through 6 (rather than by the year itself) to avoid having to relabel annually. Keep last year's tax records and related receipts in the Year 1 folder, the previous year's records in Year 2, and so on. At the end of each year, toss the contents of the bottom folder (Year 6), move each set of records back one folder, and put the records from the year just ended into Year 1. Tuck this box in the back of a closet or up in the attic. If ever the tax man cometh, you'll be ready.

---

4. Containerize

My Favorite Containers for Household Paper

• Wooden two-drawer filing cabinets—usually the perfect size for household papers. Seek attractive, wood designs; cheap metal filing cabinets bend and rust easily, and will make filing too difficult.

• Portable file boxes—a perfect alternative if you have no space for a file cabinet. They come in plastic, rattan, wicker, and galvanized steel, and easily fit on any shelf.

• Hanging pocket file—excellent for use as a tickler file on the wall, especially for visual types who suffer from the "out of sight, out of mind" syndrome (E-Z Pocket makes a popular one).

• Wood and wicker basket drawers—an effective way to store office supplies on a countertop or bureau without creating visual clutter.

• Letter trays—an attractive tool for sorting mail and messages by person in an entryway, desk, or countertop location; they come in rattan, wood, wicker, mesh, and steel.

• Wicker or wire telephone and answering machine stand—a wonderful space saver.

• Paper-covered boxes—an attractive way to sort and store receipts, kids' artwork, and banking supplies on shelves.

• Wood-rattan file bureau—an excellent storage unit for files and office supplies, disguised as a bedside table (available from Hold Everything).

• File/blanket chest—excellent for use in bedroom or living room household information centers because it provides a beautiful camouflage.

The Home Manager consolidates information for whole family
(courtesy DayRunner, Inc.).

• File trolleys—conveniently rolls files from storage space to wherever you prefer to work (e.g., the dining room table); wood, metal, and upholstered trolleys are available.

• Wall calendar/message center—great for keeping every member of your active family in the loop; consolidates all important information in one location.

Labeling

This is as important to a household information center as to any other space of your office or home so that it will be easy for you to see where files go, make retrieval a breeze, and notice if items are missing or don't belong. For tips on labeling files and containers, see Chapters 6–9. What works for office spaces can apply equally to home information centers.

5. Equalize

If others in the household will be using your system, make sure they understand it. Explain the filing system, where bills should go, etc., so they'll be able to find and put items away where they belong, too.

Encourage participation by delegating certain household paperwork duties to other family members. Give one of your children the job of sorting the daily mail into each person's In box. Give another the responsibility for keeping catalogs current and tossing out old ones. Once papers are organized, ask your spouse to pay the bills if that's a task you particularly hate.

Most important, if you want to maintain control over the constant influx of household paper, create a regular time to process it, just as you would in an office.

- **Daily.** Set aside fifteen to thirty minutes to process mail, make phone calls, and handle correspondence. If you do it every day, clutter won't build up.
- **Ongoing.** Depending on the volume, schedule thirty minutes on a weekly or biweekly basis to pay your bills. Have plenty of stamps and envelopes on hand for convenience. If you pay bills twice a month, store them according to their due date in two files, one marked "Bills Due 1–15," the other marked "Bills Due 16–31." This presorting will speed up the bill-paying process.
- **Annual tune-ups.** Set aside half a day to clean out your files, tossing warranties and instructions for any item you no longer own; placing the year's bank statements, receipts, and tax records in your six-year rotating tax file; and making labels for any new files you created during the year. Pay special attention to your "Lifestyles File" if it's begun to bulge with items—recipes, articles of interest, clippings about books and tapes—you thought you'd refer to or considered buying, but haven't. Get rid of 'em!

Attics, Basements, and Garages

ANALYZE

1. What's Working?
Examples:

> "We keep all the recycling cans and containers by the door of the garage. It's easy to dump them from the kitchen, then bring it out to curbside once per week." —*Stan and Sally B.*

> "I have two garment racks up in my attic, where I keep all off-season clothes. It's great because I don't even have to take them off of the hangers to store them." —*Bella G.*

2. What's Not Working?
Examples:

"I've got so much stuff in the attic, I'm afraid it's a fire hazard. I have no idea what's up there anymore."   —*Ron U.*

"We have a two-car garage packed with so much junk we haven't been able to park either car in there for several years. The seasons are rough on them. It's costing us a lot of wear and tear on our vehicles!"
—*the Bensons*

"I put up some shelves and some Peg-Boards in an effort to get organized. But there's so much junk piled on the floor in front of them, you can't even reach them to put stuff away. I haven't been able to work in my workshop in over a year."   —*Bob V.*

"I can never find my baseball glove, or Rollerblades or hockey sticks. And so much of my stuff gets ruined. Last week, my dad ran over my bike trying to park the car."   —*Tommy C. (10 years old)*

3. What Items Are Most Essential to You?
Examples:

• **Roberta and Rich P.,** whose active family includes five kids, needed places for seven bikes and helmets, lots of sporting equipment, gardening supplies, a workshop and tools, camping and beach equipment, baby paraphernalia, and recycling cans and crates.
• **Myra and Alberto R.,** a teacher and an engineer with three youngsters, needed places in their attic for spare bedding, holiday decorations, extra classroom props and supplies, family memorabilia, and spare household furnishings.
• **Marianne and Ron W.,** a working couple with two children, had a finished basement in which they needed places for kids' toys and games, off-season clothing, a sewing machine, cutting table and fabric, and a laundry center.

4. Why Do You Want to Get Organized?
Examples:

• "Better use of my space."
• "A place to move the clutter from the rest of my house."
• "Rediscover and enjoy family memorabilia."

- "A playroom for the kids."
- "A workroom for my hobby."
- "A place to park my car—to protect it from the harsh winters."
- "Access to all this valuable stuff we own."

5. What's Causing the Problems?
Here are some common causes of clutter in these three spaces:

- **Items have no home.** People usually just "throw" things into their attics, basements, and garages without any sense of order or design. Before long, it all piles up, and it becomes impossible to find what you need, or even know what you have.
- **Sentimental attachment.** Attics, basements, and garages are often home to many items you can't bring yourself to part with, even though you never look at them or even remember you have them after a few years. It's fine to hold on to things that have real sentimental or monetary value to you, as long as you make access to them by organizing them effectively. But holding on to old newspapers you haven't had a chance to read yet or old furniture that is just rotting away is a common waste of these valuable storage spaces.

STRATEGIZE

Plan Your Zones
Some typical activity zones, related supplies, and storage units might be the following:

Activities	Supplies	Storage Units
Sports	Bikes	
	Skates	
	Hockey sticks	Utility shelves
	Sports balls	
	Helmets, knee and elbow pads	
	Fishing gear	Peg-Board
	Camping gear	
Automobile	Car wax, polishes	Metal shelves
	Cleaning cloths	
	Oil, antifreeze, window washer fluid	
	Spare parts	
	Tools	

Activities	Supplies	Storage Units
Gardening	Seeds	Lockable cabinet
	Pots	
	Stakes	
	Hand tools	
	Garden tools, rakes	
	Fertilizers, chemicals	
Memorabilia	Family photos	Old armoire
	Scrapbooks	
	Heirlooms, kids' artwork and school papers	
	Vacation mementos	
	Videos	
Spare household supplies	Extra furniture	Far end of attic
	Lamps	
	Fans, humidifiers	
	Curtains, draperies	
	Extra bedding	Cedar chest
	Baby equipment	
Pantry	Canned and boxed goods	Utility shelves
	Paper supplies	
	Lightbulbs	
	Deep freezer	
Holiday	Decorations	Need storage
	Wrapping paper	
	Spare gifts	
Recycling	Trash cans	
	Sorting bins	
	String, can crusher	
Laundry	Detergents	Shelves
	Spot removers	
	Mending kit	
	Laundry baskets	
	Hangers	
	Drying rack	
Off-season clothing	Kids' and adults', by season and size	Storage closet
		Plastic tubs

Tips on Rearranging Furniture

By the time you're motivated to organize them, most attics, basements, and garages are simply too crammed with debris to move anything around; space must be emptied first. For attics and basements, you may need to box items temporarily just to create enough floor area to work in. For garages, the best approach is to remove everything and spread it out on the lawn or driveway in categories. This gives you the opportunity to sweep the place out and give it a good cleaning before setting up your zones and putting things back inside.

INSIDER'S TIP

When planning your space, keep in mind such factors as humidity, ground moisture, and dirt to head off any potential damage to your goods later when you begin assigning homes to everything you decide to keep. For example, in one client's basement, we located the zone for spare household goods away from a window in case rain leaked in during a storm. In another situation, we located the Sports Equipment Zone right at the garage entrance so the kids could easily grab and return bikes, skateboards, balls, and helmets as conveniently as possible.

Ideas for Stretching Space

Think Vertical

- Line walls with floor-to-ceiling utility shelves.
- Install a high loftlike shelf or platform near the ceiling for off-season, rarely used items.
- Mount hooks and Peg-Boards on walls to hold tools, gardening equipment, clothing, etc.
- Mount racks for bikes, fishing gear, and sporting equipment on walls or from ceiling.
- Stack pull-out plastic or corrugated drawers.

Break Up the Space

(These suggestions may not work for your garage if you park your car[s] inside.)

- Place shelving units, bookcases, and dressers perpendicular to the walls to better define zones and expand storage capacity.
- Line furniture and shelving units down the center of room, creating aisles on either side, like a library or bookstore.

Use Nooks and Crannies

• Openings under stairs and wall recesses in walls make excellent choices for additional shelving.

• Use spare dressers, filing cabinets, or armoires you are saving to store off-season clothing, papers, or memorabilia.

Estimate the Time
Here are some average times required for organizing attics, basements, and garages:

```
HOW LONG WILL IT TAKE?

Attack
1. Sort                16 hours
2. Purge               3 hours
3. Assign a home       2 hours
4. Containerize        3 hours
5. Equalize            5 minutes daily
```

ATTACK

1. Sort
Attics, basements, and garages are filled with a rare combination of items we currently need to use, things we used to use, and things we think we may use again some day. Take a good hard look and keep only those items that are in good condition and that have strong practical, monetary, or sentimental value to you. Limit the amount of each you keep, so that it is manageable and you will enjoy maximum access to it.

Sort your belongings into groups that make the most sense to you. Here are some options to start your thinking:

Gardening (by category—tools, seeds, soil, fertilizers)
Tools (by category—electrical, plumbing, tiling, painting, adhesives, nails and screws, power tools, hand tools)
Clothing (by person, by season, by size)
Sporting (by sport, by person, by age)
Memorabilia (by person, by year, by event)

I am a firm believer in the importance of saving memorabilia; letters, photographs, and certain objects can trigger memories that bring us joy and some perspective on who we are. The key is to keep it from becoming so voluminous that you have too much to enjoy. Be selective and only keep memorabilia that have strong emotional or financial value to you. Then organize them so they can be easily accessed and a pleasure to look through, not a burden. To save only the best of everything consider creating a family memorabilia center. Protect important photos, letters, and records in archival boxes or albums. Save memorabilia from family trips in decorative flat file boxes, one for each trip. Get a trunk and fill it with a limited number of cherished clippings and other items that keep the family history alive. Create a personal memory box for each of your children (and yourself!), filled with carefully selected items that will satisfy those periodic yearnings for a trip down memory lane. For example, I keep a single decorative shoebox filled with cherry-picked treasures from my growing-up years. The key is that all these items fit inside that one small shoebox for easy storage and access, yet they still provide all the memory triggers I need. Here are the types of things I have in it:

Julie's Childhood Memory Box

- Two autograph books from elementary school.
- Photo album from Overnight Camp Galil, summer of 1972.
- Sculpture I made with wood and nails in fourth grade.
- Receipt for a Victrola I bought in 1975, the first of my "antique" purchases that launched years of vintage collecting.
- Class pictures from third and fourth grade with my two favorite teachers, Mrs. Singer and Mr. Cohen.
- Receipt from a strange bed and breakfast in London I stayed at with my friend Gina when we were sixteen.
- Favorite letters received from friends throughout the years.
- A photo of me meeting my childhood idol, Bette Midler, backstage at the "Clams on the Half Shell" review.
- An autographed *Playbill* from another of my idols, Katharine Hepburn.
- A complaint letter from my first landlady saying I left the apartment a mess (see, I wasn't exaggerating in Chapter 1 when I told you I was once a slob!).

2. Purge

Getting rid of some stuff in your attic, basement, or garage will be pretty straightforward. No doubt there are items that have become ruined as a result of poor storage and environmental conditions.

Julie's No-Brainer Toss List

- **Rusty nails, tools, and equipment.**
- **Mildewed or moth-eaten clothing, curtains, rugs, bedding, and upholstered furniture.**

AVOIDING COMMON PITFALLS

Attics, basements, and garages are filled with a rare combination of things we continue to use, things we once used, and things we think we may use again some day. Focus on the positive to facilitate your decision-making:

More space. Think of all the room you'll have here and elsewhere in the house for all those things you really use, love, and need access to.

More money. Think of the dollars you'll save not having to replace lost or broken items, the profits you can make by selling stuff, or the tax deduction you can get by donating it. The extra cash can be used for activities or things you haven't been able to afford. Deciding in advance what you will do with the money, such as take a vacation, will increase your incentive.

More environmentally and socially responsible. Imagine an aerial view of the world in which you could see all the unused possessions piled in people's attics, basements, and garages, untouched for years. What a waste of the world's resources! Putting those "dormant" items back into circulation for use by others who need them is a good deed.

- Obsolete baby equipment.
- Old, broken small appliances and electronics equipment.
- Old birthday cards, used holiday wrapping paper, and gift boxes.
- Boxes of receipts going back seven years or more. (Check with your accountant first.)
- Old newspapers and magazines.
- **Broken furniture** with no antique value.
- **Broken garden hoses, pots, and tools.**
- **Dried-out paint.**
- **College notebooks and textbooks.** (This is a tough one for many people; I struggled with this one myself. Try to be realistic, though: do you think you will ever refer to them again? Isn't the material outdated? If you simply can't part with *all* the vestiges of your school days, keep a box of your best papers and reports, and let everything else go. It's quite liberating!)

OK, that was the easy stuff, but in cleaning out your attic, basement, and garage, you are bound to uncover a ton of objects you no longer use or want but are still reluctant to get rid of. Here are some ideas to make it easier to clear out the clutter:

- **Use off-site storage.** This is an especially good option if you have items like furniture that you're saving for a second home or to give to your kids, or if you have a home-based business and need someplace outside the home to keep important paperwork or records. Be sure to wrap furniture for safety and to mark all bins well, indicating contents. Prepare a detailed inventory of everything you send to self-storage and file it under "Storage Bin" where you keep your most current records. Some companies even have pickup and delivery service now, which makes it more convenient than ever to put things in storage. They will deliver a container to your doorstep, you fill it up, and they whisk it away.

• **Donate items to a charitable organization**—a shelter for the homeless, a library or hospital. This teaches an important lesson to kids. Also, funneling your unused possessions to a worthy cause can get you a substantial tax deduction that may net as much financial reward as selling them, with much less work. For example, my daughter donates her unused stuff to a shelter for battered women and children; I share the tax deduction with her, giving her a portion of the savings to teach her the added benefits of giving.

• **Have a tag sale.** If you've got the time and have a substantial supply of salable stuff in good condition, a tag (or garage) sale can be a fun activity for the whole family. Each person can make some extra cash selling his or her own items, or the money can be pooled and invested in something for the entire family such as a state-of-the-art computer, a holiday party, a new stereo or TV. Bear in mind, though, that you will do best if you are in a neighborhood that is big on tag sales. Also, tag sales are a lot of work. You must be realistic about how much time you will need to invest. Here's a breakdown of the number of hours typically involved:

• Survey, clean, and price items	1–2 days
• Make and put up signs and ads	2 hours
• Arrange and display your wares	4 hours
• Go to bank for change to have on hand	1 hour
• Tag sale itself	2 days
• Take unsold items to charity	3 hours

TOTAL TIME: 4–5½ days

• **Sell to a dealer.** If you have many older valuables, you may be able to sell them directly to an antique dealer; most are honest with their appraisals and will pay you a legitimate price. Or have a professional appraiser assess the value of your items and sell them through an ad in the local paper or a magazine geared to collectors.

3. Assign a Home

• **Logical sequencing.** Storing related things together is especially critical in attics, basements, and garages because they're big spaces and everybody in

INSIDER'S TIPS

Tag Sale Success

Get the best price. Be honest about the condition of the item; make sure it's clean and in good repair. For brand-new, barely used items in excellent condition try charging two-thirds of the original price, especially if you still have the warranty receipt and instructions. You can always negotiate down or drop your price to one-third if the sale is coming to a close and you haven't sold the item. Aim for 25–30 percent of the original price on older items, depending upon their condition.

Use price tags. Clearly label the cost of each item in advance; you'll avoid having to think fast on your feet to come up with a price or remember it when people try to bargain. If you're having a multihousehold tag sale, or if each family member is selling his or her own stuff and pocketing the cash, use different color price tags to indicate whose stuff is whose and prevent chaos. Each seller can even wear a matching-color shirt the day of the sale to add to the fun.

Have enough change. Start with about $25 in change, broken down as follows: $20 in singles, $4 in quarters, $1 in dimes and nickels. Keep your money in a waist pouch for security as well as convenience.

Get help. If you feel the need for more guidance to make sure your tag sale runs smoothly, and profitably, hire a professional organizer to assist you. Call the National Association of Professional Organizers (NAPO) at 512-454-1226 for a local referral.

the family needs to see the logic behind why things go where in order to understand and adhere to the system. For example, the front half of the room might house all of the currently active items, sporting goods, workshop tools, and garden supplies; the back half is then used for more archival items (off-season clothes, tax records, household furniture).

• **Accessibility.** Convenience is essential if you want to maintain your system. Make sure you don't pile boxes and containers so high or so deep that you can't see what's behind what or have to work too hard pulling stacks down to get to what's on the bottom. Keep everything arranged so you can see what you have from any angle, and get to it with a minimum of effort.

4. Containerize
Containers for attics, basements, and garages demand special consideration. Because these rooms tend to be more extreme environments than other

rooms in the house (e.g., damper, colder, warmer, dirtier), you need to select containers that are extra durable and will protect your belongings. Of course, containers need to be a good fit for what you are sorting, but since these rooms are mostly utilitarian, practicality is more of an issue than aesthetics.

My Favorite Containers for the Attic, Basement, and Garage

ALL-PURPOSE

• Metal utility shelves and bins—simplest, classic solution for sorting and displaying everything from toys and sports paraphernalia to hardware, clothing, gardening supplies, and papers.

SPORTS ZONE

• Tension-mount sport rack—protects bikes and skis by storing them off the floor.
• Galvanized bike rack—easy parking grid keeps up to six bikes upright; especially helpful for bikes without a kickstand.
• Sports equipment organizer and bench—for gathering and organizing balls, bats, skateboards, helmets, skates, and even golf clubs in easy reach for adults and kids.
• Clothespins—great for safe wall storage of fishing rods.
• Tall garbage can—excellent, easy way to store balls, bats, and hockey sticks.

GARDEN AND HARDWARE ZONES

• Lockable cabinet—provides safe storage for lawn chemicals and cleaning solvents.
• Peg-Board—keep hand tools organized and easy to grab. Outline where each tool goes for quick cleanup.
• Upright tool organizer—holds rakes, shovels, and spades if you can't mount them on the wall.
• Flip-down bins—sorts small parts, nails, and bolts.
• Battery rack—wall-mounted rack stores, tests, and recharges up to 40 batteries.
• Storage step stool—portable tool chest that doubles as a step stool.
• Pack rack wall mounts—to display and sort seed packets.

SPARE HOUSEHOLD GOODS ZONE

• Portable closet and garment racks—perfect for storing and protecting hanging clothing.

Shelving and cabinets make great use of space in garage *(courtesy of Rubbermaid)*.

- Large plastic storage bins—stores and protects folded garments and bedding from mildew and moisture.
- Luggage rack—provides wall-mounted luggage storage.

MEMORABILIA AND PAPERS

- Banker's boxes—great for tax records, kids' art and school work, but make sure to keep them off the floor (see illustration on page 72).
- Cedar-lined trunk—protects treasure chest of mixed memorabilia including clothing, papers, and objects.
- Archival photo shoeboxes—for sorting and protecting photos. Makes it easy to sort by year, event, or person.

RECYCLING CENTER

- Crate with string dispenser—makes gathering and tying up papers and magazines effortless.
- Can crusher top—allows you to crush cans before recycling; saves space.
- Trash bag dispenser—keeps bags handy on wall.

Note: Catalogs for these products include Hold Everything, Lillian Vernon, Exposures, Get Organized, and Frontgate. See Resources.

5. Equalize

Wonder of wonders, you no longer have to worry about the ceiling caving in from too much stuff in the attic. You don't have to use a mine sweeper to navigate your way across the basement. And not just one but *both* cars fit in the garage!

Don't let all that hard work go to waste. To maintain each space the way it looks now, do the following:

- **Daily.** Cleanup should take only 3–5 minutes provided it's completed each day. If children are using the space, don't allow them to postpone cleanup to another time (lazy spouses can be guilty of wanting to do this, too!); the clutter will soon return.
- **Yearly tune-ups.** As you'll probably accumulate more things for storage in these spaces throughout the year, expect the need to update your system and make some changes. You may have to do another round of sorting and purging, but it will go much easier and faster this time as long as there has been daily maintenance all year long. Schedule your tune-up to coincide with a specific time of year. For example, just before or after the holidays is a good time to reassess the volume of decorations you've amassed.

Go easy on yourself and others when trying to organize these difficult spaces. Everyone in the family is learning a valuable new skill, and it takes time.

12

Bathrooms

ANALYZE

1. What's Working?
Examples:

> "I have a hook in the wall near the sink for my blow dryer. It's very convenient since I use it every day." —*Zoe A.*

> "I color-code our toothbrushes and towels by child, to avoid confusion. John's blue, Mike is green, Sara is yellow." —*Debbie B.*

2. What's Not Working?
Examples:

> "This bathroom is so small, there's no place to put anything—towels, robes, makeup, or shaving gear! It's so inconvenient!" —*Jane S.*

> "I spend a fortune on duplicates and triplicates of toiletries because I can never find what I need. I'm embarrassed to show you what it looks like under the sink!" —*Laurie B.*

> "There's so much stuff piled on the sink, the tank top, and around the tub, I can't even clean my bathroom properly!" —*Audrey K.*

3. What Items Are Most Essential to You?
Examples:

- **Shirley F.** and her husband needed places for shampoo, soap and bubble baths, loofahs and scrub brushes, a shower cap, shaving equipment, and towels.
- **Valerie S.** and her family needed places for their robes, hair brushes and accessories, hair gels and sprays, paper supplies, tooth-care products, and cosmetics.
- **Raymond G.** needed places for prescription medicines, cold remedies, ointments, salves, and first-aid products.

4. Why Do You Want to Get Organized?
Examples:

- "Save time and aggravation getting washed up and ready for work every morning!"
- "End feeling embarrassed when guests come over."
- "Stop wasting money on duplicate purchases."
- "Reduce family friction over the mess and misplaced items."
- "Create a sense of spaciousness; I want to feel good while I'm grooming in the morning."

5. Whats Causing the Problems?
These are common causes of bathroom clutter:

- **More stuff than storage space.** Bathrooms are one of those places where we tend to lose control over how much we accumulate. Multiple containers of shampoo and hand lotion, mouthwash, toothpaste, makeup, and hair creams pile up because we often don't know what we have, and we are always buying more. Organizing your bathroom products so you can do a quick inventory can help you limit your buying.
- **Items have no home.** Due to the limited storage space available in most bathrooms, people often stash their toiletries and other items wherever they will fit—then have no idea where to look for individual items. The solution is to assign a specific home for each category of items so you can find things in the same place every time.
- **Limited space.** Most people do not know how to make the best of the limited, odd-shaped storage space usually found in bathrooms. The ideas for stretching the space and containerizing in this chapter will help you overcome this problem.
- **Uncooperative partners.** If more than one person uses the bathroom, it is likely that every time you set up a system, the other person takes it apart.

Use the guidelines for containerizing and labeling later in this chapter to make sure everyone understands and buys into your system.

STRATEGIZE

Plan Your Zones

The bathroom is a great "laboratory" for honing your organizing skills because it is one of the busiest rooms in the house as well as one of the smallest and most crowded per square inch. This challenges our ability to keep everything we need at our fingertips.

In a shared bathroom, consider dividing activity zones by person—depending, of course, on the number of people doing the sharing, and the amount of space you have available. That way, if you, your spouse, your children, or your roommate have different ideas of about what constitutes "neatness" (is that laughter I hear?), each of you can keep your own area the way you like.

These are some typical activity zones, supplies and storage units for a bathroom.

Activities	Supplies	Storage Units
Bathing	Shampoo	Shower caddy
	Soap & bubble baths	
	Loofah	
	Shower cap	
	Towels	Tall cabinet next to tub
	Robes	
Grooming	Tooth care	
	Shaving gear	Medicine chest
	Hair products	Wall-mounted cabinet
	Nail care	
	Cosmetics	
Medicine	First aid	Linen closet
	Ointments	
	Cold remedies	
	Prescriptions	
Cleaning	Cleanser	Under sink
	Sponges	
	Tile cleaner	
	Spare toilet paper	
Laundry		Hamper

Tips for Rearranging Furniture

Although most bathroom furniture (tubs, vanities, etc.) cannot be moved without a major construction overhaul, some items like hampers, wastebaskets, small tables, or stools for reading materials can be easily shifted around (or moved out entirely).

Ideas for Stretching Space

- Use storage containers and baskets under the sink; this can *triple* capacity.
- Use freestanding or wall-mounted cabinets or carts around the sink area.
- Add shelves or high cabinets in the space above toilet.
- Add hooks and/or shelves near the tub area for everyone's current towels and supplies. Keep fresh towels in a nearby linen closet, or even a spare dresser drawer.
- Install high shelving around the perimeter of the bathroom for towels or decorative objects, to save space and look attractive.
- Attach a fabric skirt to a freestanding sink for storing supplies or even laundry baskets underneath and out of sight.

Estimate the Time

Here are some average times required for organizing a bathroom:

HOW LONG WILL IT TAKE?

Attack

1. Sort	3 hours
2. Purge	30 minutes
3. Assign a home	15 minutes
4. Containerize	3 hours
5. Equalize	5 minutes daily

ATTACK

1. Sort

We tend to accumulate an inordinate volume of smaller items in the bathroom, most of which we barely, if ever, use. For example, I once helped a client clean out her parents' four-bedroom house, which was filled to the brim with a lifetime of belongings. In a third-floor bathroom, we discovered a medicine chest stuffed with old remedies, talcum powders, and beauty products from the 1950s. The expiration date had long passed on the majority of them; in fact, most of these products weren't made anymore. Anthropologically speaking, it was a fascinating find. But nothing we found in that cabinet had any current practical value and, unfortunately, no resale antique value either—because everything was opened and partially used. Remember, collectors' items are usually only valuable when in unopened packages.

Keep only those items you use regularly, or will need if an emergency strikes in the middle of the night. If you buy bulk supplies in advance, consider keeping only a current supply in your bathroom, and store the excess in a nearby closet or storage cabinet.

SECRETS OF A PROFESSIONAL ORGANIZER

Duplicates you want to keep. Pack duplicate cosmetics and toiletries you just can't bring yourself to part with in a travel bag and store with your suitcases, kept ready to go. This reduces clutter, puts the duplicates to good use, and shortens packing time for trips. Then replenish the bag each time you return from a trip.

The family first-aid kit. Many people ask me what supplies are most important to keep on hand for a first-aid kit, especially in households with children. Here are the basics recommended by the American Academy of Pediatrics that will prepare you for most household emergencies. Keep only one of each!

- Acetaminophen for pain relief (or aspirin, with doctor's approval)
- Antihistamine for allergies and bee stings
- Syrup of ipecac to induce vomiting (this should replaced every year)
- Triangular bandage for wrapping an injury or making a sling
- Elastic wraps for sprains
- Disposable instant-activating ice bags
- Various sizes of adhesive Band-Aids, including butterfly bandages
- Adhesive tape
- Scissors with rounded tips
- Safety pins
- Tweezers
- Mild antibacterial soap
- Petroleum jelly
- Antibacterial ointment
- Rubbing alcohol
- Cotton swabs or balls
- Thermometers, both oral and rectal
- Roll of gauze plus 2-inch and 4-inch gauze pads for dressing wounds
- A first-aid chart or easy first-aid book with your kit to guide you in handling injuries

Ways to Sort

By category

- Tooth care (toothbrushes, toothpaste, mouthwashes, dental floss)
- Hair care (styling gels, hairsprays, combs, brushes, blow dryers, curling irons, shampoos, conditioners)
- Hair accessories (headbands, barrettes, scrunchies)
- Cosmetics (eye makeup, lipsticks, foundation, blushes)
- Facial cleansers (scrubs, masks, moisturizers)
- Nail care (manicure tools, nail files, nail polish, polish remover, nail brush)
- Grooming tools (tweezers, nail clippers, small scissors)
- Medicines (prescriptions, over-the-counter remedies, ointments and salves, bandages)
- Body washes (bubble bath, soaps, body scrub brushes)
- Shaving supplies (razors, shaving cream, after-shave lotions)

2. Purge

Give away any duplicate quantities of beauty and grooming products you bought but ended up not liking. For example, my friend Zoe is very committed to streamlined living, and frequently comes over with small "goodie bags" of duplicate beauty products for my teenage daughter Jessi, who loves trying them out. At the same time, Zoe loves having someone to funnel her "excess" purchases to so they don't go to waste or clutter up her bathroom space.

Julie's No-Brainer Toss List

- **Expired medicines**—or any excess quantities of remedies you seldom, if ever, use.
- **Half-used bottles**—of shampoo, hair-care products, or anything else that's been opened and abandoned.
- **Rusty nail clippers, tweezers, scissors**—or anything else that's outlived its usefulness.
- **Out-of-favor nail polish**—or any other color cosmetic that no longer appeals to you.
- **Old toothbrushes**—replace every 3–6 months to maintain their effectiveness.
- **Clogged, twisted, bent tubes**—of toothpaste, ointments, or anything else that's been through the wringer so many times it no longer works, and looks "scummy" besides.
- **Tattered towels**—or anything else that's too worn, or stained.

AVOIDING COMMON PITFALLS

I know it will kill you to part with all those cosmetics, shampoos, tonics, and remedies you spent a small fortune on, even though you never use them. But that's exactly why they should go. Focus on the positive:

I'll save money. Reducing duplicate and triplicate purchases of aspirin, cough syrup, hair products, etc., will make it easier to see what you already have and prevent unnecessary buying in the future.

I'll minimize cleaning time. If there's less of everything, your bathroom will be clutter-free and so much easier to keep spotless.

I'll feel more "together." If, for example, you have easy access to all your grooming supplies, there won't be any more frantic, last-minute searches for that missing tweezer, hair gel, or comb that make you late and cause you to run out the door looking like some "wild thing."

I'll feel more relaxed. If you turn your bathroom into a functional, attractive place to relax, rejuvenate, and take good care of yourself, think how much lower your blood pressure will be.

- **Worthless bandages**—such as Ace cloth bandages that have become stretched or shapeless.
- **Duplicate blow dryers, hot curlers, curling irons, hair accessories.** How many do you need?

3. Assign a Home

- Within the medicine chest, decide which categories go on the top shelf, the middle shelf, and the bottom shelf. Around the tub and sink, decide how you will separate tub toys from soaps and washcloths, shampoo and conditioners from shaving supplies.
- Consider putting medicines in the linen closet, not the medicine chest. Unless you take medications on a regular basis, why waste that prime piece of real estate at the hub of the sink with infrequently used items? It's much more practical and convenient to reserve the medicine chest for items used every single day, such as grooming products.
- Depending on the size of your family and your personal preferences, put individual hampers for dirty clothes in each person's bedroom (where undressing usually occurs) or store just one hamper in a central spot of the bathroom for everyone to use. In either case, consider separate baskets or bags for whites and darks. Also consider keeping a basket, along with some liquid detergent, in the bathroom for clothes that must be hand-washed; each time you shower, you can wash a few garments at the same time. (A basket near the door might serve well for the dry cleaning.)

Rubbermaid pull-out drawers, fliptop bin, and bag recycler
stretch under-sink storage.

• Assign each family member a different-colored towel, toothbrush, and cup to avoid confusion. Also assign each family member a toiletries or tote bag for carrying grooming supplies to and from the bathroom each morning and night, to avoid confusion as well as clutter.

4. Containerize
When selecting containers for the bathroom, a special environment, keep in mind the following.

• **Portability.** It often helps conserve space and reduce clutter and is more convenient if all those who use the bathroom tote their containers of supplies (cosmetics, medicines, etc.) from one room to another.
• **Practicality.** Remember that bathroom humidity can warp wood. Wicker and fabric containers will be fine, as long as they're not stored in an area that may get wet. Otherwise, stick to plastic, chrome, glass, and so on.

My Favorite Containers for the Bathroom

• Chrome or glass canisters—perfect for cotton balls and cotton swabs on tank top or shelf in medicine chest.
• Acrylic organizers—great for use in medicine chest or cabinet to organize makeup and grooming supplies.
• Rectangular drawer dividers—ideal for organizing supplies on medicine chest shelves.

• Custom drawer dividers—great for organizing makeup or grooming supplies in a vanity drawer (available from Neat Way and the Container Store).

• Flip-top containers—perfect for stacking under the sink supplies that may also be toted around from time to time.

• Stackable shoebox containers—terrific for organizing medicines on closet shelves.

• Sliding two-tiered baskets—great for organizing supplies under the sink.

• Turntables—great for use under the sink, in cabinets, or in closet to store medicines, nail polishes, makeup.

• Blow-dryer caddy—easily mounted on wall or inside cabinet door.

• Plastic pull-out drawers—great for organizing supplies under the sink.

• Wall-mounted magazine file—perfect for those who use the bathroom as a library; can be attached to the wall right next to the toilet so that reading material is always available, but out of the way.

Labeling

For aesthetic reasons, you may not want to label the outside of the medicine chest and cabinets, the exposed edges of shelves or containers that may be visible to guests. Find more discreet places to label that will still do the job, such as the inside of the medicine chest, or the surface of the shelf upon which the item will be stored.

5. Equalize

There it is at last: an organized bathroom! And it really didn't take that long to accomplish, did it? But how do you keep your bathroom looking the way it does now all year long, especially if you're not the only one who uses it?

• **Daily.** Even if your bathroom does get out of hand again from time to time, getting it back into shape should take no more than 3–5 minutes as long as daily maintenance is the routine rather than the exception.

• **Ongoing.** You can even head off potential problems by making a rule not to buy any new products or supplies for the bathroom until the old ones are used up.

• **Regular tune-ups.** Every couple of months, schedule a half hour on your calendar for a mini sort and purge. Get rid of any cosmetics or other products you no longer use, as well as any medicines that have expired since your last update.

13

Bedrooms

ANALYZE

1. What's Working?
Examples:

> "I get cold at night, so I keep spare quilts in a blanket chest at the foot of my bed. It's great to be able to reach down and grab one in the middle of the night." —*Bonnie N.*

> "I keep a notepad and some pens in my night table to record ideas or even dreams when I'm in bed." —*Isaac S.*

2. What's Not Working?
Examples:

> "I can never relax in my bedroom, because it's where I dump all the unfinished household chores until I can get to them. It certainly helps me clean up the rest of the house for company, but I dread coming into my bedroom at night." —*Amy B.*

> "The side of my bed is a wreck. I can barely fit a glass of water on my bedside table, and there are piles of newspapers, books, socks, running shoes, stationery, and checkbooks on the floor. The clutter puts me on edge. I think it's why I have trouble sleeping at night!" —*Frank S.*

> "My dresser top is a mess. Ties, receipts, cuff links, change from my wallet . . . everything gets dumped there, and everything gets lost there. I lose a half hour a day just searching for what I need." —*Chris M.*

3. What Items Are Most Essential to You?
Examples:

- **Sharon D.** often folded laundry and mended clothes while watching TV, and thus needed places for laundry and mending as well as videos and her *TV Guide.*
- **Cathy M.** needed places for bedside reading materials, candles, reading glasses, hand lotion, alarm clock, phone, and water glass.
- **Carl M.** made out his bills in the bedroom while listening to music and needed places for banking supplies, envelopes, and writing implements as well as audiocassettes.

> **NOTE:** *See Chapter 14 for tips on how to organize clothing and accessories in your bedroom closets.*

4. Why Do You Want to Get Organized?
Examples:

- "A peaceful retreat!"
- "Better sleep at night."
- "Sense of control."
- "Get more reading done."

5. What's Causing the Problems?
These are common causes of bedroom clutter:

- **Inconvenient storage.** Bedrooms have become multipurpose rooms. No longer just a place to sleep and dress, they're where we watch TV, do chores, even exercise. Yet they are usually outfitted to store only the most traditional bedroom-related items. The solution is to inventory what you will keep in the room and find containers and storage units designed specifically for them.
- **Unclear goals and priorities.** Sometimes people feel that since the bedroom is not a "public" room, it does not need the same attention to detail and design as other rooms in the house. So it remains an afterthought, and a rather uncomfortable place to be. Follow the guidelines in this chapter to transform your bedroom into a mecca of relaxation and enjoyment.

STRATEGIZE

Plan Your Zones

These are some typical activity zones, supplies, and storage units for a bedroom:

Activities	Supplies	Storage Units
Reading	Magazines Books Reading glasses	Bedside table
Grooming	Hair brushes Jewelry Accessories	Vanity dresser
TV/music	Videos CDs Audiotapes *TV Guide* Remote controls	TV stand Bedside table
Sleeping	Spare blankets Pillows Eye masks	Closet shelf Bedside table
Paperwork	Stationery Bills Pens, pencils Stamps Banking supplies Greeting cards	Bedside table

Tips for Rearranging Furniture

• If you habitually read, write, or watch TV in bed, work with your habits and shift things around to keep all your bedside necessities handy.

• If the first thing you'd like to see when you enter your bedroom is your dresser, your favorite chair, or the bed, make it so.

• Empty dressers and bureaus beforehand to make the job easier. Pile their contents on the bed as well as everything strewn about the floor to allow room for moving furniture.

Ideas for Stretching Space

• Store extra bedding, off-season clothing, or even reading material under the bed.

AVOIDING COMMON PITFALLS

Scattering furniture. Many people spread their bureaus and dressers around the room just to take up wall space. This makes for inconvenience. So what if some walls show? Keep bureaus and dressers close together, preferably near your closet, so you won't have to cover so much ground getting dressed and putting things away.

Shared bedrooms. If your mate isn't as neat as you are (a not uncommon situation), clearly define zones for each of you. Keep yours the way you like; let your mate keep his or her zones the way he or she likes. One of my clients accomplished this feat by arranging the room so that her neat side of the bed faced the open doorway and her mate's cluttered side (floor strewn with papers, magazines, running shoes, clothes) was hidden from view.

• Buy bedside furniture that stores. For example, I have a small bookcase on one side of my bed for books and magazines and a closed cabinet on the other for my journal, writing materials, hand lotion, pens, etc.

• Drape an attractive cloth over your bedside table to add storage space underneath yet conceal it from view.

• Store extra bedding and linens at the foot of your bed in a space-saving chest or trunk.

• Mount shelves above or beside the bed for books, reading material, and your alarm clock.

• Use dressers more creatively if you have a number of them. For example, reserve space in one of them for videos, paperwork, mending, and craft items instead of clothes.

• Make use of often overlooked storage space by flanking doorways and windows, floor to ceiling, with easy built-ins such as bookshelves, cabinets, or closed cabinets. Window seats can also be used for storage; they add an elegant touch to the bedroom.

Estimate the Time

Here are some average times required for organizing a bedroom:

HOW LONG WILL IT TAKE?

Attack
1. Sort   4 hours
2. Purge   1 hour
3. Assign a home   1 hour
4. Containerize   3 hours
5. Equalize   10 minutes daily

ATTACK

1. Sort

If, like Sharon D., you use your bedroom as a catch-all in order to keep the rest of your house neat and ready for guests, you're just robbing Peter (that's you) to pay Paul. Remember that even though your bedroom is the least public room in your house, it's the quality of your privacy that counts.

It's OK to use your bedroom as a chore room; just be sure to sort your items into their various categories and give each group a home.

If you are going to keep videos, CDs, and books in your bedroom, as well as other parts of the house, it's best to assign particular categories of each to keep in the bedroom. For example, Rebecca C. read junk novels before going to sleep, so she only kept that category of books in her bedroom. Nonfiction and classic literature were kept in the library in her living room.

Ways to Sort

Videos—by category: comedies, action, romances, drama, science fiction, classics

Reading material—by type: magazines, books, clippings

Accessories—by category: belts, ties, jewelry, handbags, wallets and keys, scarves

Accoutrements—by category: hand lotion, reading glasses, water glass

Chores—by category: paperwork, laundry, shopping returns, mending, crafts

2. Purge

Keep too much of anything in your bedroom and the value of its presence is lost. You can't get at or even find, much less use most of it. Limit the quantity to what you need and reroute or dispose of the rest.

Maybe some things you currently store in your bedroom, such as off-season clothing or luggage, could be stored in a hall closet or another room, freeing up bedroom space for more immediate necessities.

Store paperwork in your bedroom only if that's where you do it. For example, one of my clients had a desk taking up space in her bedroom though she actually did all her paperwork in the kitchen. Working with her habits, we created ample storage in the kitchen for her paperwork, removed all papers from her bedroom desk, and transformed it into a wonderful vanity for her jewelry, makeup, and hair products.

Julie's No-Brainer Toss List

- **Belts, bags, shoes, ties, scarves** that you haven't worn in two years or more

- **Bed linens** that are old or tattered beyond repair, or that you don't use anymore
- **Books and magazines that you'll never read**

3. Assign a Home

- Don't use a deep drawer for jewelry or belts; it's a waste of too much space; use it for folded sweaters or even handbags. Assign smaller accessories to shallow drawers where you won't have to rummage to find them.
- Consider assigning underwear to the top drawer of your dresser, dress socks and stockings to another drawer, athletic socks to another, workout wear to another, and pajamas to the bottom drawer.
- If you have two dressers, consider using one for items worn all year long (socks, underwear, workout wear, etc.) and the other for seasonal wear (sweaters, pants, T-shirts, shorts). Another option: use one dresser for work-related clothes, the other for casual clothes.
- Reserve extra high shelves in bedroom cabinets for off-season clothing, memorabilia, or valuable items not needed daily. One of my clients used the back portion of her bedroom's deep closet to store silverware and old hat boxes that had previously been taking up bedroom space. (For more on closets, see Chapter 12.)
- Protect jewelry from getting tangled up by storing it in a divided box rather than out in a pile. Don't place videos, audiocassettes, or CDs too close to a heat source. TVs, VCRs, and stereos placed inside a closed cabinet should have plenty of ventilation. And if you have young children who come into your bedroom, be sure cosmetics, spray perfumes, and toiletries are stored out of their reach.

4. Containerize

My Favorite Containers for the Bedroom

- Jewelry stackers—their velvet-lined dividers keep jewelry protected and neatly organized in shallow drawers (available from Lillian Vernon).
- Bureau-top jewelry organizers—neatly organize earrings, bracelets, and necklaces on dresser top; it's like having our own jewelry shop display case.
- Wicker three-drawer chest—great for use as a bedside table or for storing videos, grooming supplies, etc.
- Wicker baskets & trunks—ideal for storing blankets.
- Under-bed bins—perfect for under-bed storage; permit fast, easy retrieval.
- Fabric, leather, or metal boxes—great for loose change and other pocket items placed on dresser top.

Square carousel displays
and organizes earrings
in small space
(*courtesy of Ginny's
Ear Nest*).

• Photo or fabric screens—great for attractively hiding exercise equipment, hobby supplies, or that desk you decided to keep in your bedroom
when not in use, and concealing unfinished chores.

• Large plastic bins—excellent for storing off-season folded clothes by type
elsewhere in your bedroom such as a deep closet or shelf; gets them out of
your dressers and makes seasonal rotation a snap.

• Clothes tent—just the thing for attractively concealing garments stored
openly in the room because of limited closet space (available from Hold
Everything).

Labeling

Obviously you don't want to go overboard with too many labels, especially
external ones, or you'll spoil the look of the room. But labeling some things
will prove beneficial to help you and/or that other person sharing the bedroom stick to your system until it becomes habitual.

Label the inside of drawers and surfaces of shelves. Likely candidates for
external labels include such things as jewelry boxes, where it is a helpful time-
saver to write a description of the contents on the outside of the box.

5. Equalize

Give yourself a pat on the back. You've completely streamlined your bedroom so that everything you use and love is attractively and conveniently stored. To keep it that way, do the following:

- **Daily.** A well-organized bedroom should take no more than five minutes to straighten up no matter how messy it gets in the course of a day or evening. As the bed is usually the centerpiece of most bedrooms, get into the habit of making it every morning so that the first thing that greets you as you enter your hideaway after a busy day isn't an unfinished chore but a symbol of your newly acquired organizing skills.
- **Ongoing.** Keep a box in another room (perhaps a nearby hall closet) for items such as clothing, jewelry, books, and magazines you subsequently decide you no longer want or need and wish to give away. When the box is full, take it to your chosen recipient, then start filling up a new box.
- **Regular tune-ups.** Undoubtedly you will accumulate more accessories, grooming supplies, books, tapes, and so on in your bedroom as the months go by. Go through them once a year and decide what to purge. In fact, you may want to do this twice a year, at the change of seasons, to coincide with rotating seasonal wear.

14

Closets

ANALYZE

1. What's Working?
Examples:

> "I keep all of my evening clothes in a separate closet upstairs because I rarely wear them, and I don't mind the inconvenience."   —*Becky M.*

> "I hang my pajamas and sweats on the inside of the closet door. I wear them a lot and it's easier to get to than opening a drawer."   —*Gwen T.*

> "I keep running and exercise gear in a crate on the floor of my front coat closet. I like having it close to the front door."   —*Bill M.*

2. What's Not Working?
Examples:

> "I'm always losing things in my closets. I can't find what I urgently need and spend enormous amounts of time looking. I start every day rushed, late, and with my nerves frayed."   —*Dolores R.*

> "I'm afraid to open the closet doors. Stuff always comes toppling down on me. It's dangerous!"   —*Fred S.*

> "My closets are so chaotic I have no idea what's in there. It's costing me money because I actually go out and buy new things to avoid the agony of looking inside to see what I own."   —*Perry M.*

> "I don't have enough room for all my coats. I keep some upstairs, some downstairs, and never know where to find what I'm looking for."
>
> —*Agnes D.*

3. What Items Are Essential to You?

Before organizing one individual closet or another, I suggest you do a Master Storage Plan and consider everything you need places for in the closets throughout your home.

How to Create a Master Storage Plan

As there are typically four different kinds of closets in a house—clothes, linen, utility, entry hall—it's a mistake to organize one closet without thinking of the others. Making them work in relation to each other is critical so that all your belongings will have a logical home. It's like doing a jigsaw puzzle; all the pieces must fit together.

Use the following worksheet to take an overview snapshot of your storage needs and available closet space. It will help prepare you to make the best use of each closet when you start tackling them one by one.

• On your worksheet, check off all the categories of items (clothes, linens, memorabilia, luggage, etc.) you need places for in your home.

• Go room by room and do an inventory of the number of closets you have available for storage and the number of shelves, rods, and containers in them.

• Assign a category to each closet based on function rather than fit. Be specific. You can combine categories within a closet (e.g., clothing, memorabilia, luggage), but functions like "General Storage" or "Miscellaneous" are useless; they make it very hard to know what to put into or find in that closet, and will lead to chaos and confusion in a matter of weeks.

This master storage plan is flexible. It may and probably will require slight changes when you begin cleaning out individual closets. For example, you may discover you have more of one category and less of another than you anticipated, or you may unearth a whole new category you never considered. So it's okay to adjust your plan as you go. Its primary objective is to give you a foundation from which to work.

4. Why Do You Want to Get Organized?

Examples:

• "Gain control over my wardrobe."
• "Confidence that I can find what I need."
• "Spend less money on duplicate purchases."
• "Get more use out of my storage space. Make room for the clutter that's piled all over my house."

Maximize Your Storage Space

❶ List what you need places for:

☐ Clothing — Hanging	☐ Books	☐ Dishes, Glasses, Flatware
☐ Clothing — Folded	☐ Collections	☐ Pots and Pans
☐ Coats/Outerwear	☐ Memorabilia	☐ Serving Pieces
☐ Shoes and Bags	☐ Photo Albums	☐ Groceries
☐ Jewelry	☐ Records, Tapes, CDs	☐ Cleaning Supplies
☐ Toiletries	☐ Sports Equipment	☐ Pet Supplies
☐ Linen, Blankets	☐ Toys and Games	☐ Stuff to Go Out Center
☐ Luggage	☐ Hobby/Craft Supplies	☐ Dry Cleaning
☐ Holiday Decorations	☐ Gift Center	☐ Laundry
☐ Files	☐ Repair Center	☐ Mail, Packages
☐ Mail (Incoming)	☐ Utility/Hardware Center	☐ Recyclables
☐ _____	☐ _____	☐ _____
☐ _____	☐ _____	☐ _____

❷ Do a room by room inventory:

Room	Storage Unit	Function	(Shopping List) Sub-Dividers Needed
_____	_____	_____	_____
_____	_____	_____	_____
_____	_____	_____	_____
_____	_____	_____	_____
_____	_____	_____	_____
_____	_____	_____	_____
_____	_____	_____	_____
_____	_____	_____	_____
_____	_____	_____	_____
_____	_____	_____	_____
_____	_____	_____	_____

❸ Sketch your floor plan.

Master Storage Plan Worksheet

- "Better access to my belongings."
- "Room to put my guests' coats."

5. What's Causing the Problems?
These are common causes of closet clutter:

• **Limited space.** People tend not to know how to make the most of their closet space. Things get thrown around in a haphazard way, with lots of wasted space and unused nooks and crannies. It takes a lot of skill to make the most of every inch of closet space. This chapter will give you lots of ideas.

• **Complex, confusing system.** Another common mistake people make is not assigning a specific function to each closet, resulting in many closets of an "all-purpose" nature. This often results in that awful feeling, "I know I put it someplace special where I would be sure not to lose it—but where?"

• **Inconvenient storage.** Impractical physical design is another problem that causes cluttered and disorganized closets; keep this external reality in mind when you're assessing what's not working. With all due respect to the architects and contractors of the world, they seldom put much thought into how people actually live when they design closets. The single rod-and-shelf configuration of most clothes closets is impractical for most wardrobes and wastes huge amounts of storage space. Some closets are designed "double deep" with a second rod behind the front one—and for most people, clothes hanging on the back rod are so hard to reach that they wind up forgotten. In addition, many wide closets have doors that are so narrow you can neither see nor reach half the storage space inside. And shelves in closets are often too far apart, too deep or too high to be practical. I'll give you some suggestions in a moment how to compensate for a poorly designed closet and make the most of every inch inside.

STRATEGIZE

Plan Your Zones

You don't really have "activities" in a closet, but you do have broad categories of belongings as identified in your Master Storage Plan. Itemize what will go into each closet based on that closet's function. In assessing storage units, count all shelves and hanging space available in each closet. Consider any supplementary pieces of furniture nearby that might hold some of the spillover.

For example:

Activities	Supplies	Storage Units
Clothes closet	Short hanging	Double rod 6 ft.
	Long hanging	Single rod 3 ft.
	Folded jeans	6-drawer dresser
	Sweaters	
	Robes & PJs	Inside door
	Shoes	Closet floor
	Ties & belts	Inside door
Linen closet	Sheets	Armoire
	Towels	
	Extra bedding	
	Spare toiletries	

Activities	Supplies	Storage Units
Entry hall closet	Long coats	Right pole
	Short jackets	Left pole
	Guest coats	
	Gloves, hats, scarves	Shelves
	Boots	
	Sporting gear	
	Backpacks, totes	
Utility closet	Tools	Door hook
	Extension cords	
	Batteries	
	Cleaning supplies	
	Spare paper goods	
	Tape, glue, string	
	Wrapping paper	

Ideas for Stretching Space

1. Reposition Clothing Rods

• If you have a lot of short garments (jackets, pants, suits) to hang, you can literally double your storage space by double-hanging your clothing rods.

• If the floor space where you keep your shoes and accessories is dark and hard to reach, measure your longest hanging garment, then lower the rod so that the garment falls one inch above the floor. Install a low-pile rug or carpet on the floor to keep clothes dust free, then you can add a shelf or two at eye level above the rod for shoes and accessories.

• If your closet doors are so narrow when opened that they hide a significant number of your hanging garments from view, you can have them widened, of course, but an easier solution is to turn your rod from front to back. This way you'll not only bring all your garments into full view but often quadruple your space.

2. Remove Rods

• If you need more space for folded rather than hanging clothing, replace the hanging rod with shelving or fill the space beneath the pole with a dresser.

• If you have several hanging rods configured one behind the other, use the back one for off-season clothing and the front one for current wear. Or remove the front rod entirely; install shelves for sweaters, shoes, folded wear, handbags, and accessories in its place; and reserve the remaining back rod for all your hanging garments.

• If you have some closets so shallow that long garments hang askew, making them hard to see and manage, reserve them for shirts. Or remove the rod and install shelves for storing folded garments.

3. Raise or Lower Shelves

• If your closets have more space than needed between shelves, wasting huge storage opportunities, you may be able to fit a significant number of extra shelves inside by moving the shelves closer to each other, closing the gap between them. If they can't be moved, containers (see Step 5) are available for doubling the available space on them.

4. Use Doors and Walls for Storage

• By attaching hooks, shelves, sorters, and rods on your closet walls and doors, you can create storage space you never knew you had. Use them to keep your bathrobe, pajamas, etc., from taking up needed space, for hanging up dry cleaning or your next day's outfit, or for your kids to hang up coats in their rooms or entry hall closets.

5. Rearrange Clothing

• If your off-season apparel takes up too much space needed for current wear, move it to another storage area such as your attic, basement, or garage (see Chapter 11). Dress clothes used only occasionally could be consigned to another storage space or area as well. One client of mine used a cedar closet in her attic for rarely used evening clothes.

• If you group long-hanging garments on one end of the rod and short-hanging garments on the other, you will open up a significant amount of floor space below the short garments. Place a small dresser or large shoe rack in that space to maximize storage.

• Unused hangers take up a significant amount of rod space. Remove them and place them in a basket on the floor for convenience.

Estimate the Time
Here are some average times required for organizing a closet:

HOW LONG WILL IT TAKE?

Attack
1. Sort   3 hours
2. Purge   1 hour
3. Assign a home   30 minutes
4. Containerize   3 hours
5. Equalize   5 minutes daily

ATTACK

The nice thing about closets is that you can do them quickly; the feeling of reward and satisfaction you get from so short an effort can enliven you to tackle other areas of your house. For example, one of my clients had a five-bedroom house that needed so much organizing it took us almost a year to complete the entire job. But the first area we tackled was the entry hall closet because I wanted her to see results immediately. In less than a day we transformed that closet from chaos to perfect order, providing a specific home for every jacket, coat, mitten, glove, hat, and umbrella. My client felt relieved and inspired. No matter how gargantuan the rest of the project seemed, all she had to do was look at that neat, tidy, and now functional closet, and she knew if she had accomplished that, she could transform the rest of her house as well. And she proceeded to do just that.

1. Sort

As you pull things out of your closet, sort them onto the floor or bed into piles that make logical sense to you, based on your own associations.

Ways to Sort

Clothes—by garment type (pants, shirts, jackets, suits)
      by color, season, use (work, dressy, casual, sports)
      by person (in shared closets)
Accessories—by category (belts, scarves, shoes)
      by season (summer, winter)
Household items—by category (lightbulbs, tools, adhesives, paper goods,
      toiletries)
Linens—by size
    set
    color, or pattern.

AVOIDING COMMON PITFALLS

Though closets are small in comparison to many other disorganized spaces, they can begin to look like the Grand Canyon when it gets down to the nitty-gritty of cleaning them out. It's easy to fall into numerous traps that impede or destroy progress. Here are the major ones, and what to do about them.

Doing an incomplete job. Sorting and purging closets is hard work physically and mentally because it involves so much climbing, stretching, reaching, and tough decision-making. Many people give up 80 percent of the way through because they get too exhausted to press on. The work will go faster, you'll be less inclined to skip those hard-to-reach spaces, and you'll do a more thorough job if you pace yourself.

Keeping more than you have space for. Even if the space can be stretched, many people are too unrealistic about how much can be stuffed into their closets, and they keep stocking up on items in the belief there's enough room. This is a sure recipe for a cramped and cluttered existence. If you buy in bulk, split the cost and share the excess with a friend.

Saving unused things because you spent good money on them. What to do with that expensive suit you bought but never wear or that extra sewing machine you never use? These are killer questions. Getting rid of them feels like throwing money down the drain. But keep in mind how much more they're costing you in wasted space, frustration at not finding what you *do* need because your closet is filled with so much you *don't* need, and in bad feelings you have about yourself each time you look at all those "mistake" purchases. Do yourself a favor: clear them out of your closet *and* your mind.

---

2. Purge

You will inevitably find lots of surprises in your closets—among them items that are obviously such useless junk, you don't need to hesitate about getting rid of them.

Immediately relegate the following items to your giveaway box or trash bag.

Julie's No-Brainer Toss List

- **Clothing that doesn't fit anymore.** (Many people's closets are stuffed with clothes of different sizes due to frequent weight changes. If you want to keep several different sizes on hand "just in case," store only current size clothing in the closet; box the others and store them under the bed or in the attic, basement, or offsite.
- **Stained clothing, towels, and linens**—or things ripped beyond repair.

- **Shoes that hurt your feet.**
- **Stockings and socks with runs** or holes in them.
- **Any item whose elastic has stretched.**
- **Anything broken** that's gone unrepaired or unmended more than two years.
- **Mangled wrapping paper, ribbon, and gift boxes.**
- **Outdated, nonworking appliances.**
- **Duplicates and triplicates** of anything nonconsumable.
- **Cleaning supplies** you haven't used in a year.
- **Rusty tools, nails, hooks, bolts.**
- **Acidic batteries.**
- **Old, dried paint.**

As you group similar items, you may be surprised by how many of one item or another you actually own. One of my clients was astounded when we found sixteen almost identical black cardigan sweaters scattered throughout her closets. How did she accumulate so many? Every time she found herself in a department store or boutique wondering what she needed, when nothing caught her eye, she figured, "I could always use a basic black cardigan," and bought one. She simply had no idea she had so many.

Like her, you may rediscover items you haven't seen in years that, even though you haven't missed them, you may still have difficulty parting with because they're perfectly good. Think of your closets as a place to "retrieve" items rather than "store" them. This small mental shift can make all difference in the world in how you go about deciding what to save (the stuff you use) and what to get rid of (the stuff you don't).

Here are some ways to feel good about getting rid of those perfectly good, albeit unused, items you don't want.

- **Adopt-a-friend.** Give them to someone you care about who will use and enjoy them. For example, my friend Judy, who loves to shop for new clothes, regularly makes room in her closets for her latest acquisitions by delivering to me and several of her other friends bags full of beautiful designer suits and shoes she no longer wants. I regularly purge my own closets by giving things I don't use to my friend Eneida and her two daughters. It's a happy a day for all of us; I'm thrilled that what I spent money on will continue being used, they get lots of goodies, and my closets stay clutter-free
- **Have an Annual Clothing Exchange.** My friend Valerie came up with a brilliant tradition of inviting a group of friends to her house each year for a morning brunch and some fun swapping unused clothes. Each guest brings clothes she no longer wears, wants, or fits into, and, after bagels and coffee, everything is dumped into the middle of the floor so everyone can rummage.

People try things on and keep whatever they like. There's never even any squabbling; it all seems to work out. At the end of the gathering, anything that hasn't been claimed is taken to a charity for donation. Try this with your unused clothes and/or your family's.

3. Assign a Home

• Remember that in order to be able to use an item, two things must happen: you have to be able to see it, and you have to be able to reach it. Unless they're intended for long-term storage (e.g., old tax records), things stuffed into the dark recesses of your closet are as good as gone forever.

• In a utility closet, consider putting all "adhesives" (tapes, glues, strings, etc.) together. In a clothes closet, you might assign work clothes to one area, casual clothes to another. In a linen closet, you might earmark a precise spot on each shelf for pillowcases, flat sheets, and fitted sheets. Or group your linens in sets according to which bedroom they belong in.

INSIDER'S TIP

Sharing Closet Space

Clothes closets. Give each person one side of the closet for all his or her hanging and folded garments and accessories. Extend this pattern to dressers.

Entry hall closets. Work around your family's habits rather than fighting them. Inventory what gets dumped where—mail, keys, coats, backpack, sporting equipment—and make sure each has a clear and accessible home.

---

4. Containerize

My Favorite Containers for Closets

FOR CLOTHES CLOSETS

• Small wood, corrugated, or plastic dresser—for putting in closets in space under short-hanging garments.

• Battery-operated closet light—attaches easily to interior wall, helping you see.

• Shelf dividers—a must for separating stacks of sweaters, jeans, or handbags to prevent them from spilling over into each other (available from Lillian Vernon Catalog).

INSIDER'S TIP

Measuring Properly

As you may be adding or deleting rods and adding or moving shelves to expand space in your clothes closets, it's important to know how much space your garments will take up. Measure the height of each stack of folded garments (jeans, sweaters, etc.) to know how much space is required between shelves. (Limit the height of each stack to no more than 12 inches.) Measure the length of all your shoes also, as some footwear racks are designed primarily for large-size shoes, and your smaller ones may slip through the cracks. Count the number of short- and long-hanging garments to be stored, and allow one-half to one inch of rod space per garment; this will tell you how much total hanging space you need.

• Fabric boxes—excellent for organizing accessories, bathing suits, and hats on shelves neatly and attractively.

• Shelf baskets—perfect for storing underwear, socks, and stockings.

• Shoe racks and bags—good for storing shoes neatly on floor, wall, or door.

• Scarf stand—works like a coat tree, keeping scarves accessible, decoratively displayed, and wrinkle-free.

• Floor baskets—great for dry cleaning or gym clothes.

• Rotating floor rack—ideal for expanding hanging storage in walk-in or extra deep closets (available in clothing display stores and catalogs).

• Wood or sturdy plastic hangers—wire hangers get easily tangled. Sturdy hangers are neater and help you retain the shape of your clothes.

FOR ENTRY HALL CLOSETS

• Stacking plastic drawers—perfect for storing each family member's own supply of mittens, gloves, and hats.

• Narrow shelving—great for holding rows of hats, gloves, and scarves on doors, keeping them within easy reach.

• Plastic containers—good for storing supplies on upper shelves.

• Laminated checklist—just the thing to help family members remember those last-minute items they need to take with them (e.g., keys, wallet, backpack, briefcase) before leaving the house.

• Hallway cabinet—good for keeping items bound for the mail, the repair shop, to be returned to the store, or mailed together at point of departure.

• Floor bins—good for sports equipment.

• Mudroom shoe/boot rack—perfect for keeping filthy footwear out of clean closets.

Stretch closet space with a combination of hanging rods and shelves or a dresser *(courtesy of California Closets)*.

• Wood hangers—great for your heavy coats and those of guests because they withstand heavy weight and don't get tangled.

FOR LINEN AND UTILITY CLOSETS

• Turntables—perfect for shelves; brings items to you with a flick of the wrist.

• Plastic bins—ideal for keeping groups of items separated (sewing materials, hair care stuff, bathing products, medicines) and easy to find.

• Wire "add-a-shelf" products—stand one on a shelf to double storage space for linens, towels, and toiletries.

• Pocket bags—fantastic for organizing toiletries and paper products on the door, saving shelf space for linens and towels.

• Wire or acrylic shelf dividers—a must for keeping stacks of towels and sheets from toppling over.

• Plastic or wire sliding drawers—great for keeping paper products, and cleaning supplies organized and separated.

• Wrapping paper containers—perfect for keeping all those expensive rolls of holiday/birthday gift wrap and related supplies together, damage-free, neat, and tidy.

• Milk crates and bins—just the thing for grouping and storing painting and electrical supplies, tools, etc., on floor or shelves.

• Plastic bins—great for separately storing groups of batteries, candles, lightbulbs, cleaning supplies, etc.

• Step stool tool box—sturdy and very handy; insert checklist of good basic tools to keep always on hand and tape it to lid of box (available from Rubbermaid).

Labeling

Labeling containers, edges, and surfaces of shelves in linen, utility, even entry hall closets is important so that everybody who uses these spaces will be able to understand and follow your system. In your own closet, you may wish to be less blatant so as not to spoil the aesthetics. Here's how:

• Use colored plastic hangers rather than labels to distinguish work clothes from casual clothes, dress shirts from informal wear, or to cue some other distinction you want to make. Color-coding makes getting dressed in the morning quicker and easier; it also shows if your wardrobe is out of balance (e.g., too much of one thing, not enough of another) so you can shop more wisely.

• Tie a colored ribbon on the hangers of navy blue suits to easily distinguish them from black.

• Tape a Polaroid picture of shoes to the front end of shoe boxes so you don't have to open them to see what's inside.

5. Equalize

Wow! Look at those closets now. No more things falling on your head. No more frustration over not being able to find what you want. And no more guilt about the money you wasted on unused items. Feel more in control of your life already, don't you?

To maintain that feeling, and your neat closets, do the following:

• **Daily.** Put things away as you use them; hang up clothes every night.

• **Ongoing.** Keep a giveaway container on the floor of the entry hall or clothes closets. When items are no longer needed or wanted, drop them in the container; every six months or so, give the unused stuff to friends who would like to have it, or donate it to a favorite charity.

• **Regular tune-ups.** Every system requires an occasional adjustment as additional items accumulate from month to month. Schedule a half day to give your closets a timely tune-up. Go through linen, utility, and entry hall closets once a year and flush out the unneeded old to make way for the valuable new. For clothes closets, I recommend two tune-ups a year. Key them to a change of seasons, the perfect opportunity for shifting around current and off-season wear.

15

Kids' Rooms

ANALYZE

INSIDER'S TIP

Working Together

The key to successfully organizing a kid's room is involving the child in the project as much as possible. As tempted as you may be to sneak in there with a Dumpster to clear out all the "junk," long-range success comes only through allowing your child to participate in the design, transformation, and maintenance of his or her own space. Kids love to solve problems—which is what organizing is all about. And provided you stay calm and supportive, rather than judgmental, your child will enjoy the special attention and time together with you.

Working together also presents you with a unique opportunity to stay in touch with your child's emerging and evolving personality. As you observe and help your children make decisions about what to keep and what to toss, you will gain insight into how their minds work, and where their values lie. You will learn about new interests, and what's become passé. And together, you can create a room that is a true reflection of who they are and what is important to them.

---

1. What's Working?
Examples:

> "We have all the blocks in a big wicker basket. It's easy for Billy to dump them out to play with and put them away when he's done."
>
> —*Diane W., mother of a four-year-old*

"We use a series of accordion hat racks on the wall where we hang up Jennifer's huge collection of stuffed animals. She rarely uses them, and it keeps them off the floor and bed."   —*Loni S., mother of a seven-year-old*

2. What's Not Working?

Ask your child what problems she or he is experiencing in order to create a list based on her or his frustrations, not yours. Carefully pose questions that speak to your child's concerns and needs so that your child will have her or his *own* reasons for tackling this project. Let's compare two different lists of what's not working.

The Parent's Frustrations

- "The room is a pigsty!"
- "I'm tired of cleaning up after you."
- "Someone's going to trip and kill themselves in here."
- "We spend too much money on toys and clothes you just lose."
- "It's embarrassing for people to see."

The Child's Frustrations

- "My favorite toys get broken."
- "I can't play my favorite games because the pieces are lost."
- "I get in trouble at school for always losing my homework."
- "There's no room in here to play with my friends."
- "Cleaning up is too hard. I don't know where to put anything."

3. What Items Are Most Essential to You?
Examples:

- **Lauren,** age eight, needed places for her arts and crafts supplies and an easel, dress-up clothes, dollhouses, stuffed animals, and Barbie dolls and their accessories.
- **Sam,** age five, needed places for his dinosaur collection, Sega Genesis games, model kits, books, and his rock collection.
- **Erin,** age twelve, needed places for her schoolbooks and computer; candle collection; sewing supplies; video games; stationery, stamps, and address book; and bedtime reading materials (books and magazines).

4. Why Do You Want to Get Organized?
Examples:

- "Less fights with Mom."
- "Easier to have friends over."
- "No more broken or lost toys."

- "Bigger allowance." (It's OK to offer your children rewards.)
- "It'll be faster to clean up."
- "Better grades in school."

5. What's Causing the Problems?

These are common causes of clutter in a kid's room:

- **Organizing is boring.** Remember the kindergarten classroom model? If it's not fun to clean up, kids are even less likely than adults to do it. Yet kids love fitting things into all kinds of neat spaces. (Watch them at play sometime.) If the containers are attractive and a perfect fit for what goes inside, kids will often find it gratifying to put things away.
- **Items have no home.** Kids seem to accumulate new belongings faster than they can keep up with them. It's hard to find places to put all these items, and very frequently, they never actually give them a home. Naturally, if there is no place to put things, you can't expect the child to clean up.
- **Inconvenient storage.** Frequently, storage in a kid's room is impractical and difficult, thwarting even the best organizing intentions. Shelves are too high, drawers are too tight, cabinets are too far removed from where items are used.
- **Complex, confusing system.** Kids' rooms are often set up according to someone else's (i.e., their parents') idea of logic and placement, which may not make sense to the child. Use the methods in this book to help your child create a system space according to her or his own logic. This will make it easier for the child to maintain that system.

STRATEGIZE

Plan Your Zones

Ideally, your child's room should be a reflection of his or her own unique personality, dreams, and aspirations—a place to develop, to reflect, to thrive, as well as a peaceful place to sleep and a pleasant place to work.

Some typical activity zones, supplies, and storage units for a kid's room are:

Activities	Supplies	Storage Units
Sleeping	Blanket, pillows	Bed
	Stuffed animals	
	Books	Small bookshelf
Schoolwork	Backpack	Desk
	Paper	
	Pens, pencils	
	Reference books	

Activities	Supplies	Storage Units
Games & floor play	Puzzles Board games Dolls Blocks	2 open shelves
Arts & crafts	Paper Crayons, markers Watercolors Brushes Paste, tape	1 open shelf
Dressing and grooming	Clothes Shoes Brush, comb	Dresser

Tips for Rearranging Furniture

If your child reads before going to sleep, move a bookcase next to the bed. Create a convenient dressing/grooming zone by placing the dresser near the closet door. Better yet, move the dresser *into* the closet if there is enough floor space.

Instead of lining furniture against walls, use it as room dividers to delineate zones by turning a dresser, bookshelf, or even the bed perpendicular to the wall.

Ideas for Stretching Space

• Use vertical space for rarely used items. Mount a high shelf that goes around the room near the ceiling for decorative or sentimental items your child rarely uses but won't part with, such as special collections, an oversupply of stuffed animals, decorative objects, or souvenirs.

• Mount storage racks, hooks, shelves, or pockets on the backs of doors and inside closets.

• If your child doesn't have much hanging clothing, install shelves in the closet and use them to store toys and games.

• Use under-the-bed storage for extra bedding, toys and games, and off-season clothing.

• If the room is small, build a loft or bunk bed. This frees up enormous storage and floor space underneath for a desk or play area.

Estimate the Time

Here are some average times required for organizing a kid's room:

HOW LONG WILL IT TAKE?

Attack

1. Sort	12 hours
2. Purge	2 hours
3. Assign a home	1 hour
4. Containerize	4 hours
5. Equalize	5 minutes daily

ATTACK

1. Sort

Group items according your child's associations to make it easier to find and put things away later. But don't be afraid to make suggestions. Consider the following groupings.

Ways to Sort Baby's Room

Interactive toys
Musical toys
Stuffed animals
Changing paraphernalia

Ways to Sort Six-Year-Old's Room

Games and puzzles
Activity kits (science, art)
Fantasy sets (playmobile kits, dollhouses, GI Joe trailer)
Dress-up clothes, bags, and jewelry
Computer games

Ways to Sort Twelve-Year-Old's Room

Schoolbooks
Homework files
Supplies
Reference books

Bedtime reading (books and magazines)
CDs and audiotapes
Old toys from childhood

AVOIDING COMMON PITFALLS

Being judgmental. Remember: the goal is to get your child to buy into the organizing process—not to steamroll Mary or Frank into cleaning up the room because *you* can't stand it anymore. This requires the ultimate in diplomacy and tact. In working with your child, you become the Organizing Consultant. You have to ask questions to find out what is going to work for your "client." Remember and respect how overwhelming the project can be. Your job is to guide, motivate, and stay supportive—not be critical.

---

2. Purge

Inevitably, you'll come across outgrown toys, things that are broken or worn out, gifts that were received but never used, objects that simply no longer have a place. Yet many kids (and parents!) get wrapped up in memories and have a hard time letting things go.

Save the best of these memories and conserve space by doing the following:

• **Create a childhood memory box.** Select a limited number of treasured baby clothes, favorite toys, and books, and store them in a cardboard banker's box. Add to it over the years, but always keep the volume confined to what will fit in the box. You'll be creating a wonderful time-capsule of treasures that will someday move easily from your house to your child's first apartment.

• **Open a school-and-art archive.** The best of your child's schoolwork and artwork can also be saved in a single banker's box (see illustration on page 72), outfitted with a pocket folder for every year of school. During the year, all of your child's potential treasures can go into a plastic crate on the closet floor. Then, in June, spend an hour or two sorting through the crate, picking only as many highlights as will fit in a folder. By the end of high school, you'll have a wonderful, hand-picked history of your child's development.

• **Design a memory book.** For those borderline gems that you ultimately decide to get rid of, you might appease your child by taking pictures of them before tossing and compile them in a book. This is especially helpful if you have an industrious, creative child on your hands who is churning out more three-dimensional objects than you have room to display. Let your child compose some accompanying text and give the book a title like "Wendy's Artistic Creations" or "Philip's Best Buildings."

• **Set up a rotation box.** To save space, keep cleanup simple, prevent over-stimulation, and allow your child to get the most out of his or her possessions, consider keeping only a limited number of items available in your child's room at any given time. Put the rest away in a "rotation box" in the closet. Once every month or so, when your child has begun to lose interest in what's familiar, you can pull things from the box and stow the familiar items away.

3. Assign a Home

• It's not enough to say, "These are clothes," and stuff them in a drawer. Assign a precise drawer for socks, another for sweatshirts, and so on.

• On a bookshelf, you might group all the reference books on the top shelf, all the poetry and storybooks on the second, and coloring and activity books on the bottom.

• If you want your child to be responsible for his or her belongings, it is essential to store them in places he or she can reach, not just you. Nothing's more frustrating to a child than a toy that can be pulled from a high shelf but not put back.

• For more tips on organizing clothing and closet space, see Chapter 14.

INSIDER'S TIP

Toy Chests

For the most part, I do not like toy chests. On one hand, they make cleanup a breeze—just dump everything inside. On the other, they make retrieval a nightmare. Toys get lost, broken, forgotten. If you want your child to use a toy chest, give it particular function so that it won't be a "catch-all." For example, relegate to it a specific category of extra large items, such as balls, blankets, play stations, or building blocks.

---

4. Containerize

Useful containers for kids' rooms can be found anywhere: houseware and hardware stores, office and art supply shops, catalogs, your own attic or basement. The material you choose is a matter of taste; select textures and colors that appeal to your child and fit the decor of the room whether you opt for plastic bins, woven baskets, or shoeboxes covered with contact paper. A few points to keep in mind.

• The containers you select should be tough enough for a lot of wear and tear by your child. Don't be tempted to economize with egg cartons that will disintegrate in a few months.

• Containers should be easy for small hands to handle, preferably with some sort of handle or grip. Also consider the container's weight when full. Your child should be able to slip the bin easily off the shelf, dump and play with the contents, refill the bin, and carry it back to its rightful place with ease.

• Color-coordinating containers (e.g., red for toys, blue for arts and crafts) can help your child stick with the system, but try to avoid multicolored containers or ending up with a riot of hues. Even when organized, kids' rooms are busy places; uniform containers and colors can help calm the space down.

My Favorite Containers for a Kid's Room

• Stuffed animal hammock—a clever way to get stuffed animals off the floor.

• Plastic see-through bins—great for storing toys on a shelf. They come in attractive, totable sizes ideal for little hands; the tops snap on and off easily to keep contents dust-free.

• Small-parts sorters—great for storing collections such as marbles, coins, Barbie accessories, or matchbox cars.

• See-through plastic shoe bags—hang on back of door to neatly organize art supplies; coloring books, crayons, markers, modeling clay, paints, and brushes fit into pockets, yet remain visible.

• Basketball hoop over laundry basket—encourages kids to get dirty clothes off the floor by making cleanup fun.

• Plastic dishpan or tub—use on bookshelf to gather and store flat-edged books face out, so kids can flip through and see what they've got.

• Magazine file—place on a bookshelf to visually separate periodicals from library books so that it will be easier for the child to find the latter when it's time to return them.

• White picket fencing—provides a practical, attractive place to hang up hats, backpacks, even stuffed animals.

• Stationery trays—use on a desk or bookshelf to separate and store different types of paper for art projects and homework.

• Cleaning caddy—everyday plastic bin that's perfect for toting markers, crayons, and glue.

• Wooden puzzle trays—the child uses them in the classroom; use them at home, too. Store each puzzle in a separate groove to simplify taking them out and putting them away.

• Clothesline and clothespins—string across a high corner to display artwork and star schoolwork.

Over-the-door pockets
create additional toy storage
*(courtesy of Lillian Vernon
Catalogs).*

Labeling

For young children, especially preschoolers, every container, drawer, and shelf should be labeled. Add pictures. The combination of words and pictures will enable them identify contents easily, as well as help them learn to read! Solid, brightly colored contact paper can be cut into shapes and stuck to drawers and bins to label contents.

Older children may not want the exteriors of their drawers labeled, but remind them that labels make cleanup more fun. Encourage them to make their own labels; they may prefer to do this anyway in order not to see your labels as a nagging voice of authority.

5. Equalize

You and your child can now step back and enjoy the results of your work. But is it possible to maintain it? The answer is "yes" because when a child's room has been organized from the inside out, maintenance becomes a much more natural course of action.

Of course, new habits are not established overnight. The key is to create an easy, realistic maintenance plan you and your child can live with. Parents need to accept the fact that they must stay involved beyond the initial organizing process to help kids establish these new habits. Children require ongoing gentle but consistent reminders, along with periodic help readjusting their space to keep up with changing needs. Do the following:

• **Daily.** Expect your child to clean up completely every day, either before dinner or before bedtime, and never put it off to the next day. No matter how messy the room might get, cleanup in a well-organized kid's room should take no longer than 3–5 minutes. With younger kids, give them a hand at first by setting aside a specific time for cleanup and working with them on the job. Set a tone of fun and simplicity by making cleanup a game or a race. Put on some music and see if you can finish together before the song is over—but don't let the excitement of beating Mom or Dad tempt your child to take shortcuts. Once children get the hang of it, your job is simply to schedule cleanup time and provide them with a gentle but firm reminder. Kids often have no sense of time when they are playing or focusing on homework; giving them a nudge about ten minutes before cleanup is scheduled will give them enough time to finish whatever they're doing and still clean up.

INSIDER'S TIP

Stay Supportive

Remember that your child is bound to make mistakes along the way, causing chaos to resurface. That's okay. Just calmly ask questions to determine the cause of the slippage and come up with possible solutions. Did he or she develop a new interest that has caused an invasion of stuff that hasn't yet found a home? Did something in the family schedule change, making cleanup time a forgotten ritual? Is something you set up in need of adjustment because it's not working out as planned? (This happens to all of us.) Perhaps your child is simply getting bored with cleanup and needs some extra fun put back into the process. Whatever the cause of the slippage, don't take it as a personal affront. Keep in mind your role as Organizing Consultant, and help your "client" get back on track.

• **Regular tune-ups.** Plan to spend a full day at least once a year to update the room with your child. Kids are growing and changing all the time, and a yearly review will ensure that the room keeps up with their developing selves.

In addition, possessions have a way of multiplying like weeds, and yearly pruning is necessary. Consider scheduling the annual tune-up just after your child's birthday or the December holidays, when an influx of new toys and gifts may have invaded the room. Purge items your child no longer wants, and assign a home to every new item your child has acquired. If necessary, buy and install new containers, though it is likely you will be able to recycle those you already have in place.

16

Kitchens

ANALYZE

1. What's Working?
Examples:

> "Our everyday drinking glasses are in the cabinet next to the sink. It makes it easy to grab a glass of water."   —*Stella G.*

> "I keep two trash cans under my sink, one for regular garbage and one for recyclables."   —*Lilly K.*

2. What's Not Working?
Examples:

> "I spend a fortune on food buying the same things over and over because I can't see what I've already got in the fridge and pantry."
>   —*Jeanne C.*

> "My cabinets are jammed to the point of uselessness. My husband and I were both married before. We've got multiple sets of everything—utensils, crock pots, dishes, glassware, pots and pans, toaster ovens, you name it. We have too much stuff!"   —*Marian C.*

> "Dishes, glasses, pots and pans are just heaped in my cabinets. They are clumsy and difficult to pull out, and I break at least one thing a week."
>   —*Fran B.*

> "My kitchen is so cluttered that the idea of cooking anything is overwhelming to me. We end up going out to dinner or getting take-out five nights a week! What a waste of money."   —*Rose K.*

"I could really use help cleaning up after dinner, but nobody else knows where anything goes. The kids even have to ask me where the snacks are."   —*Sue N.*

3. What Items Are Most Essential to You?
Examples:

• **Sara M.** needed places for pots and pans, two sets of dishes, drinking glasses, wine glasses, bakeware, and kids' snacks (within reach).
• **Melissa E.,** who had very little counter space, needed places for her herbs and spices, food processor, microwave oven, toaster, coffeemaker, vitamins, telephone book, message pad and pencils, and paperwork.
• **Ric M.** needed places for his bread-baking supplies, steamer, juice maker, pet food, pantry items, and cleaning supplies.

4. Why Do You Want to Get Organized?
Examples:

• "Speed up cooking and cleanup time."
• "Get more help from family in meal preparation and cleanup."
• "Improve health by cooking at home more often."
• "Make it easier to entertain."
• "Stop wasting money on duplicate purchases."
• "Reduce breakage of items."

5. What's Causing the Problems?
These are common causes of clutter in kitchens:

• **Complex, confusing system.** Very often, items are put away according to where they fit, not where they're used. So you end up with all "big" items in one set of cabinets, small items in another, medium ones somewhere else. Problem is, related items end up scattered all over the kitchen, and remembering where each one is can be challenging.
• **More stuff than storage space.** The kitchen is one of those spaces where we tend to accumulate huge volumes of items we never use. We collect vast quantities of mugs, dishes, souvenir glasses, food, pots and pans, serving platters, odd utensils, and plastic containers with missing lids, and rarely have enough storage space to keep them all.
• **Need for abundance.** One reason we accumulate such excess is it can give us a real sense of "fullness" and "bounty." We feel comforted and secure that we are prepared for anything—for a family of ten to drop by for dinner unexpectedly, for being suddenly housebound for months with no access to a

store, for our favorite glass, plate, or our frying pan to break—because we've got backups.

STRATEGIZE

Plan Your Zones

Arrange your zones around the natural flow of activity that goes on in your kitchen, using existing storage units. Some suggestions:

• **Food Preparation Zone.** For this zone, look for the longest uninterrupted counter space between either the sink and refrigerator or the sink and oven. This gives you all the room you need to do all the washing, chopping, mixing, and seasoning involved in food preparation, with easy access to water, food, and cooking sources.

• **Daily Cooking Zone.** Naturally, this zone should be built around your oven and stovetop. In kitchens where the oven and cooktop are in different locations, store pots and pans in the cabinets near the cooktop, and bakeware near the oven. Use the nearby countertop or drawers for cooking utensils and pot holders.

• **Daily Dishes Zone.** Locate this zone as close to the dishwasher and sink as possible so that everyday dishes, glassware, and flatware can be washed and put away with a minimum of effort.

• **Food Serving Zone.** Look for storage cabinets near where the family generally eats (i.e., the kitchen or dining room table) for convenient access to place mats, tablecloths, napkins, trivets, breadbaskets, salt and pepper shakers, sugar bowls, and serving pieces.

• **Food Storage Zone.** Consists of the refrigerator and, if you're lucky, a separate pantry. If you have no pantry; there are several options for food, depending on your available space and your own sense of logic. You might use the cabinets nearest the fridge to keep all food together, or utilize the cabinets in the food preparation zone for easy access when preparing meals.

Your activity zone, supply, and storage unit plan might look like this:

Activities	Supplies	Storage Units
Food preparation	Cutting boards, knives, mixing bowls, spices, food wraps, mixers, blenders, measuring cups, and spoons	Above & below long counter Microwave cart

Activities	Supplies	Storage Units
Daily cooking	Pots, pans, cooking utensils, potholders, bakeware	Cabinet next to oven
	Recipes, cookbooks	Bookshelf
Daily dishes	Everyday dishes, bowls, mugs, glasses, flatware	Above sink 2 drawers
	Detergent, dishtowels, scrub brushes, scouring pads	Under-sink cabinet
Food serving	Serving platters, place mats, napkins, tablecloths, serving utensils, breadbaskets, salt/pepper shakers, candlesticks	Buffet
Food storage	Canned goods, bottles, and boxed food and paper products	Jelly cupboard

Other possible zones in a kitchen might be:

• **Arts & Crafts.** In households with small children, it is common to assign a cabinet or two near the kitchen table for crayons, paints, brushes, and clay so kids can do these messy activities where cleanup is easiest.

• **Cooking Hobby.** If you're into baking or pasta making, for which you have a lot of special equipment, you may want to create a specific zone just for this activity, so that everything you need is consolidated and at your fingertips.

Tips for Rearranging Furniture
Typically, there's little or no furniture to move around in a kitchen, but you may have a table or freestanding cabinet you can shift to its new zone and see the jigsaw puzzle begin to take shape.

Ideas for Stretching Space

• Add open shelving for cookbooks, displays of attractive serving bowls and dishes, stemware, vases, or baskets.

• Display pots and pans by hanging a wall grid or a ceiling rack above stove. This option works best if you keep pots and pans clean and attractive.

• Install under-the-cabinet models of appliances such as coffeemakers, toaster ovens, microwaves, and blenders to free counter space.

• Mount magnetic strips along backsplash for hanging knives and cooking utensils—a popular European design.

• Install a freestanding pantry or shelving unit in a corner or under a window to add storage without taking up much floor space.

• Buy a wheeled cart with a butcher block top and cabinet space below for use as a portable Food Preparation Zone (it can hold spices, mixing bowls, measuring cups and spoons); when not in use, just roll it out of the way.

• Install racks, hooks, and shelves on the inside of cupboard doors or the back of the kitchen door to expand storage capacity considerably.

• Adjust shelving to eliminate wasted "air" space between shelves and create room to add an extra shelf or two. If cabinet shelves are not adjustable, see "Containerize" section of this chapter for wire racks that stand on shelves and double storage capacity.

• Use a cutting board over the sink to expand counter space during food preparation.

• To free up cabinet space in the kitchen, move stemware and serving pieces used only for company or on holidays to the dining room; shift pantry extras to a shelf in the basement or garage.

Estimate the Time

Here are some average times required for organizing a kitchen:

HOW LONG WILL IT TAKE?

Attack
1. Sort	6 hours
2. Purge	2 hours
3. Assign a home	1 hour
4. Containerize	2 hours
5. Equalize	15 minutes daily

ATTACK

1. Sort

As you sort through items, group them into categories that make sense to you. Here are some suggestions:

Dishes, Flatware

Dinner plates
Salad plates
Cereal bowls
Soup bowls
Forks
Knives
Teaspoons
Tablespoons

Pots & Pans (nested w/lids separate)

Saucepans
Frying pans
Stock pots
Rectangular casseroles
Square casseroles
Baking sheets

Utensils

Cooking utensils
Mixing utensils
Serving utensils

Food

Soups
Pastas and rice
Snacks
Beverages
Dairy
Fruits and veggies

Spices

Savory (basil, oregano, thyme)
Sweet (cinnamon, ginger, vanilla)

2. Purge

This is the tough part. Sure, those dozens of pots and pans from several different sets, eighty-seven coffee mugs, sixty-two glasses, two and a half sets of dishes, and scads of plastic containers (with and without lids) give you a sense of bounty and wealth. But think how such "plenty" is robbing you of valuable space, time, money, calm, and control. Focus on keeping only what you use and love, and let the rest go. Find a charity or friend to give your excess away to—get it back out into the world for use!

Julie's No-Brainer Toss List

- **Chipped or broken dishes, glasses, and mugs.**
- **Duplicate sets** of items, especially if they're missing parts or pieces.
- **Pots, pans, utensils, and bakeware** that are burnt or rusty.
- **Ugly serving pieces,** even if they were wedding gifts; save the thought instead.
- **Excess stemware**—how many glasses have you actually used in the last five years? Let the rest go.
- **Excess plastic containers, bags, and jars.** Keep 5–6 of each. Let the rest go.
- **Ugly souvenir glasses and mugs.**
- **Plastic tumblers,** if your kids are all grown. Save a couple for memories or visiting grandchildren.

AVOIDING COMMON PITFALLS

As you consider which items to get rid of think about the following impulses that may get in your way.

Fantasy. Many of us imagine ourselves whipping up wonderful gourmet meals for the family night after night, if only we had the time to become that great chef we feel we could and should be. That's why we've kept all those barely used bread makers, exotic pots and pans, juicers, soufflé dishes, sprout makers, strange spices with stranger sounding names, and weird cookbooks we wishfully bought. Face it, if you haven't found the time yet, that's because you prefer investing it in other quality-of-life interests that are more important to you. Accept that fact and give away or donate all your Wolfgang Puck paraphernalia to someone who'll use it.

Sentimentality. We all inherit flatware, dishes, silverware, and stemware that, for emotional reasons, we want to hang on to even though we never use it. That's fine. But you won't be dishonoring any memories if you store those things away in a box in your attic or closet rather than keeping them front and center in cabinets where often-used items belong.

- **Broken or never used appliances and gadgets.**
- **Pantry items you haven't used in one year or more.** Give them to a shelter for the homeless or housebound.

3. Assign a Home

As you assign specific homes for items within their zones, keep the following tips in mind.

- Reserve tall cabinet space for oversize boxes such as cereal.
- Reserve shallow drawers for flatware, spices, wraps and bags, candlesticks, and dish towels.
- Use deep drawers for bulky appliance accessories, pots and pans, or large serving dishes.
- Minimize breakage by storing dishes and fragile items like glassware in upper cabinets; lower cabinets are likelier to get kicked or bumped.
- For safer knife storage in a drawer, wedge a heavy metal spring into the drawer, then insert a knife in the space between each coil.
- In households with small children, be sure to use a safety latch if storing fragile items, cleaning supplies, detergent, garbage bags, sponges, etc., in lower cabinets.
- Reserve upper cabinet space for lightweight items, lower cabinet space for heavy things like mixers, blenders, heavy serving platters, pots, and pans.
- If you have designated a particular cabinet for bakeware, and you have a little space left over, resist the temptation to fill the space with an unrelated item, like spare paper towels. That sort of placement defies logic, and makes retrieval and return a brain twister.
- Group items according to your own associations. For example, coffee, tea, and sugar could be stored near the coffeemaker and teapot because that's where you use them, or in the pantry, because you consider them food staples. Place them where you would look for them.
- During a seminar on kitchen organizing, I divided the class into four groups and asked them to decide where they would place certain items in the kitchen. Four groups came up with four different, equally logical places for the coffeemaker. Group 1 said, "Near the sink to make it easy to fill the pot with water." Group 2 said, "Near the kitchen entrance for convenience in turning it on and remembering to turn it off." Group 3 said, "Near the breakfast table, for convenient serving." Group 4 said, "In the Food Preparation Zone, grouped with other small appliances."
- Instead of placing tall glasses in back and short glasses in front, which requires you to reach behind one row to get to another, try placing glasses of different heights in columns from front to back of the cabinet. This is the system used by restaurants and bars, which gives you front-row access to each of the sizes you own.

• Keep plates and bowls of different sizes in separate stacks on cabinet shelves, to avoid having to lift one stack to get to another.

• To save space, try nesting pots and pans by type (frying pans, saucepans, stock pots). Group all lids in a nearby plastic container or lid organizer. This is especially helpful in locating lids quickly if several pots share the same size lid.

• Use high pantry and cabinet shelves for seldom used items and duplicates you can't part with. One of my clients had triplicates of spices she was unwilling to part with. We kept one of each within reach in a cabinet in her Food Preparation Zone, and stored the rest in a high cabinet directly above the same zone, to make it easy for her to remember where to look when she ran out of an item.

4. Containerize

My Favorite Containers for the Kitchen

• Wire expand-a-shelf racks—place on shelves to double storage capacity in cabinets.

• Door-mount spice racks—keeps spices handy for cooking and food preparation, freeing counter space.

• Sliding utility baskets—great for organizing cleaning supplies under sink so items in back of cabinet are accessible.

• Cleaning caddy—terrific for organizing cleaning supplies under sink and toting them from room to room for cleaning purposes.

• Lazy Susans and plastic turntables—perfect for organizing spices, canned goods, and glassware on cabinet shelves; brings everything in deep cabinets within easy reach.

• Pot lid basket—a simple solution for keeping all those different pot lids together so you can nest pots and pans to save space. Allows you to grab the right size pot lid in seconds.

• Plastic lid holder—ideal for keeping all those different-size tops together and conserving cabinet space by nesting plastic containers.

• Grocery bag recycler—neatly holds and dispenses plastic grocery bags for reuse. Mounts inside cabinet door.

• Maple rack—conveniently stores baking sheets and trays upright in cabinet, saving space.

• Custom drawer dividers—just the thing for keeping utensils and small items neatly organized, separate, and distinct in drawers while expanding space.

• Packet organizer rack—ideal for holding seasoning packets and drink mixes, keeping them out of the way in cupboards.

Maple rack for neatly storing baking sheets *(courtesy of the Container Store®)*

• Wicker drawer units—great for capturing mail, bills, duplicate keys, etc., neatly in one place that's easy to get at.

• Step rack with folders—a terrific way to keep frequently referred to papers stored in kitchen organized by category (e.g., schoolwork, phone lists, invitations, take-out menus, shopping coupons).

Labeling

Obviously you don't want to label the outside of your kitchen cabinets, but you should label shelf edges and surfaces, drawer rims, and all the containers that go inside so that your family will understand and be able to stick with your system. For example, by labeling the shelf edges in her pantry with the types of foods that went there (e.g., sweet snacks, salty snacks, beverages, rice/pasta, canned goods), one of my clients was able to comfortably delegate putting groceries away to her husband and children without having to guide them each time.

5. Equalize

Well done! Your kitchen's no longer cramped and cluttered, but a model of efficiency. Here's how to keep it that way.

• **Daily.** The key to keeping your kitchen organized is to put things away in the same place all the time, preferably as you work. Get into the habit of cleaning the kitchen up after meals. Don't leave the dishes stacked up in the sink until the morning. Awakening to a clean kitchen is a gift you'll appreciate. Of course, dishwashing is a boring task. Try doubling it up with a more rewarding task to make sure it happens. For example, you can "Wash and Learn"—play some music or study a foreign language on tape while you do the dishes. Or you can "Wash & Chat"—I use dishwashing time to call my friends. They are used to the sound of running water and clinking pots when I call. It keeps me in touch, helps pass the time, and gives me something to look forward to.

• **Regular tune-ups.** Schedule a day once a year before the holidays or in the spring to go through your cabinets and weed out any dishes, pots, utensils, cookbooks, plus that inevitable accumulation of plastic shopping bags. Toss, give away, store elsewhere, or recycle. Expand storage space where possible if "keepers" grow significantly.

17

Living Rooms

Working Together

People often ask me how to get the rest of their family to respect and maintain the system they've set up. The solution is to involve everyone in the process. Start by holding a family or house meeting and have everyone brainstorm the answers to the five Analyze questions together. If everyone in the family finds his or her own reasons for wanting the living room organized, each will have a higher stake in keeping it that way. You'll be surprised to find that even those family members who generally don't mind looking at clutter, *do* mind the family tension and frustration it creates, and *do* mind wasting time and money on items that they frequently lose.

ANALYZE

1. What's Working?

Examples:

> "My bookshelves basically work. They are roughly grouped by category— all the novels together, autobiographies together, classics together. It's not perfect, but it works for me."   —*John R.*

> "I keep the *TV Guide* on the end table. When the new one comes in, I throw the old one away. That's one thing I don't save."   —*Sharon P.*

2. What's Not Working?
Examples:

> "The place is always such a mess that I'm too embarrassed to invite people over. My social life is becoming nonexistent."   —*Jerry S.*

> "When I come home from work, I want a nice peaceful place to relax and unwind. But when I walk into my living room, all I see is piles of clutter screaming at me 'Clean me! Clean me!' I can't relax."   —*Sally M.*

> "This room is so filled with knickknacks and clutter, it's virtually impossible to keep clean. It takes hours to dust, and I just don't have that kind of time."   —*Ramona B.*

3. What Items Are Most Essential to You?
Examples:

- **The Clarks,** a musical family, needed places for a large collection of sheet music, CDs, and cassettes; a variety of musical instruments with their cases; and photo albums and books.
- **Mary V.,** a single mother who loved reading and knitting in her spare time, needed places for newspapers, magazines, books, her reading glasses, knitting yarns, needles, projects-in-process, and her son's homework supplies and books.
- **The Bells,** a family of five that included two toddlers, needed places for videos, CDs, and audiocassettes; three remote controls; baby toys; family games; and the daily newspapers.

4. Why Do You Want to Get Organized?
Examples:

- "A place to spend quality time with my family."
- "Rebuild my social life. Invite people over more frequently!"
- "Reduce cleaning time." (Cleaning professionals say that getting rid of excess clutter reduces housework by 40 percent.)
- "Have the confidence to say yes to unexpected visitors, without having to panic and throw everything into the closet."
- "Read and listen to music more often."

5. What's Causing the Problems?

These are common causes of living room clutter:

• **Items have no home.** Living rooms are usually multifunction spaces, where we spend time with family and friends, pursue hobbies, watch TV, listen to music, do paperwork, entertain guests, and even iron and fold laundry. With so many items to store, and a desire to keep the place nice looking for company, we often don't assign specific homes for many items, hoping that we and our family members will carry them elsewhere. Or we accumulate so much that we run out of storage space altogether. The challenge is to find storage that not only fits with the decor of our room, but enables us to attractively store everything at its point of use.

• **Sentimental attachment.** Living rooms are often homes to vast quantities of books, videos, CDs, audiocassettes and knickknacks. And although most people would agree with the 80-20 rule (i.e., we only use about 20 percent of what we own), they are quite reluctant to part with any of it. Some people seem to attach enormous meaning to these objects and often feel the need to hold on to everything as a way of defining themselves, or who they think they "ought" to be.

• **Need for abundance.** Why does it feel almost criminal to get rid of books, tapes, or CDs, even if we never look at or listen to them? Because some of us have ingrained the belief that these items represent knowledge we always have at our disposal. We want to feel secure that there will always be plenty on hand to read, listen to, or do should we become housebound for a time.

STRATEGIZE

Plan Your Zones

The living room presents special challenges because as one of the most visible rooms of the house, it sets a tone for the rest of our home, and says much about who we are. It's where we play with our children, hold family gatherings at holidays, and entertain guests, as well as kick back and relax. How to accommodate the enormous amount of stuff related to these various activities and different people without spoiling the decor and causing family friction or embarrassment?

Your activity, supply, and storage unit plan might look like this.

Activities	Supplies	Storage Units
Reading	Books, magazines, newspapers, reading glasses	Built-in bookshelves

Activities	Supplies	Storage Units
Family games/leisure	Board games, cards, photo albums, scrapbooks	Armoire
TV/music	Videos, CDs, audio-cassettes, remote controls, *TV Guide,* headphones, cleaning cloths and sprays	Entertainment center
Napping	Spare blankets and pillows	Trunk
Entertaining	Serving dishes, cocktail napkins, tablecloths, place mats, candles and matches, liquor, bar glasses, mixers, snacks	Console

Be creative in using existing storage units in nontraditional ways. For example:

• Use a hutch or buffet to store papers, files, or hobby supplies.
• What about using one bookcase to display your collectibles and adding some lighting to dramatically highlight them?

Tips on Rearranging Furniture

• Shift seating to face a window, a fireplace, or an entrance to the room.
• Place the sofa or a desk perpendicular to the wall, or in the center of the room, to serve as a room divider.
• Put two bookcases back to back to separate living room from dining room. Store books in the living room side; vases, serving bowls, or decorative objects in the dining room side.
• Put small tables next to chairs or sofas for people to set down drinks, food, and reading glasses.
• Don't feel restricted by a lack of electrical outlets. You can always use extension cords.

Ideas for Stretching Space

• Switch to furniture (coffee tables, end tables, hassocks, etc.) that can do double duty as storage units.

• Make use of the often overlooked spaces between and under windows; they're ideal for extra bookshelves.

• Use that spot behind the sofa for a low cabinet or short bookcase; they won't take up much floor space.

• Flank doorways or windows with easy built-ins such as floor-to-ceiling bookshelves, closets, or enclosed cabinet windows.

• Use window seats for storage; they can be built in if you don't have them, and they'll add an elegant touch.

• Install wall-mounted shelving or storage units in your zones.

• Adjust shelves so there is no wasted space between them; this will give you room to add an additional shelf or two.

• Sacrifice an extra window, door, or radiator if you have many in your living room (as most older homes do).

Estimate the Time

Here are some average times required for organizing a living room:

HOW LONG WILL IT TAKE?

Attack

1. Sort	5 hours
2. Purge	1 hour
3. Assign a home	30 minutes
4. Containerize	3 hours
5. Equalize	5 minutes daily

ATTACK

1. Sort

Ways to Sort Books

By size, subject, or author
By hardcover vs. paperback

Ways to Sort CDs/tapes

By genre (classical, jazz, show tunes, movie soundtracks, rock, etc.)

Alphabetically by artist
By mood (upbeat vs. mellow)

Ways to Sort Art Objects and Collectibles

By look, texture, and origin.

2. Purge

Each item you keep increases the time you have to spend cleaning and dusting, and takes up precious storage space needed for things you use and value more. If you are not using an item, get rid of it. You won't be breaking any laws. Here's how:

• Create your own book-of-the-month club by shipping packages of books you've read to faraway relatives who might enjoy them, or pass them along to interested friends.

• Share the pleasures of a good book by donating those you've enjoyed to senior citizen centers, schools, libraries, or hospitals. (And get a tax deduction to boot!)

• Keep a log of the books, videos, and CDs you get rid of and where; if you ever do need an item again, it will be easier to locate.

Julie's No-Brainer Toss List

• **Books**—that are out of date or been read, with no plans to reread.

• **Prerecorded videos**—that haven't been viewed in two years or more.

• **Orphaned video boxes**—especially if they're crushed or torn.

• **CDs and cassettes**—that you've owned more than a year and never listened to, or just once or twice.

• **Extraneous furniture**—stick with key pieces, especially if the living room is small.

• **Serving pieces**—that are broken, chipped beyond repair, or out of fashion (like that old fondue set).

• **Excess stemware**—that hasn't been used in five years or more.

• **Photos**—that are blurry, boring, make the person in them look awful, or are duplicates.

• **Outdated newspapers**—they're old news.

• **Magazines**—that are more than a year old unless part of a collection you refer to often.

• **Old *TV Guides***—what could be more useless?

• **Games**—that you and your family haven't played in several years, or that are missing pieces.

3. Assign a Home

• Don't use a deep drawer for audiocassettes; it wastes too much space. Instead, use the deep drawers for bulky items like cables and headphones,

---

AVOIDING COMMON PITFALLS

Fighting personal preferences. In an effort to eliminate clutter, we often try to change bad habits by retraining ourselves to do everything differently even if it runs counter to our personality style and preferences. This doesn't work. It's like fitting a square peg in a round hole. If you like to read in the living room but it takes you days to go through the newspapers or finish a book, don't try to retrain yourself to read faster or elsewhere. Use a wicker basket or ottoman to create a spot for your reading material. If your children like playing in the living room so they can be with you, keep a basket or bin there for a few playthings instead of relegating all toys to their room.

---

and assign audiotapes to a shallow drawer, or, if there isn't one, to a special audiocassette holder mounted on the wall or shelf.

• If you are arranging your books by category and the art books take up one and a half shelves, put an attractive bookend or decorative object in the unused space, and start biographies on the next shelf. Similarly, in a buffet cabinet or a hutch, assign everyday dishes to one side of the cabinets and company china to another.

• Place related items near each other based on your own associations. For example, I group my CDs by the mood they set for me, assigning music to relax by (mellow jazz, soft rock, vocalists) to the top three drawers of my CD storage unit and up-tempo music (dance, show tunes, and world-beat) to the bottom three.

• High bookshelves should be reserved for classics and infrequently read books, while lower shelves are best for everyday reference books and novels. Likewise, place holiday serving dishes on the top shelf or back of your cabinets, with everyday ware within easier reach.

• Bolt bookcases to the wall if they seem unsteady. Don't assign videos, audiocassettes, or CDs a home too close to a heat source. Make sure there's plenty of ventilation inside those closed cabinets if that's where you want your TV, VCR, or stereo to go.

4. Containerize

My Favorite Containers for Living Rooms

• Camouflage cassette holder—a clever way to store videos on a bookshelf so they look like books.

• Wood remote control caddy—the perfect thing for *TV Guide*s and multiple remote units.

INSIDER'S TIP

- -

Book Storage

If you have an extensive library of books, keep a log of what you assign to those harder-to-reach high shelves; this will facilitate inventory and retrieval.

When you finish a book, place a small adhesive dot on the spine to indicate this. Later, when you're looking for something new to read, you'll be able to see at a glance what to consider without having to ask yourself, "Did I read this one or not?"

One or two oversized books can interfere with your ability to bring an entire set of shelves closer together for increasing space. Rather than waste space, try laying them flat on their own special shelf, so you can raise or lower shelves closer together.

- Galvanized box—an attractive way to hide CDs on shelf.
- CD/audiotape towers—ideal for fitting many CDs or audiotapes in a small space.
- Stacking media storage unit—holds a huge library of mixed-media items (CDs, videos, audiocassettes); its sliding dividers enable you to categorize on shelves.
- Wicker storage chair and ottoman—ideal for keeping blankets, newspapers, and magazines out of sight when not in use.
- Clown CD cabinet—perfect for CDs; comes in a whimsical hand-painted design.
- Planter photo tower—a beautiful unit for storing large quantities of snapshots and slides.
- Wicker baskets—great for storing toys, blankets, and reading material in the living room.

Labeling
Label containers that go inside a drawer or a cabinet, but restrict external labels to the edges/surfaces of shelves inside cabinets and drawer rims. Brass library tags are a classy way to identify book categories on shelves.

5. Equalize
Hard to believe, huh? But there it is, that clutter-free oasis amid all the chaos of the world you've always wanted. Here's how to keep it that way.

- **Daily.** House rule: schedule cleanup before dinner or bedtime. It will only take a few minutes and you'll be greeted each new morning by a wonderful, relaxing space.

A cabinet like this can attractively double as both end table and filing cabinet in a living room *(courtesy of Lillian Vernon).*

• **Ongoing.** Keep a box in a nearby hall closet for books, tapes, and CDs you decide you no longer want as the months go by. When the box is full,

---

INSIDER'S TIP

My daughter does her homework in the living room and was getting into the habit of leaving it a mess. Because it's important to me that the room always be an uncluttered and peaceful retreat, I started charging her $2 every time she left the house in the morning without cleaning it up. I called it my "maid's fee." She called it "highway robbery." But it put a quick end to the mess.

---

give them away, and start filling up a new box. Schedule family time on a weekly basis to get caught up on those unfinished photo albums. Then, as more family photos accumulate, schedule one Sunday night every month to stay caught up.

• **Regular tune-ups.** Schedule these right before the holidays or at spring cleaning time. Go through your books, tapes, photos, and videos, and clean out again; expand storage if "keepers" grow significantly.

PART 4

Tackling
Time and
Technology

18

Conquering the Clock

"Time is like a circus, always packing up
and moving away."   —*Ben Hecht, 1957*

I have left organizing time for this point in the book for two reasons. One, I believe it is imperative to organize your space and paper first, because that naturally frees up time. It is only then that you will know how much time you actually have available to organize.

Two, in my own journey from chaos to order, time was the last element I learned to organize. I think this is typical for many disorganized people. Time is much more elusive than space and paper. You can't see it or hold it in your hand. It's not something that piles up or that you can physically move around.

But is time really so intangible? Jerry Seinfeld said in one of his monologues, "What is this concept of 'saving time,' anyway? I mean, if you save an hour a day for five years, do you get to add it on to the end of your life?"

The answer is, no, of course not, because in fact, time is much more finite than it first appears. Time is measurable, and we all get exactly the same amount: 24 hours a day, 7 days a week, 365 days a year. Therefore, it is not time we need to organize, but the tasks we fill it with.

My biggest organizing breakthrough occurred when I realized that organizing time is exactly like organizing a closet. And the same principles and techniques can be applied to each.

Let's compare a disorganized closet to a disorganized schedule. Both are

- Limited either in space or hours.
- Crammed with more than will comfortably fit.
- Haphazardly arranged, with items or tasks appearing in different places all the time.
- Inefficient in their use of organizing tools.

The good news is that my foolproof formula and centerpiece Kindergarten Model of Organization work just as well for your time as they do for your closet. With each, the way to de-clutter is to clearly define the function of the space or time period and then organize the "contents" to reflect your goals.

By applying the same techniques you used to organize your home or office, you can take a chaotic, out-of-control schedule and turn it into one that puts you in command, full of purpose, and feeling gratified at the end of each day.

ANALYZE

1. What's Working?
Examples:

> "As long as the time is structured for me, I do fine. Work hours, appointments, meetings. It's the unstructured time I have trouble with."
> — *Banker*

> "My favorite day of the week is Sunday. No pressure, I get to do whatever I want. I enjoy fixing up the house, repairing things, working in my shop."
> — *Salesman*

2. What's Not Working?
Examples:

> "My days are a whirlwind of nonstop activity, but it all seems so trivial: dumb, 'have-to-do' stuff that leaves me with no time for the people and projects I really care about."
> — *Freelance Writer*

> "I am constantly making to-do lists, yet most days I don't even look at them. I'm too busy dealing with crises and putting out fires. I feel I have no control over my time."
> — *Stockbroker*

> "It is so hard to keep my life in balance. Between my job, kids, spouse, friends, and time for myself, I am in perpetual motion, and still always feel like I'm neglecting something important."
> — *Interior Designer*

> "My business is exploding, so I hired an assistant. Problem is, I don't have time to stop and train her!"
> — *Entrepreneur*

> "I get no exercise because I'm stuck at my desk all the time just trying to catch up. I'm getting out of shape, and it shows. I don't feel well, but can't even fit in time to go to the doctor."
> — *Real Estate Broker*

3. What Items Are Most Essential to You?
Examples:

• **Theodore H.,** an engineer who wanted to increase his business knowledge and maintain his income level, needed time in his schedule for taking courses, attending conferences, reading, studying, and going over his investment portfolio.

• **Sheila K.,** a working mom to whom home and children were very important, needed time for doing home chores, helping her kids with homework, taking them on cultural outings, exercise, work time, and one-on-one time with her husband to keep the romance going.

• **Albert G.,** a retiree who wanted to remain active, needed time in his schedule for swimming, spending time with his grandchildren, taking photography classes, going to museum lectures, reading novels, and managing his weekly paperwork and finances.

• **Peggy S.,** head of a growing nursing agency, needed time to do paperwork and phone calls, write proposals and speeches, meet with her staff, deal with crises, and attend off-site meetings with strategic alliance partners.

4. Why Do You Want to Get Organized?
Examples:

• "Free up time to spend with family."
• "Increase my client base. Boost income."
• "Handle more work in less time."
• "Feel a sense of accomplishment at the end of each day."
• "Feel like I'm doing something worthwhile."
• "End procrastination."
• "Reduce my stress level. Feel more in control."
• "Pursue my dream of starting my own business."
• "Make the most of my life."

5. What's Causing theProblems?
These are common causes of disorganized work schedules:

• **More stuff than storage space.** One of the most obvious causes of time management problems is that we simply try to fit more things into our schedules than we have time for. This entire chapter is geared toward helping you purge your schedule of unnecessary activity.

• **Need to retreat.** Much has been written lately about how we use work as a way of running away from personal problems—a troubled marriage, difficult relationships. A busy schedule can keep you both physically and mentally distracted from tough issues you may not be ready to face.

• **Conquistador of chaos.** Many people subconsciously leave things until the last minute or pack their schedules impossibly tight because they thrive on "conquering the impossible." In fact, if they have too much free time, they become listless and remarkably nonproductive, and can spend a whole day just trying to get one thing done. People like this need to replace the clutter in their schedule with meaningful activities of their own choosing, creating as much structured time for leisure activities as they do for work, and self-imposing deadlines to keep themselves feeling stimulated and alive.

• **Unclear goals and priorities.** One of the biggest causes of a scattered schedule is not being sure what your goals and priorities are. Perhaps you are having a hard time selecting a small handful of goals to concentrate on in today's high-speed world. Or, like a recent client of mine, you may be trying to do something to which you are not completely committed. He was having a hard time organizing his time to go job hunting because he was unclear about what kind of job he actually wanted. In order to build a logical schedule, you have to be sure what your priorities and goals are.

STRATEGIZE

Plan Your Zones

The beauty of my Kindergarten Model of Organization (see Chapter 4) is that you can use it to organize time as well. Your schedule must be set up in activity zones that allow you to accomplish the goals you have in the various areas of your life.

List the core activities you need to accomplish your goals. Let's use a married working mom as an example. Some typical zones:

• **Self time.** (Exercise, medical care, leisure reading, taking baths, getting haircuts and manicures, visiting friends, spending time on a hobby.)

• **Family time.** (Dinners, cultural outings, helping the kids with homework, vacations, reading time, bathing, household chores.)

• **Work time.** (Paperwork, meetings, business reading, seminars and conventions, field visits, strategic planning, writing, assembling reports.)

• **Relationship time.** ("Dates" with spouse, quiet time each evening, weekends away.)

• **Financial time.** (Paying bills, studying investments, doing tax returns, reading the *Wall Street Journal.*)

• **Community time.** (Volunteering, attending religious services.)

• **Education time.** (Reading, watching the news, taking classes, studying a foreign language, learning to play an instrument.)

When it comes to organizing time, your storage units are the hours you are awake. On a piece of paper, fill out a schedule of your day as follows, beginning with when you wake up each morning and ending with the time you go to sleep at night, including regular mealtimes. Everything in between is what you have to work with.

7 a.m.	Wake	Wake	Wake	Wake	Wake	Wake	Wake
12 noon	Lunch	Lunch	Lunch	Lunch	Lunch	Lunch	Lunch
7 p.m.	Dinner	Dinner	Dinner	Dinner	Dinner	Dinner	Dinner
11:30 p.m.	Sleep	Sleep	Sleep	Sleep	Sleep	Sleep	Sleep

This is what I call a "Time Map." It allots specific spaces in your schedule for tending to the various core activities of your life. It serves as a foundation from which to work that forces you to keep your life in balance, giving you all the time you need to accomplish your goals. The details of what you do within each space, or zone, will be developed more fully in the Attack stage, but here's an example, a completed Time Map from one of my clients.

Ideas For Stretching Time

• **Layer activities.** Try to accomplish several goals at once by combining activities logically. For example, if one of your goals is to make a certain income, which requires you to commute one hour every day to your job, and another goal is to learn to speak French, combine commuting time with listening to French lessons on tape. Combine developing your business presentation skills and becoming better recognized at the office by offering to run one of the weekly staff meetings each month. Combine staying in touch with your friends and keeping your house clean by calling someone on the phone every night while you do the dishes. Combine spending quality time with your kids, teaching them life skills, and eating healthy by preparing dinner together every night.

• **Increase your fees.** This tip is mostly relevant to entrepreneurs and business owners who have control over what they charge for their services, but can also apply to employees in a position to increase their value in the job market. One client of mine was a very successful writer who was working 12–14 hours a day, 6–7 days a week to keep up with the demands for her work. She was exhausted and frustrated that she never had time for her husband, her health, or some independent projects she had been dreaming about doing for years. Obviously, her work was in high demand; her busy schedule was testimony to that. But she wasn't charging as much as the market in her field would bear. Doubling her fees allowed her to make the same income in half

Schedule Template

Time	Monday	Tuesday	Wednesday	Thursday	Friday	Saturday	Sunday
4:30	Wake Up →					FAMILY	FAMILY TIME
4:30–6:00	SELF-TIME—Reading, Running →					House Cleaning and Errands	Outings, Fun
6:00–7:30	FAMILY TIME—Dressing, Breakfast, Clutter pick-up, Fun time →						
7:30–8:30	COMMUTE—½ hour with kids, ½ hour dictation for work →						
8:30–	WORK AND SCHOOL →					FAMILY FUN TIME	
5:00							
5:00–6:00	COMMUTE—½ hour dictation for work, ½ hour with kids →						
6:00–	FAMILY TIME—Dinner preparation, Dinner, Relaxation →					MARRIAGE TIME—	FAMILY PROJECTS
9:00–10:00	MARRIAGE TIME—Quiet time together →					Date night	Repairs, Mending, Organizing
10:00–11:00	SELF-TIME—Read, Relax, Lay out clothes →						
11:00	Sleep →						

Working Mom's Time Map

the time—and freed up 36 precious hours per week (6 hours per day), which she easily filled pursuing her other goals.

• **Add something fun to keep you energized.** No matter how busy you are, if you add something enjoyable to your schedule, your productivity will increase—which, in effect, will expand your available time for other activities. I discovered this personally several years ago when I added swing dancing as a hobby to my packed schedule. Knowing I had this purely fun activity to look forward to every Sunday boosted my energy level all week long, and I got considerably more accomplished with both my business and my daughter; it was astounding.

• **Postpone some goals.** You don't have to accomplish all your goals at once. Try spacing them out over time. Focus on achieving one this month, another next month. My friend Gordon, for whom acquiring knowledge is a big goal, selects a different topic to study in depth each year. One year it was the history of jazz, another year the space program, the next year American poetry. Be realistic about what you can accomplish at once, and keep in mind that you can save some projects and tasks for future dates to free up time today.

• **Find shortcuts.** If you talk faster than you write, dictate memos and letters rather than roughing them out on paper. Organize your space (if you haven't already done so) to make tasks simpler, more convenient, and less time-consuming to achieve. For example, keep file cabinets within easy reach of your desk rather than in another room. (See the various chapters in this book on organizing home and office spaces for more tips on this.)

• **Change activities.** To offset boredom and perfectionism—the two greatest time killers—plan to change activities every thirty minutes to two hours. You'll stay fresh and get more done.

Estimate the Time

The schedule required to organize our time is a little different from what we use for space, because we are dealing with something less concrete. Whereas with space, it is often desirable to work as quickly as possible, with time, I always suggest you take it more slowly. By working gradually over a month, you are in the best position to replace old habits with new ways of thinking and behaving. Here are some average times required for getting the job done.

HOW LONG WILL IT TAKE?

Attack

1. Sort	1 week
2. Purge	1 week
3. Assign a home	2 hours
4. Containerize	2 weeks
5. Equalize	15 minutes daily

ATTACK

OK, now that you've planned out your ideal schedule on paper, take your Time Map into the real world and use it to sort, categorize, purge, and arrange the activities and tasks you are bombarded with on a daily basis. It will be your guide in making decisions about what to do, when to do it, and what to say "no" to.

It will take a while to refine your Time Map and get used to the time management tools you will be learning about in this chapter, so I suggest you spread the work out over a month or two, setting aside an hour every week to evaluate, adjust to your new tools, and get comfortable with the new habits you're developing. Going from a chaotic to an organized schedule can be a huge change that needs to be integrated gradually, requiring a period of adjustment.

1. Sort
Keep a copy of your Time Map posted on the wall of your office, or on an index card in your wallet or handbag. Refer to it whenever you are planning your specific to-do's or when you get hit with a request from someone to do something for them.

Try to direct each task to its proper place on your schedule. If you decide you need to go shopping for shoes with your kids, plan to do it on an upcoming Saturday during Chore Time. If someone hands you a special report you want to review, put it in your reading basket to hit later in the afternoon during Reading Time. If you just found out you need to write a proposal, plug it into your Writing Time later in the afternoon or the week. If you work from home and a business call comes in during Family Time, let the voice-mail pick it up and return the call during Work Time. If something urgent comes up that cannot wait, it's OK to periodically switch one zone in your schedule for another, but now you will know what you have missed and be better equipped to make up the lost time elsewhere. A Time Map puts you in control, so that you can make informed, thoughtful decisions about what you will do when, while keeping your eye on the Big Picture.

If "crises" come up on a daily basis, constantly interfering with your planned activities, you may need to create a special Time Map for Crisis Management that builds in plenty of "empty" time to quickly handle these crises as they arise, while still enabling you to handle all your other tasks.

The following Time Map was developed for the head of the global marketing division of a bank, who manages a staff of twenty people and was constantly having to juggle phone calls, meetings, and unexpected urgencies brought to him by staff members. It allowed him to accomplish all his goals by having a place to funnel every activity of the day, while never requiring any staff member to wait more than thirty minutes for his attention.

Time Budget for Crisis Managers

Time	Monday	Tuesday	Wednesday	Thursday	Friday	Saturday	Sunday
8:30	Meeting		Meeting		Meeting		
9:00	Phone		Phone		Phone		
9:30	Open Door		Open Door		Open Door		
10:00							
10:30	Meeting		Meeting		Meeting		
11:00	Phone	←	Phone	←	Phone		
11:30	Open Door	Field	Open Door	Field	Open Door		
12:00		Visits		Visits			
12:30	Lunch/Meeting	and	Lunch/Meeting	and	Lunch/Meeting		
1:00		Project		Project			
1:30	Phone	Work	Phone	Work	Phone		
2:00	Open Door	→	Open Door	→	Open Door		
2:30	Open Door		Open Door		Open Door		
3:00	Meeting		Meeting		Meeting		
3:30	Phone		Phone		Phone		
4:00	Open Door		Open Door		Open Door		
4:30							
5:00	Sacred Time		Sacred Time		Sacred Time		
5:30							

Crisis Manager's Time Map

2. Purge

Your Time Map allows you to assess every task that competes for your time by measuring it against your goals. Before automatically performing any task, you can now ask yourself if it is worth doing. Does the task even merit a place in your schedule? If not, get rid of it. You'd be surprised at how many things you are doing by rote that have nothing to do with your current goals. Most likely, they apply to some previous goal that is no longer important to you.

One client, the head of national marketing at a major bank, realized after creating her Time Map that a special project she had been doing for the past four years was no longer relevant to her company's goals. She immediately let go of the project, regaining three solid months of work time every year. At her salary, this discovery saved her company more than $50,000 annually.

A Time Map highlights how limited your time is for tending to each area of your life and job. This awareness will make you much more selective about the tasks you choose to keep and perform. Purging doesn't always mean tossing, however. Sometimes it can mean "giving away" tasks, another word for which is "delegating." You may discover that although some of the tasks you're performing are indeed helping you achieve your goals, they could be done just as well, more quickly and easily, by your support staff, or another member of your household.

Some common examples of tasks that you might be able to delegate are cooking, cleaning, or bill paying. This frees you up to attend to those tasks only *you* can do, such as reading to your kids, spending time with your spouse, or taking care of yourself by going to the gym. Be honest with yourself in determining what those tasks are. You'll be surprised at how much you needlessly take upon yourself just to prove how "indispensable" you are.

3. Assign a Home

At this point, you have worked with your Time Map for a week or two, and it is time to reevaluate the placement of certain zones and activities in your schedule. For example, you may have discovered that a certain time slot you've allotted to phone calls never seems to work out. Or that you have not allowed sufficient time for creative writing. Now is the time to adjust and refine where various activities in your schedule are assigned so that they better reflect the realities of your life. Keep in mind the following guidelines as you assign certain activities a single, consistent home:

• **Group similar tasks.** Just as you group similar items in a closet (e.g., all the short jackets together, all the jeans together), you can batch tasks within your schedule to save time and reduce your chances of "losing" or overlooking them. Errands, phone calls, and meetings are likely candidates for tasks that can be grouped and done all at once.

- **Measure how long things take.** A common mistake people make in creating their schedule is being unrealistic about how long certain activities take. Good time managers are excellent estimators, so they always set aside the right amount of time for each activity. To improve your estimating skills, keep a log for a week or two, noting how long each task takes you to accomplish. This information will help you plan your days better from now on and look for shortcuts; it will come in handy when deciding what tasks you may be able to give away.

- **Work with your energy cycles.** For example, if exercising is important to you, and you wake up each day full of vim and vigor but come home late at night tired and sapped of strength, assign your workout a home first thing in the morning when you're motivated, at your best, and more inclined to follow through and sustain it.

- **Other people's schedules.** In your schedule, you may need to assign certain activities slots that accommodate other people's schedules and availability. For example, if you are a night person and the members of your family are day people, schedule Family Time early in the evening, then get back to work after everyone else has gone to bed. In searching for the best time to write this book without interfering with the running of my business, I assigned Writing Time from 7 a.m. to 10 a.m. every day, which still left me practically a full working day to make business calls and meet with clients.

4. Containerize

In time management terms, containerizing involves evaluating and selecting time management tools, learning how to use their features, then customizing them to your personal style. Spread this step out over time as well.

The most basic storage container essential to any time management system is a daily planner. It is where you capture and track all of your appointments, to-do's, phone calls, and important information for running your business and your life in a single, reliable place.

There are so many styles, brands, and formats on the market that the selection process can be overwhelming. Apply my "Select One Rule." Don't hedge your bets by buying two or three different planners for fear of making a wrong decision. Select one planner, use it for everything, and stick with it at least three months to give it a proper chance to work for you. Juggling several planners at once or constantly going back to the store to find that "perfect" one are sure bets for losing information, forgetting appointments, overlooking to-do's, and frustration. There is no "best planner" out there. The key is to choose one you will feel comfortable using because it reflects the way you think and will make it easy for you to keep on top of your life and work.

So how do you choose the right planner? You must first decide whether you want a paper-based, electronic, or computer-based planner. Canadian time management expert Harold Taylor wrote an excellent article comparing different planners. Here are some of his thoughts.

• **Paper-Based Planners (At-a-Glance, DayRunner, DayTimer, Franklin-Covey Planner, FiloFax).** These are among the easiest to use and least expensive to buy. You can access them almost anywhere, jotting down appointments while standing in line or adding items to your to-do list as they occur to you. They come in many sizes, from small pocket formats that are lightweight and extremely portable, to large desktop formats that give you lots of room to write and are fast to use. A flip of the wrist and any page of your calendar is right there in front of you. You don't have to turn anything on, so they won't "crash." They offer a great overview of your schedule, both past and future weeks, allowing you to flip back and forth between pages quickly and easily, and are completely nonthreatening for people who relate best to the old-fashioned paper-and-pen method of writing down their appointments and thoughts. Furthermore, they can be filed like books at the end of each year, with all your past history intact for future reference.

• **Electronic Planners (Newton, Palm Pilot, Wizard).** These are extremely portable and can hold a tremendous amount of information in a small, lightweight container. They are excellent for people who are on the road frequently and need to bring a lot of information with them in a compact manner. Unlike paper-based planners, they can move unfinished to-do's from one week to the next. One entry can schedule repetitive meetings throughout the year, and carry reminders of birthdays, anniversaries, and other special events from one year to the next. You can set alarms to remind you when to leave for an appointment, make a phone call, or take your medicine. You can look up names and addresses alphabetically, by city or town, or by category—client, prospect, friend, vendor. Most electronic planners can transfer information to and from your computer's contact manager or database, saving you lots of rewriting time. They are great for people who enjoy working with an electronic interface. PDAs (personal digital assistants), which operate with a stylus pen instead of a keypad, allow paper-and-pen aficionados to use their natural mode of writing. Many electronic planners serve as communication tools as well, allowing you to receive messages and e-mail and to download computer files through a built-in modem. The disadvantages of them are that you can only view one screen at a time, which prevents you from getting a good overview of your past and future schedule; you can't file them on a bookshelf for reference; and, of course, they do crash from time to time. But you can minimize the loss if a crash occurs by diligently backing up data on your computer daily, or investing in a second backup unit that you can keep fully loaded and ready to come to your rescue, if needed.

• **Computer-Based Planners (ACT!, DayRunner, DayTimer, Lotus Organizer).** These are usually integrated into software packages, either in the form

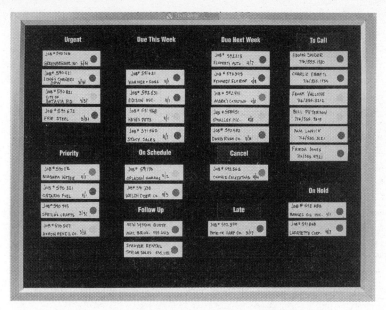

Data board with card slots allows for easy organizing of tasks
(courtesy of Time Wise).

of a Personal Information Management (PIM) program or a Contact Management program. The main difference between the two is that the first organizes your to-do's around what they are and when you have to do them; the latter is more of a sales tool that organizes to-do's around the people with whom you do business. Computer-based planners share most of the advantages of electronic planners, but come with some additional power. For example, clicking on a "call Mary Simpson" action item will pull up Mary Simpson's contact page or telephone log to the screen, complete with telephone number and pertinent data. It'll even dial the phone number or e-mail address for you, and see that any action items that result from the call go onto your to-do list. A record of the call is automatically entered on your contact history page.

In short, a computer-based planner does a lot of the recording work for you. However, it only works if your job is fairly stationary, allowing you to sit in front of your computer all the time, because the calendar program must be switched on and available at all times. Otherwise, you will be writing notes and appointments on scraps of paper everywhere, with the good intention of entering them in the computer when you get to it, but those items will too easily fall through the cracks. Computer-based planners often team well with electronic planners for people who are on the road a lot, but you have to make transferring information between them a daily ritual.

Other considerations to keep in mind when selecting a planner:

• **Your view of time.** In choosing your calendar format, consider whether you want to view your schedule in a linear, vertical, or horizontal manner, or whether you want to be able to view it in a grid format. How big or small a picture of your schedule do you want to be able to see at a glance: a year, a quarter, a month, a week, or a day? You might need two formats, a monthly one for the Big Picture, a daily or weekly for a close-up snapshot.

• **Quantity of information.** The more information or activities you want to record for each day or week, the more space you will need. For example, a busy entrepreneur with three or four appointments to keep, a dozen or more phone calls to make, and six action items per day probably needs a two-page-per-day format, while a person with the same number of appointments, phone calls, and action items *per week* could use a week-at-a-glance format.

• **Aesthetics.** As with any organizing tool, be sure you like the design of the planner you choose, whether it's paper-based, electronic, or computer-based. The features of the planner will make little difference to you if its looks don't appeal to you enough to make you want to use it. Ask yourself if the planner reflects your self-image: elegant, classy, sporty, lively, professional, sharp? Do you like the layout, color, typeface on the pages? Do you like the case, the shape, and the material the planner is made of? You want to be proud to pull your planner out, and enjoy using it every day.

5. Equalize.

Congratulations! You've finally gained mastery over that intangible called time by turning it into something concrete: a schedule that works for you.

But keeping your schedule on track requires constant vigilance. Do the following:

• **Daily.** Take just fifteen minutes every evening to go over the next day's activities, keeping in mind your priorities when considering conflicting alternatives (e.g., taking the kids to the museum tomorrow vs. working on that important proposal). Even this small amount of advance preparation will better equip you to deal with the different demands you must face daily.

• **Ongoing.** Keep your goals visible; post them on your refrigerator or your desk at work. Run every interruption, distraction, request, demand, and tempting activity by this filter, asking yourself, "Will it help me reach my goals?" If not, find a way to avoid the interruptions and distractions, politely decline the requests and demands, and resist the temptations. Follow the "one in, one out" rule. Recognize that when you want to add an activity to your full schedule, you can only do so by subtracting another. This will make you think long and hard about what new activities to take on. Will they really be worth your time?

INSIDER'S TIP

Making the Most of a Planner

• Color-code entries in your planner (e.g., red for work, blue for family) for a quick visual picture of whether you are keeping your life in balance.

• Treat action items and phone calls like appointments to ensure they get done and avoid placing unrealistic expectations on yourself. For each to-do and phone call, ask yourself three questions: "What zone does this belong in?," "Which day will I do it?," and "How long will it take?" Then earmark the time directly in your planner.

• Learn how long you can concentrate on single tasks and then break larger projects into manageable chunks. Schedule backward from their due date, leaving a cushion, just in case things take longer than expected.

• When writing appointments in your planner, include any related addresses and phone numbers in the same spot for convenient, instant reference. Also, make sure you schedule travel time to and from appointments, an often overlooked item.

• Write a small "B" in a circle next to any appointments, events or meetings for which you have to "bring along backup material" (e.g., a file, invitation, or directions). This little reminder will ensure you arrive with everything you need.

• Set aside a separate page in your planner for each of the key people in your work or personal life. Use it to capture all the items you want to talk to them about as these items occur to you. During your next phone call or meeting, you will have your complete agenda instantly at your fingertips.

• Be prepared to take advantage of impromptu free time—by keeping a list in your planner of short (five- to fifteen-minute) but meaningful tasks that could productively fill this time when it pops up.

• **Regular tune-ups.** Review your goals and activities at least twice a year but preferably more often (perhaps bimonthly) to allow for any changes in priorities, responsibilities, and interests. Then revisit your Time Map to make sure it reflects what is most important to you.

This is all it will take to keep time a friend rather than an enemy—an ally that will help you achieve your ultimate goal: living your life the way *you* want, according to your own agenda, not someone else's.

19

Taming Technology

Technology has created a whole new dimension in which to organize, presenting challenges for which we have no historical precedent. As powerful and potentially liberating as technology is, it can also be incredibly overwhelming. It is not uncommon to feel as if you are drowning in a sea of information, surrounded by stacks of faxes, e-mails, voice-mails, and computer files that you have no idea how to organize—adding to the chaos of your paper files. Because previous generations cannot give us any guidance based on their experience, many of us have no framework for how to deal with technology, no system for integrating it smoothly into our lives, and thus we are floundering.

So, instead of just including some tips for how to use technology in each of the practical chapters, I decided to give technology a special chapter of its own, here at the end of the book, the purpose of which is to provide you with that framework: a new, yet simple, straightforward way of thinking about technology that will allow you to organize and tame it just like any other space in your office or home.

To accomplish this, I called on Terry Brock, a leading international expert on technology and president of Achievement Systems in Orlando, Florida. For more than fifteen years, Terry has been teaching business people all over the United States, Canada, Europe, and Asia about the practical uses of technology to boost productivity. (If you'd like to contact Terry directly for more technology information, you may reach him at his web site: **www.terrybrock.com** or call 407-363-0505.) Together, Terry and I offer you the following tips for taking control of technology.

TECHNOLOGY IS A TOOL

One of the biggest mistakes people make is thinking of technology primarily as a time-saving device. It's more accurate to think of it as a set of power tools for helping you do your work faster, more efficiently and effectively. Each tool should have the ability to give you more power than you can imagine to do that work, but it takes a lot of time to research, understand, master, and maintain each tool you buy. So think long and hard before you invest in any new technological tool, and be prepared for a significant, ongoing involvement of time and money.

Technological tools are options: it is your choice whether to use those options or not. You're not obligated to use them simply because they exist. Let the need drive the purchase, not the other way around. Don't buy cool-looking gadgets, gizmos, and software packed with features without understanding whether they'll really be useful to you. If you have a manual system that works for you, there is absolutely no need to change it. Look to technology only if there are processes and projects that seem too time-consuming or difficult to accomplish by hand (like addressing a 2,000-piece mailing once a month). There may be a technological solution out there, and the more specific your need, the easier it will be to find the right tool.

USING MY FORMULA

Technology will not organize you; in fact, it is almost impossible to manage if you aren't organized first. To make the most of what's available, you must start with an organized office, home, paper files, and calendar. Then you can add technology to enhance and interact with your system. After all, in terms of the clutter problems it can present, information generated by technology is really no different from information that comes to your office or home on paper. Therefore, having applied the Analyze and Strategize parts of my formula to the organizing problems encountered in your office and home spaces, you already have the essential information—what's most important to you and your needs, wants, goals, and plan of action—to adapt to your technology problem. You're ready to launch into the Attack stage, where you will decide how to use technology and what new tools to buy to solve your problem based on your individual situation and the way you think.

GENERAL PRINCIPLES FOR ORGANIZING TECHNOLOGY

Information now comes to us from many different directions and many different sources at once: e-mail, c-mail, faxes, voice-mail, regular mail, express mail, Internet research, memos, newsletters, notes from meetings, seminars, and conferences. According to the Gallup Organization, the average Fortune 1000 worker sends or receives 178 messages and documents per day.

The key to tracking it all is to create one logical place to look for any piece of information, regardless of how it was received. Process and file electronic information the same way you do your paper files, according to subject, not method of delivery. In other words, instead of creating file folders labeled "E-mail," "Faxes," "Downloads," and "Voice Messages," file all the information you need to save in folders by topic—e.g., "Investment Tips," "Customer Service," or "Travel Information"—so that in a given folder you will have all your e-mail, faxes, downloads, and voice messages related to that topic regardless of how they were received.

ATTACK

A good way to think of your computer is as a filing cabinet that gets cluttered and overstuffed even faster than a paper-filing cabinet. It is necessary to clean out those files frequently—once a day to once a week is advisable, depending on the volume of work you do.

If you're thinking about buying a larger computer because there's no more room on your hard drive, I suggest you wait because that would be like going to the expense of buying a neat new set of filing cabinets before you've had a chance to sort and purge the contents of your current ones, to find out if you're really out of storage space. After a good sort and purge, you will probably find that you have all the space you need on your hard drive already. Furthermore, with a cleaned-out hard drive, you'll be able to find documents more quickly, and your purged computer will operate faster.

Apply the same sorting and purging criteria to all forms of information, no matter how they come to you. Ask yourself, "Does this tie in with the core activities of my life or business? Will this help me complete a project I am working on right now? Does this represent a viable business opportunity? Do I have the time to take action on this? Under what circumstances would I refer to this again? Do I need to keep it for legal or tax reasons? Would my life change dramatically if I got rid of it?" Then act, file, or toss accordingly.

Note: Terry Brock points out that you can actually stretch storage space on your hard disk by using a FAT 32 instead of a FAT 16 filing system. FAT stands for File Allocation Table and is how computers decide how much space on the hard drive each file will consume. The FAT 16 system will consume significantly more space per file than the highly efficient, compact FAT 32 system.

1. Sort

Ways to Sort

• If you have a huge backlog of files to sort through, approach it the same way you did your paper files, by tackling the most recent, active documents first. In your file directory, sort files by date, working backward. You may want to quickly free up storage space on your hard drive by temporarily transferring elsewhere data more than a year old, such as onto diskettes. Then plan to sort through it in a month or two, after you've gotten your current files organized and under control.

• Although many people store their documents according to which program created them, try sorting according to subject instead. This way, all the spreadsheets, invoices, and letters created for Project 2000 can be more efficiently filed together in a single folder called "Project 2000."

• To decide which documents should be saved on the computer and which should be saved in hard copy, determine first whether your computer will be your primary record-keeping source. If you have a scanner, a very large capacity hard drive, and an excellent backup system, or if you work for a company that has a paperless office policy, then you will use your computer as your main file cabinet. Terry calls scanners the intermediary between the paper-centric and the computer-centric office because they can be used to transfer articles, handwritten notes, memos, business cards, photos, drawings, and charts directly into your computer, where they can then be filed by subject. Once in the computer, these items have more power than they do on paper because you can automatically e-mail or fax them to colleagues and friends and even integrate them into reports and presentations. Using the keyword, lookup, and search functions, it's also quicker and easier to locate a document on your computer than in a paper file. But Terry warns not to automatically toss the paper versions of everything you scan in because they have value too—for tax and legal purposes, and in the event technology changes and today's software can't be read by future computers.

• If your computer will serve as your main filing cabinet, save on paper only original documents such as contracts and paid invoices. You may also want to print out drafts of documents you're working on until they're complete, as hard copy is sometimes easier to work on in these situations.

• If your paper files are going to be your main reference cabinet, save on the computer only those documents and forms you might revise and or reuse. Customized letters and other one-time-only documents can be printed out and stored in your paper file records, then deleted from your hard drive.

2. Purge

As mentioned above, a way to make room on your hard drive without permanently tossing documents is to save data on diskettes, organized by category. Terry also recommends the use of external backup devices like Zip and Jaz drives from Iomega Corp. These are boxes that hook into your computer and allow all your files to be "squirted" into them. The data are stored on cartridges that hold 10–50 times more than a single diskette. These cartridges take up very little space, and can be organized and labeled to make retrieval of data as easy as it is with a diskette.

Julie's No-Brainer Toss List

- **Working drafts**—of documents that have long since been completed.
- **Empty files** you created but never filled.
- **Identical documents** with different names.
- **Files too old to be reused.** (**NOTE:** Do NOT remove .BAK files)

3. Assign a Home

• On Windows 95 (and earlier) operating systems, you can make it easier to find what you're looking for quickly, without having to wade through documents and applications scattered and mixed in with each other: use File Manager or Windows Explorer to organize your hard drive directory into three main subdirectories—"Software" (for all your applications); "Utilities" (for all the maintenance tools on your computer); and "Files" or "Data" (for all your documents, regardless of which program created them). Terry points out that new operating systems such as Office 97 do this automatically with a built-in place on the hard drive called "My Documents."

• Under your directory called "Files" or "My Documents," assign subdirectories (computer file folders) to reflect the categories (zones) of your filing system: e.g., "Advertising," "Clients," "Personnel," "Marketing," "Proposals," "Financial." These subdirectories should mirror your paper file categories as closely as possible. Then each document you decide to keep can be dragged and dropped into its proper subdirectory.

• If you have more than one drive on your computer, you will also have to assign which drive the document should be stored on. If you have a networked computer, your company may have policies as to what is kept on each drive. Otherwise, keep it simple. For example, store work-related documents on one drive, personal projects on the another.

• Save two copies of your archival and working files, one as a master, the other as a backup. Keep your backup data diskettes or cartridges off-site, not in the same place as your master, to reduce the risk of loss or damage to both in the event the worst happens.

4. Containerize

Here are some favorite computer and software tools for containerizing computer data that Terry and I recommend:

Our Favorite Computer Tools

• Explorer—the built-in file manager for Office 97 for creating subdirectories and making finding and filing documents a snap.

• Scanners—insert information directly into your computer, and help you find, file, and print it, but not necessarily edit it. You can edit typewritten text documents that have been scanned, but not pictures and handwritten notes. Software that can convert handwritten notes into text on your computer is on the horizon, but that is not a function you should be currently looking to your scanner to provide. PaperPort is an excellent inexpensive, compact scanner for basic needs.

• Business card scanners—scans and arranges the information directly into your computer's Contact Manager (see Favorite Software Tools). Excellent for quickly indexing and categorizing those piles of business cards in your top desk drawer. CardScan is the best known.

• File indexing program—since it is often easier for a computer to search for a file by keyword than for you to rifle through drawers of folders to find what you're looking for, there are several software programs that allow you to enter documents and file names into the computer to create a sophisticated but easy-to-use index, and virtual file cabinet for them. One such program is Paper Tiger by Barbara Hemphill, another is PaperMaster by Documagix.

Our Favorite Software Tools

• Financial management programs—these can help you do everything from balance your checkbook to pay bills, and even run a small business. Perhaps the most popular and easy to use are Quicken and Quickbooks Pro. Used in conjunction with tax preparation programs such as Turbo Tax, you can file your taxes with the IRS directly from your computer, with the software guiding you as to what papers and forms you need.

• Contact managers and PIMs—these software categories are often confused with each other, because their functions overlap slightly; both help you organize your addresses and contacts, your to-do's and your appointments. However, a Contact Manager organizes the information by person while a PIM organizes it around you and your schedule. A contact manager is primarily a business tool that allows you to customize letters, e-mail and faxes by person, keep a detailed history of all contacts and meetings with that person, and schedule follow-up alarms. Popular contact managers are ACT!, Maximizer, and Ascend (see Favorite E-Mail Tools). A PIM focuses primarily on you, your to-do's, reminders, and phone calls. It has an address book feature and can produce labels and letters, but the information in a PIM works more like a date book or planner. In fact, the most popular PIMs are Lotus Organizer, DayTimer, and DayRunner—which are virtual date books.

• Personal digital assistants (PDAs)—these are electronic intermediaries between the convenience of a paper-based appointment and address book and the power of your computer. You write notes on the small electronic

PDA's like the Handspring Visor bridge the gap between handwritten notes and electronic power *(courtesy of Handspring, Inc.).*

screen with a stylus pen, and the device converts it into text. Any information you enter can be uploaded into your computer at the end of the day. You can also download information from your computer onto the PDA. They are lightweight, brilliant machines that bridge the gap between handwritten notes and the power of the computer. The Palm Pilot is the best selling PDA on the market, due to its compact size and ease of use. Many additional software packages are being designed for it. Other popular PDAs include Casio's Psion and the Newton.

• Project management programs—ideal for guiding you through the steps of large projects by helping you break things into smaller tasks and setting deadlines for each one. Excellent for networked computers where many people are involved in the execution of a project.

• Cookbook, family tree maker, and home inventory programs—all can be very helpful in indexing information that can be hard to categorize. Remember, a computer can do cross-referencing more easily than you can do it manually. Many of these programs guide you through all the steps required to complete a project, yet all require discipline in entering the data. If you don't enjoy data entry, they may not be the best tool for you.

More Tips for Taming Technology

Here are some specific suggestions for organizing several key technologies that are playing an increasingly important role in most offices and homes today. Each is followed by some favorite tools Terry and I recommend for taming the technology and staying in control.

E-MAIL

• There is rarely a reason to save e-mail. You need to treat it like regular paper and either toss it or take action on it. If you do want to save it with the records for a project or for sentimental reasons, simply print and file it. If your computer is your main file cabinet, file it there by subject. If your paper files are your primary source, print and file it. Check to see if your online service automatically files your read e-mail; for example, America Online (AOL) offers an online file cabinet. If you receive a lot of e-mail, it's important to do frequent purges because those filing cabinets quickly get overstuffed and clog your hard drive.

• Schedule specific times during the day to check and process your e-mail—e.g., 8 a.m., 11 a.m., 2 p.m., and 4 p.m.

• Put your full message on the subject line to make it easier for recipient to know what you need, e.g., "Schedule Meeting 11/4 10 a.m.?" or "Send packet by snail-mail today."

• Start long documents with a description of "ACTION REQUESTED." This saves time and helps the reader focus her or his thinking.

• Note reminders to follow up on e-mails in your day planner, not online.

• Send yourself a copy of important e-mails to be sure they went through, or save a copy until everyone has responded.

• Receiving: (1) Sort incoming e-mail by subject, keyword, or person so you can process related mail collectively. This prevents your brain from having to jump around from subject to subject. (2) Use screening devices (such as the Finder tool in Microsoft Exchange) to prioritize incoming e-mail; they will separate e-mail you "carbon-copied" to someone, junk e-mail, notices of meetings, and general information sent to everyone, and process it in order of importance. (3) Screen and process mail for your boss in the following manner: delete, respond, file, print out and file, print out for review.

• Keep your e-mail address book up to date online. File addresses individually and by group. Store e-mail addresses by person in your key address file as well, right alongside their regular address and phone numbers.

• Don't save files in "Incoming Mail." Delete them, or file them in "Personal File Cabinet" by category; this is usually done automatically, so that you only have to create folders and drag and drop.

Our Favorite E-mail Tools

• Contact managers, such as ACT! and Maximizer, can be programmed to send e-mail directly from the program. In other words, you look up "John Smith," click on "Write," then click on "E-mail" and the program automatically logs you on and sends the e-mail.

• Internet providers, such as AT&T, can accomplish this as well.

• PDAs (see Favorite Software Tools). Some, like PalmPilot Professional, will allow you to log on and send and receive e-mail from anywhere in the world.

VOICE-MAIL

• First decision: Where will you record your messages other than on loose scraps of paper? I recommend a two-part telephone message pad, or your calendar. I use a special section of my calendar to record calls I receive when I'm out of the office.

• Record immediately, then delete. Save a minimum number of messages—for example, only those someone may actually need to hear for her- or himself due to some nuanced or emotional content. It takes more time to listen to a voice-mail message than to read a written one.

• Forward voice-mail intended for others if your system allows you to.

• If you want to save a message for record-keeping purposes, write it down and include it in its proper subject file.

• Schedule specific times during the day to check and process your voice-mail—e.g., 8:30 a.m., 11:30 a.m., 2:30 p.m., and 4:30 p.m.

• Put routine requests, e.g., for your fax number, on your outgoing message. Ask caller to leave best times to call him or her back.

• Use a two-part telephone message pad to record messages, then delete them. Use the white slip to track whether the person has taken care of the message, and make sure she or he returns it to you when done.

• Start your outgoing message with your name and what you need from the recipient. Elaborate after that. Give best times to call you back.

• Save yourself time by (1) providing as much detail as possible so that everything can be handled by voice-mail; (2) leaving messages during lunch hour, after work, and early in the morning to avoid time-consuming conversations; and (3) creating an agenda for phone conversations. Reserve a page in your planner for each person, and jot down in it all items you want to discuss with that person so you'll be prepared to just go down the list. Remember that a planned phone call always takes less time than an unplanned one.

• Don't ramble. Be sensitive to the other person's capacity for information overload, too.

• Always conclude your message by giving your phone number clearly and slowly enough for the other person to be able to hear and write it down.

• If your company uses voice-mail for all incoming calls, make sure the message encourages the caller not to hang up in frustration by promising an upcoming live voice if needed, and a company directory so the caller can find what she or he needs even when calling after business hours.

Our Favorite Voice-Mail Tools

• **Voice-mail service by local telephone company.** A relatively recent phenomenon, this service has replaced answering machines and call-waiting for many happy converts. The advantages are many: there is no limit to the number of messages you can receive, many people can leave messages at the same time, no one ever receives a busy signal, your conversation doesn't get interrupted by call-waiting, and you can retrieve, repeat, and save messages from anywhere in the world. The disadvantage is, you don't know if someone is trying to reach you when you're on the phone.

• Answering machines. Still the technology of choice for those who like to screen their calls before picking up the phone.

• Alphanumeric pagers. Callers speak to a live operator, who transmits their text message to your beeper. Their advantage over numeric pagers is that you can find out the nature of the request before returning the phone call, and then decide when and how to respond: a real time-saver.

• Cell phones and beepers. Both are now available with voice-mail so that callers can leave a more detailed message for you than a seven-digit number. Less expensive than alphanumeric paging.

PAPER MAIL AND FAXES

• Presort your boss's mail into bright-colored folders that offer visual cues—e.g., red (for Urgent Action Items), blue (for Nonurgent Action Items), green (for Needs Signature), white (for Reading Material); read first and highlight the important information if you can.

• File mail and faxes in relevant subject folders, not in a "Faxes File."

• If you report to more than one person, simplify communication by keeping a separate In box for each person. Use a vertical sorter with labeled slots for completed work and messages.

• Have separate Out boxes labeled "To Be Filed," "Fax," "Copy," and "Mail" to make processing easier for you.

• Binders take up the same amount of space whether empty or full. Use them if (1) you must often flip between several sections of material, as is the case with projects; (2) there are several users frequently referring to the same information. Bindertek and the Levenger's catalog offer particularly high-quality, attractive binders.

Our Favorite Paper Mail and Faxing Tools

• In and Out boxes—to sort incoming and outgoing mail by person.

• External fax machines—best for offices that handle a high volume of faxes, and people who want to fax magazines and non-computer-generated documents. A fax machine can also serve as a small-volume copier for single-sheet feed.

• Faxing software—to send faxes directly from your computer. If you have a scanner, you can scan in and fax articles and handwritten notes from the computer as well, eliminating the need for an external fax machine.

• Fax stand—adds storage under fax machine for blank fax coversheets and paper supplies.

• Highlighter—Read through mail with highlighter in hand. Highlight items that require action, and due dates on bills. This makes it much easier to identify each document's relevance the second time you read it.

• Article clipper—to cut out articles from magazines and journals that you want to keep. Throw the publication away.

INTERNET

• "Surfing the Net," which is just wandering from one web site to another in an exploratory frame of mind, is one of the great pastimes of the Cyber Age. Make sure you'll be able to return to any sites you discover that pique your interest by bookmarking them, or saving them under "Favorite Places." You can then create folders under "Favorite Places" to categorize and group the sites you like to frequent, e.g., "Personal Development Sites," "Research and News Sites," "Business Sites," etc.

• There is a tremendous amount of information available on the Internet, and you can easily go overboard downloading all kinds of stuff, just because it's free. Learn to be discerning about what you download to keep your hard drive from becoming a cluttered junkyard of files, software programs, and research you never look at.

• The Internet has also become a tremendous source for services. For example, you can now do all of your banking on the Internet through Security First Network Bank and probably others—paying bills, checking balances, doing transfers (www.sfnb.com).

• You can also subscribe to an Internet service for about $15 per month that will automatically back up your entire hard drive on a daily basis to several locations around the country, as an extra security measure. (Enter "Internet Backup" in one of your search engines [see below] to locate a choice of backup services.)

Our Favorite Internet Tools

• Search engines—one of the greatest inventions of the twentieth century for helping you locate information you want from the vast possibilities of the Internet. Insert a couple of keywords or phrases, and they do a speedy search all over the Internet and come back with a list of places where you will find that information. Study the instructions provided by each search engine for narrowing your searches so you don't end up with 3,672 entries. Examples of popular search engines are Yahoo, Hotbot, Excite, and AltaVista.

• Push technology—differs from search engines in that it can be programmed by you to constantly scan the Internet for information on topics of special interest to you. Once it finds something relevant, it delivers it to your "mailbox" for you to pursue if and when you so desire. For example, you can enter the topics "chess," "dominoes," and "beagles," and your Push program will deliver lists and information on those topics gleaned from the Internet every time you turn your computer on. This can be helpful, but easily overwhelming too, clogging up your hard drive with "stuff."

• Internet browsers—the little cyber-spaceships that provide a way on the Net, and cruise you from site to site at your beck and call. Microsoft Internet Explorer and Netscape Navigator are popular browsers.

Labeling

This is as important to do with computer files as it is with paper files, and often more challenging. If your program limits the length of the document name, you can use extension letters to add identifiers, though, as Terry Brock points out, this is becoming an archaic problem, relevant only to older computers. For about $100, owners of such computers can upgrade to a version that will allow them to use more than eight letters to name their documents. But if you don't want to spend the $100, here's how one of my clients named a "proposal for smith" and a "thank-you" letter for Smith, respectively, using extensions: "Prpsl.smi" and "Thanks.smi."

To speed retrieval, be sure to put the name and path of the document (and diskette/cartridge, if applicable) in the header so that you remember what you named each document. This can be automatically done on Office 97 by first clicking on "View," then "Header and Footer," then "Insert Autotext," then "Filename and Path."

5. Equalize

Remember, your computer is, in many ways, just another filing cabinet (granted, a very smart one). Yet, of all the filing cabinets in your office, it is probably the one that is *most* prone to being overstuffed with clutter. Auto-backup and multiple drafts accumulate quickly; they can get confusing and take up unnecessary storage space.

Frequent maintenance is critical to keep your electronic file cabinet clean and uncluttered so that it can work smart and fast—even more frequent maintenance than is required of file cabinets storing your paper files.

• **Daily.** As often as possible, save documents directly to their proper subdirectory the moment you create them. This will prevent you from having to take extra time to file later on. Otherwise, at the end of each day, file any new documents you have created from their originating software application to their appropriate subject folders in your directory.

• **Monthly.** I suggest having a computer "doctor" come in every month or two to check for computer viruses and scattered bytes and to clean out unnecessary files and your system. Let him or her get to know you, your needs, and your system well.

- **Regular "tune-ups."** Selecting the right software to match your needs is a challenge because even when you find the "right" program, it may often be flawed in some way. Reevaluate your software programs every six months to see if they're both doing the job and making life easier for you. If not, there may be some unexplored features in the software you should learn. Or maybe now is the time to consider whether or not to go with that upgrade offered by the software manufacturer. However, be sure to ask if the upgrade will address the problems you've been experiencing. If not, you may want to look into a new software program. Remember, each new program you buy not only costs money but takes time to learn and maintain. So do your homework before making a switch. If you decide to upgrade equipment, such as your computer or printer, Terry counsels you not to throw out your old one. Having a backup can be a lifesaver, especially if you're in business, which is why he advises those with deep pockets to buy two of every technology they deem critical to their needs.

Avoiding Information Overload

The volume of information we're bombarded with today far exceeds that of any previous generation, and will only increase thanks to the "information superhighway." Here's how to avoid being struck down:

- Be realistic. You can't read everything available to you. Limit subscriptions to those publications, paper and electronic, you read thoroughly and regularly.
- File articles in appropriate subject files—e.g., articles from *Business Week* should go in your "Financial Planning" folder, not in a *Business Week* file.
- Collect all physical reading material in one place—in a basket under your desk, perhaps, or a drawer, shelf, or tray. You can easily grab some of it to read during your commute, for example. Clean out weekly. Never let it overflow.
- Keep the source, toss the paper. Information is updated all the time. Don't save anything that will be outdated soon. Use the Internet to access current information on a wealth of subjects.

Resources for Organizing Products

CATALOGS:

Office/Home Office

Bindertek	www.bindertek.com
Reliable	www.reliable.com
Quill	www.quillcorp.com
Office Depot	www.officedepot.com
Staples	0800 141414/www.staples.co.uk
IKEA	www.ikea.co.uk
Levenger	www.levenger.com
Mobile Office Outfitter	www.mobilegear.com
Reliable Home Office	(800) 869-6000
TimeWise	(613) 728-6777/www.timewise.net
20th Century Plastics	(800) 767-0777

Home

Container Store	www.containerstore.com
Get Organized	(800) 803-9400
Exposures	www.exposuresonline.com
Frontgate	www.frontgate.com
Hold Everything	(800) 421-2264
Ikea	www.ikea.co.uk
Levenger	www.levenger.com
Lillian Vernon	www.lillianvernon.com
Neat Way	(800) 418-9239
Pottery Barn	www.potterybarn.com
Trifles Spaces	(800) 456-7019

Time

At-A-Glance	www.ataglance.com
DayRunner	(714) 680-3500/www.dayrunner.com
DayTimer	01992 824360/www.daytimer.com
Franklin Covey	0870 600 0226/www.franklincovey.co.uk

STORES:

Office

Staples   0800 141414/www.staples.co.uk
Office Depot   www.officedepot.com
Office Max   (800) 788-8080

Home

Bed, Bath and Beyond   www.bedbathandbeyond.com
Container Store   www.containerstore.com
Home Depot   www.homedepot.com
Lechters Housewares   (800) 605-4824
California Closet Co.   www.calclosets.com

ADDITIONAL RESOURCES

Public Storage Self-Storage
  (pickup and delivery)   800-44-STORE
The To-Do Book & Paper Tiger Software   800-427-0237
Ginny's Ear Nest (jewelry organizers)   www.ear-nest.com
Flex Sort (expanding desktop sorter)   800-499-5043
Client Valuation Services (guide to
  making money on used clothing)   800-875-5927
The National Association of Professional
  Organizers—Information and Referral
  Hotline (for names of organizers in
  your area)   www.napo.net

Suggested Further Reading

OFFICE/HOME OFFICE

The Organized Executive, Stephanie Winston, Warner Books, 1983.
Organized to Be the Best, Susan Silver, Adams Hall, 1991.
Organizing Your Workspace, Odette Pollar, Crisp Publications, 1992.
Making the Most of Workspaces, Lorrie Mack, Rizzoli International, 1995.
Taming the Paper Tiger, Barbara Hemphill, Random House, 1997.
Working from Home, Paul and Sarah Edwards, Jeremy P. Tarcher, Inc., 1990.
Working Solo, Terri Lonier, Portico Press, 1996.

HOME

Children's Rooms, Jane Lott, Prentice-Hall, 1989.
The Complete Home Organizer, Maxine Ordesky, Grove Press, 1993.
Get Your Act Together, Pam Young and Peggy Jones, HarperPerennial, 1993.
Getting Organized, Stephanie Winston, Warner Books, 1978.
The Family Manager's Guide for Working Moms, Kathy Peel, Ballantine Books, 1997.
Making the Most of Storage, Debora Robertson, Rizzoli International, 1996.
Storage, Dinah Hall and Barbara Weiss, DK Publishing, 1997.

TIME

The Seven Habits of Highly Effective People, Steven R. Covey, Fireside, 1989.
It's About Time! The Six Styles of Procrastination and How to Overcome Them, Linda Sapadin and Jack Maguire, Viking, 1996.

Acknowledgments

Writing this book was an incredible journey for me. The task seemed so monumental, an impossible dream way out of my reach. I will be forever grateful to every individual who encouraged, supported, inspired, and guided me along the path, and there were many.

I draw my energy from an extraordinary circle of friends and family who provide me with a steady stream of love, community, and belonging, no matter how isolated I get when doing my work. Heartfelt love and appreciation goes to my family: David and Sonia Morgenstern; Steve and Sue Morgenstern; Rhonda Morgenstern; Myra, Alberto, Amanda, Jasmin, and Adam Rios; the Bayuk family; and Gerry and Lillian Colon. For their remarkable friendship, I thank Judy Wineman; Zoe Anderheggen; Camille, Peter, Hanna, and Zoe Ehrenberg; Cati Sorra; Richard Soll; Liz and Bill Derman; Ellen and Drew Driesen; Susan and Richie Sporer; Marilyn and Joel Duckoff; Debra Barchat and Martin Bernstein; Sonia and Gustavo Blankenberg; Robin Goldfin, and Eneida, Yvette, and Cynthia Rada.

Tremendous gratitude to all the people who have been a part of Task Masters, the breeding ground for all the material found in the pages of this book. First and foremost, I am grateful to my clients, whose courage to conquer their chaos inspires and teaches me, and to all of the students who attend my seminars and help me develop the clarity of my message.

I am grateful to all the organizers at Task Masters who understand the power of organizing from the inside out and have helped me test and develop the techniques you read about in this book: Deborah Kinney, Ron Young, Loretta Maresco, Judith Green, Lisa Sack, Judy Stern, Carol Crespo, Frank Acevedo, Kathy Soffer, Valerie Soll, Lori Marks, and Christine Brooks. A very special thank-you to one of my original organizers, Valerie Soll, who deftly showed me how to use my own organizing techniques to tackle the chaos of writing this book.

I am blessed with a circle of advisors who have guided Task Masters through the trials and tribulations of building a business with generous doses of wisdom, encouragement, and very practical help. My most heartfelt thanks go to Urban Mulvehill, Harry Lowenstein and Irwin Coplin at SCORE, Anthony Graffeo, Walt Taylor, Gerry Scattaglia, Lisa LaVecchia, Rae Retek. I am also deeply grateful to my colleagues at NAPO; especially Barbara Hemphill, Paulette Ensign, Harold Taylor, and Gloria Ritter; NSA, especially Terri Lonier, Nancy Rosanoff, Mark LeBlanc, Bob Frare, Darren LaCroix, Ed Brodow, and Dr. John DeMartini; and at Toastmasters, especially Mary Bryant, Marilyn Lundy, John Shrawder, Amelia Abad, Mark LaVergne, and Ray Frier, all for their pivotal words of encouragement and advice at just the right moment.

My most heartfelt thanks go to Terry Brock for believing in the success of this book and so generously sharing his special wisdom in the "Taming Technology" chapter.

I am extremely fortunate to have in my life a number of very special people who have been so pleased with my work that they have gone out of their way to help spread the word about my company. From the bottom of my heart, I thank Spencer Christian, Mandy Patinkin, Jacques D'Amboise, Lesli Kappel, Paul Argenti, Gordon Rothman, Kim McCabe, Gordon Mehler, Charlie Monheim, David Hochberg, Mike McCormack, Susan Scheuing, Marianne Wascak, Harriet Wohlgemuth, Larry Winokur, Robin Weitz, Emily Tufeld, and Tony Grillo for their wonderful enthusiasm and generous support of my work.

Bryan Oettel gave me the experience of a lifetime the day he called from Henry Holt and Company to ask if I would like to write a book for them. The patience and encouragement that Brian first extended me were just the beginning of the regal, caring treatment I have received from the incredible folks at Henry Holt and Company. I extend my deepest gratitude to publisher Wendy Sherman for enthusiastically believing in this project from the minute she heard about it and for guiding the project so expertly from afar. I most especially want to thank my incredibly talented editor David Sobel, and his assistant Amy Rosenthal, who in their gentle, wise way helped me bring my material to a brilliant focus and shine.

Ironically, the hardest part about writing this book was organizing the material. I sincerely thank writers Laura Salas, Cynthia L. Cooper, Barbara Warton, Barbara Spiridon, Carol Milano, Matthew Sartwell, and Katherine Cavanaugh for their help and guidance along the way.

Most importantly, I am deeply indebted to John McCarty, who expertly and patiently worked hand in hand with me to structure the manuscript, all the while instilling in me confidence in my own talent for writing.

I feel very lucky to be blessed with my wise agent, Faith Hamlin, who had an incredible knack for knowing just when to nurture me and when to put a gun to my head, to make sure I got the book done on time, and made the most of all the resources available to me.

I send a deeply felt thank-you to my readers, Kathryn Grody, Ron Young, John Gillespie, Ellen Driesen, and David Morgenstern for so generously sharing their time, unique points of view, and invaluable feedback on the manuscript.

Behind the scenes, I thank my computer doctor Chris Behnam, who came to my rescue several times; Arthur Cohen, for his photographic talents; and Jean-François Pilon, who keeps taming the chaos of my curly hair.

From the depths of my heart, I thank three very special people who basically acted as doctor, midwife, and birthing coach during the often challenging labor of delivering this book. To Faye Cone, whose masterful guidance and tireless support were a major catalyst in the transformation of this book from thought in my head to completed manuscript. To Linda Jacobs, who in her elegant, gentle way helped me draw from my center to find expression for the truth I had inside.

And to Ric Murphy, whose perspective on life, poetry of soul, and sense of humor always make me howl with laughter just when things are looking their most bleak.

Finally, I thank my extraordinary daughter Jessi, who is the greatest blessing in my life, my ongoing source of inspiration, and a wise soul who has been my closest business advisor and companion in the journey of Task Masters and this book.

—Julie Morgenstern
February 1998

Index

abundance, need for, 26–27, 191–92, 203
accessibility, 64, 145, 185, 175
accessories, 162, 163, 172
acrylic organizers, 156
ACT! (software), 224, 233, 235
"action" box, 61
action items, 227
action titles, 81
active projects, 108
activity zones, 50
    attics, basements, and garages, 138–39
    bathrooms, 151
    bedrooms, 160
    children's rooms, 181–82
    closets, 169–70
    and containers, 67
    cubicle workstation, 104
    defining and mapping, 53–55
    home-based office, 93–95
    home-office files, 98–99
    household information center, 124–25
    kitchen, 51, 192–93
    living room, 54, 203–4
    mobile office, 112–13
    rearranging furniture for, 55–56
    time management, 216–17
    traditional office, 75–76
addresses, 235
adhesives, 175
aesthetics, 66, 226
air-train travel, 112, 118
AltaVista, 238
American Academy of Pediatrics, 153

America Online (AOL), 234–35
analyzing, 15, 71
    attics, basements, and garages, 136–38
    bathrooms, 149–51
    bedroom, 158–59
    children's rooms, 179–81
    closets, 166–69
    cubicle workstation, 102–4
    defined, 39–46
    home-based office, 90–92
    household information center, 122–24
    kitchen, 190–92
    living rooms, 201–3
    mobile office, 110–12
    time management, 214–16
    traditional office, 73–75
Annual Clothing Exchange, 174
"annual giving" file, 130
answering machine, 236, 237
appliances, 143, 174, 194, 197
appointment books, 128; *see also*
    planners
archives
    boxes, 142
    computer files, 232
    photo, 147
art, 186, 206
articles, 83, 97, 130, 238, 240
arts and crafts zone, 182, 193
Ascend (software), 233
assigning a home, 18
    and accessibility, 64
    and appropriate sizing, 63

assigning a home (*cont'd*)
  attics, basements, and garages, 144–45
  bathrooms, 155–56
  bedrooms, 163
  children's rooms, 185
  closets, 175
  computer files, 232
  cubicle workstation, 107–8
  defined, 50–51, 57, 59, 63–64
  home-based office, 96, 99–100
  household information center, 130–33
  kitchen, 197–98
  living rooms, 206–7
  mobile office, 117–19
  and safety, 64
  and single-function storage, 63
  time management, 222–23
  traditional office, 84–86
ATM slips, 128
attacking, 15, 71
  attics, basements, and garages,
    141–48
  bathroom, 152–57
  bedrooms, 162
  children's rooms, 183–89
  closets, 172–78
  cubicle workstation, 105–9
  defined, 58, 59–68
  home-based office, 97–98
  household information center, 126–35
  kitchen, 194–200
  living rooms, 205–9
  mobile office, 114–21
  time management, 220–27
  technology, 230–40
  traditional office, 79–89
attics, basements, and garages, 136–48
audiotapes, 107, 117, 163, 203, 205–8
auto-desk, 120
automobile
  mobile office, 113, 119, 120
  records, 99, 128
  zone, 138

baby, 23, 143, 183
backup files, 232
  external devices, 231
banker's boxes, 72, 98, 133, 147
banking, 79, 99, 128, 129
  online, 238

baskets, 163, 208
  floor, 176
  sliding, 157, 198
bathing zone, 151
bathrooms, 56, 149–57
batteries, 146, 174
bed, 160, 163, 182–83
bedding, 161, 163
bedrooms, 55, 126, 133, 158–65
bedside table, 161, 163
beepers, 237
before and after photos, 65
belts, 40, 163
beverages, 72
"big picture goals," 44
bikes, 140, 146
bill-paying, 125, 131, 134, 135
binders, 107, 237
Bindertek, 237
bins, 177
  flip-down, 146
  floor, 176
  large plastic, 147, 164
  overhead storage, 107
  plastic, 177, 178, 186
  under-bed, 163
blankets, 163
blow dryer, 114, 155, 157
bookends, 89
books, 22, 162, 203, 205, 207, 208
  children's, 186
  in several rooms, 162
  office, 80, 95
  purging, 83, 143, 163, 206
bookshelves, 24, 95, 207
  containers, 89
books on tape, 117
boss
  disorganized, 21, 23–24, 103
  mail, 237
boxes
  dresser-top, 163
  fabric, 176
  flat file, 142
  galvanized, 101, 208
  paper-covered, 133
  for sorting, 72, 165
briefcase, 86, 117, 118, 119, 120
brochures, 99, 130
Brock, Terry, 228, 230, 231, 239

buffet cabinet, 207
built-in units, 55, 161
bulk supplies, 153
bumper clothing protector, 120
business card scanners, 233

cabinets, 24
  bathrooms, 152
  garden and hardware, 146
  kitchen, 194, 197
calendar
  household, 126
  message center, 134
  /planner, 117, 120
  voice-mail messages, 236
call-waiting, 236
can crusher, 147
canisters, 156
cart, rolling, 96, 194
CardScan, 233
carousel displays, 164
carry-on tote, 118
catalogs, 128, 130, 134
CDs, 119, 163, 203, 205–8
cell phones, 237, 120
childhood trauma, 26, 30, 32
checklist
  laminated, 176
  packing, 114
chair, office, 93
conquistador of chaos, 27–28, 216
creativity, 31
charity, 63, 144, 175, 206
  solicitations, 130
checks, 130
children, 21, 134
  bathrooms, 151
  daily cleanup, 148
  kitchen, 197
  homework mess, 209
  memory box, 142
  rooms, 179–89
chores, sorting, 162
cleaning
  caddy, 186, 198
  daily, 68
  supplies, 72, 174
  time, 51, 57, 155
  zone, 151
client files, 97

closets, 56, 166–78
  dividers, 24
  portable, 146
  See also specific types
clothes
  hampers, 155
  off-season, 139, 140, 141, 162, 171, 182
  purging, 173–74
  sorting, 172
  See also laundry
clothes closets, 40, 167, 169
  children's rooms, 182
  containers, 146, 175–76
  no-brainer toss list, 162
  ongoing give-away, 165
  purging, 173
  rearranging, 171
  rods, 170–71
  shared, 175
  sorting, 115, 141
  travel, 113–14, 115, 118
clothesline, 186
clothespins, 146
coat closet, 41
collapsible tote, 120
collectibles, 204, 206
color-coding
  children's rooms, 186
  closet, 178
  filing system, 31, 86, 87
  planner entries, 227
community time zone, 216
commuting time, 217
"complete picture" tip, 43
complex, confusing system, 19
  children's rooms, 181
  closets, 169
  home-based office, 92
  kitchen, 191
computer
  cart, 95
  "doctor," 239
  home-based office, 100
  monitor position, 77, 95
  planners, 224–25
  supplies, 79
  tools, for containerizing, 232–34
  upgrades, 20, 240
  zone, 53, 55, 76, 94

computer files, 228, 230–34, 239–40
  labeling, 239
  purging, 231–32
  sorting, 230–31
  upgrades, 240
confidential files, 84
consignment shops, 63
Contact Manager program, 83, 224, 233, 235
containerizing
  advantages of, 64
  attics, basements, and garages, 145–47
  bathrooms, 152, 156–57
  bedrooms, 163–64
  children's rooms, 185–87
  closets, 175–78
  cubicle workstation, 108
  defined, 57, 59, 64–67
  electronic/technology files, 232–39
  home-based office, 96, 100–101
  household information center, 133–34
  kitchen, 196, 198–99
  living rooms, 207–8
  mobile office, 119–20
  time management, 223–26
  traditional office, 86–89
containers, 12, 25, 146
  buying and labeling, 66–67
  flip-top, 157
  plastic, 176
  office file, 88–89
  See also specific types
conventions, 121
cooking
  software, 234
  utensils, 194
  zone, 51, 52, 192, 193
correspondence, 117. See also e-mail; faxes; mail
cosmetics, 118, 154, 157
creativity, 25, 31
credenza, 75
credit card records, 128, 129
crisis, 27–28, 57
cubicle workstations, 102–9

daily files, 84
daily maintenance
  attics, basements, and garages, 148
  bathrooms, 157

bedrooms, 165
children's rooms, 188
closets, 178
computer and technology files, 239
cubicle workstation, 108
home-based office, 101
household information center, 135
kitchen, 199–200
living rooms, 208
mobile office, 121
time management, 226
traditional office, 89
data board, 225
DayRunner, 224, 233
DayTimer, 224, 233
deadlines, 20
dealers, 144
death of loved one, 23, 33
delegating tasks, 222
designers' swatches files, 88
design zone, 94
desk
  area under, 104, 108
  file drawers in, 84
  position, 76, 77, 95
  home-based office, 93, 95
desktop
  containers, 105
  files, 89
  mobile travel, 119
  pigeon-holer, 100
diaper bag, 10–11
dining room, 55, 126
  storage units, 53
  zones, 53
dishes
  assigning home, 197, 198, 207
  doing, 199–200, 217
  purging, 196
  sorting, 195
  zone, 51, 192, 193
dishpan or tub, 186
diskettes, 88
  holders, portable, 119
  vs. Zip and Jaz disks, 231
dislike space, 32–33, 92, 123
disorganization, reasons for, 16–17
distraction, need for, 32
dividend payment records, 128
Documagix, 233

door, storage on, 96, 119, 171, 182, 187, 194
downsizing, 20, 21
drafts, previous, 83, 99
drawers
  bedroom 163
  dividers, 24, 156, 157, 198
  kitchen, 197
  living room, 206
  pull-out, 140, 157
  sliding, 177
  stacking, 140, 176
  wood and wicker basket, 133
dress clothes, 171
dresser
  assigning homes in bedroom, 163
  boxes for top, 163
  children's rooms, 185
  closet, 170–71, 175
  creative use of, 161
dressing zone, 55, 182
  mobile office, 112, 113
dry cleaning basket, 155
dual purpose rooms, 95
duplicates, 57, 83, 106, 153, 174, 196

education zone, 216, 219
Edwards, Paul and Sarah, 92
80-20 rule, 44, 203
electronic information, 229–40
electronics equipment, 143
e-mail, 20, 22, 228, 230
  and contact manager, 233
  and PDAs, 120, 224
  taming, 234–36
employee, 21, 24, 93
energy cycles, 223
entertaining zones, 53, 204
entry hall closets, 167, 170, 175–77
equalize
  attics, basements, and garages, 147–48
  bathrooms, 157
  bedrooms, 165
  children's rooms, 187–88
  closets, 178
  computer files, 239–40
  cubicle workstation, 108–9
  defined, 57, 59, 67–68
  home-based office, 96, 101
  household information center, 134–35
  kitchen, 199–200
  living rooms, 208–9
  mobile office, 120–21
  technology, 239–40
  time management, 226–27
  traditional office, 89
expense report, 120
expensive items, 62–63
Exposures, 147
external realities, 17, 20–24

family, 20, 24
  attics, basements, and garages, 136
  closets, 175
  Fun Zone, 54
  Games/Leisure Zone, 204
  household information center, 134
  living rooms, 201
  time zone, 216, 223
family tree maker program, 234
fantasy pitfall, 196
FAT 32 vs. FAT 16 system, 230
faxes, 20, 22, 228, 230
  and contact manager, 233
  machine, 100, 237
  number requests, 236
  tools, 237–38
fear of losing creativity, 31
fear of success/fear of failure, 29
fees, 217–19
file/blanket chest, 133
file boxes, portable, 100, 120, 130, 133
file cabinet, 53
  home-based office, 93, 95
  household information center, 126, 130, 133
  lateral, 77, 88
  location, 75, 77
  online, 234–35
  wood-rattan bureau, 133
file divider, self-adhesive, 89
file drawers, 84
file folders, 72, 86, 87, 88, 120
  classification, 89
  electronic information, 230, 231, 232
  mail and faxes, 237
  See also hanging files
file frame, self-standing, 108
files and filing system
  categories, 62, 81–82, 84, 85

files and filing system (*cont'd*)
  cause of problems, 75
  color coding, 86, 87
  containerizing, 86–87
  e-mail, 234–35
  folder thickness, 81
  grouping, in hanging folders, 87
  home-based office, 97–98
  household information center, 125, 130–33
  index, 85–86
  indexing program, 233
  insider's tip, 86
  keeping within arm's reach, 77
  labeling, 86, 89
  paper vs. computer, 231
  planning zones, 78–79
  purging, 82–83, 116
  off-site, 84
  sorting office, 80–82
  storage, 124
  straight-line, 87, 88
  tab coding, 87–88
  titles, 80–81, 85–86
  zone, 98, 104
  See also computer files
file trolleys, 134
FiloFax, 224
financial management software, 233
financial papers, 88, 98, 130
  sorting, 127–28
Financial Time Zone, 216
first-aid kit, 153
fishing gear, 140
floors, 100, 108, 176
food, 195, 197
  Preparation Zone, 51, 52, 192, 194
  Serving Zone, 192, 193
  Storage Zone, 51, 52, 192, 193
Franklin-Covey Planner, 224
free time, 227
frequent flyer numbers, 114
friends, 63, 174
Frontgate, 147
fun, 65, 219
  ideas file, 98
furniture, 63
  attics, basements, and garages, 140
  bathrooms, 152
  bedrooms, 160, 161

children's rooms, 182
home-based office, 93, 95
household information center, 125–26
kitchen, 193
living rooms, 204
off-site storage for, 143–44
purging, 143, 206
rearranging for activity zones, 55–56
traditional office, 76–77

games, 204, 206
  zone, 53, 182
garage, 56, 136–48
garbage cans, 146
gardening, 140, 141, 143
  containers, 146
  zone, 139
garment racks, 146
Get Organized, 147
giving items away, 72, 143. *See also* charity; friends
glasses, kitchen, 197
glove compartment, 119
goals
  combining activities and, 217
  for getting organized, 45–46
  posting, 65
  postponing, 219
  time management, 226
  See also unclear goals and priorities
"Golden Nuggets" binder, 98
grocery bag recycler, 198
grocery receipts, 129
grooming, 151, 154, 160
grouping similar items, 60, 64
  electronic information, 230
  office files, 81–82, 87
  publications, 89
  time management, 222

habits and preferences, 54, 55, 207
hair care items, 154, 155, 157
hallway cabinet, 176
hand-washed items, 155
hangers, 171, 176, 177, 178
hanging files, 87, 88
  box-bottom, 87, 88
  pocket, 133
hard copy, 231

hard drive, 231–32, 238
hardware zone, 146
Hemphill, Barbara, 128, 233
highlighter, 238
hoarding, 106
hobby supplies, 204
Hold Everything, 133, 147, 164
holiday wrapping, 139, 143, 174, 177
home-based businesses, 21, 90–101
   boundaries between work and home,
     95
   increasing fees, 217–19
   mobile office, 116
   multiple careers, 94
home improvement receipts, 129
home inventory programs, 234
Homework Zone, 209
hooks, 77, 140, 152
Hotbot, 238
hotel room, 119
hot files, 77, 89
household information center, 51, 52,
   122–35
household inventory, 128
household repair records, 129
hutch, 207

important items. see what items are most
   essential
incomplete projects, 61
information, 41, 99
   core, 82–83
   Internet, 238
   overload, 22, 240
   planner selection, 226
   technology taming and, 228, 229–30
In/Out basket, 89, 100, 105, 108, 237
insurance
   claims, 125, 131
   policies, 128, 130
Internet, 235, 238–39, 240
interoffice communication zone, 76
interruptions, 20
investment records, 128, 130
invisible stuff, 61
"is it worth the time?" tip, 57
items have no home, 18, 42
   attics, basements, and garages, 138
   bathrooms, 150
   children's rooms, 181

household information center, 123
   living rooms, 203
   mobile office, 112
   traditional office, 75

jacket pocket, 118
Jaz drive, 231
jewelry, 163, 164
job search, 23
judgmental, how to avoid being, 184
junk mail, 129

key people, 227
keys, hotel, 119
kindergarten model of organization,
   49–56
   and activity zones, 50–54
   and time management, 213–14, 216
   See also activity zones
kitchens, 51, 125–26, 190–200

labeling, 66–67
   bathrooms, 157
   bedrooms, 164
   children's rooms, 187
   closets, 178
   computer and electronic information,
     239
   cubicle workstation, 108
   files, 86
   household information center, 134
   kitchen, 199
   living rooms, 208
   mobile office, 120
   traditional office, 89
Lagan, Connie, 11
laptop computer, 113, 120
Laundry Zone, 139, 151, 155, 186
law of visible, dramatic results, 60–62, 84,
   116
layering activities, 217
leather sleeve, 120
legal papers, 82, 89, 106, 128
letters, 83, 142, 231, 233
letter trays, 133
Levenger's, 237
Library Zone, 94, 100, 162
lid holders, 198
lifestyle papers, 127–28, 135
lighting, 93, 175

Lillian Vernon (catalog), 147, 175
limited space, 24
    bathrooms, 150
    closets, 168
    signs of, 24–25
linen closets, 167, 169, 175
    containers, 177–78
linens, 172, 173
literature, 115, 116
    containers, 77, 101, 108
living rooms, 53, 54, 133, 201–9
loan records, 128
logical sequencing, 64, 144–45, 172
Lotus Organizer, 224–25, 233
luggage, 118, 162
luggage rack, 147

magazines, 22
    holders, 89, 100, 147, 157, 186
    purging, 83, 107, 128, 130, 143, 163,
        206
    sorting, 80
magnetic strips, 194
mail, 14, 77, 89, 108, 124
    sorting boss's, 237
    taming, 237–38
    See also e-mail; faxes; voice-mail
mailing assembly zone, 53
Mailings/Literature Zone, 94
maintenance, 67–68. See also daily
        maintenance; ongoing
        maintenance; tune-up
Main Work Zone, 94
maple rack, 198, 199
mapping space, for activity zones,
    54–55
master storage plan, 167, 168
Maximer (software), 233, 235
maybes, 84
meal planning, 125
measuring, 66, 176, 223
media storage unit, 208
medical records, 129
medicine chest, 155, 156
medicines, 154, 155, 157
    zone, 151, 153
meetings, 76, 222
memorabilia, 141–42, 147
    zone, 139, 141
memory book, 184–85

memory box, 142, 184
mesh baskets/stationery trays, 89, 96
messages
    voice-mail, 236
    zone, 105, 125, 126, 134
metal file frame, 88
Microsoft Exchange, Finder tool, 235
Microsoft Internet Explorer, 239
milk crates, 177
"miscellaneous" category, 127, 167
mobile office, 110–21
Mobile Office Catalog, 120
monthly maintenance, computer files,
        239, 239
more stuff than space, 18–19, 24
    bathrooms, 150
    closets, 173
    cubicle workstation, 103
    kitchen, 191
    mobile office, 111
    time management, 215
mortgage records, 128
motivation, 46, 65
moving, 20, 23
mudroom shoe/boot rack, 176
Music Zone, 53, 54, 160, 204

nail care items, 154
Napping Zone, 67, 204
National Association of Professional
        Organizers (NAPO), 145
needs assessment questions, 39–46
Netscape Navigator, 239
newspapers, 107, 143, 206
    recycler, 147
Newton, 224, 234
no-brainer toss lists, 62
    attics, basements, and garages, 142–43
    bathrooms, 154–55
    bedrooms, 162
    closets, 173–74
    computer files, 232
    cubicle workstation, 107
    home-based office, 99
    household information center,
        129–30
    kitchen, 196–97
    living rooms, 206
    mobile office, 116–17
    traditional office, 83

nooks and crannies, 141
notes, 41, 97, 98

Office 97 (software), 232, 239
office
   activity zones, 53
   equipment, 80
   storage units, 53
   supplies, 79–80, 84–85, 99–100
   time to organize, 56
   tools, 80
   See also cubical workstation; files;
      home-based business; mobile office;
      traditional office
"one in, one out" rule, 226
ongoing maintenance
   bathrooms, 157
   bedrooms, 165
   closets, 178
   cubicle workstation, 109
   household information center, 135
   living rooms, 209
   mobile office, 121
   time management, 226
   traditional office, 89
organizing
   analyze, strategize, and attack strategy,
      15
   estimating time for, 56–58
   and SPACE formula, 59–68
   frustration of, 3–4
   impossibility vs. sustainability of, 11
   from inside out, defined, 13–15
   kindergarten model of, 49–56
   mantras, 12
   misconceptions about, 9–12
   motivation for, 65
   new way of looking at, 9, 13–15
   as nonproductive vs. productive use of
      time, 11–12
   obstacles, 16–35
   from outside in, 12–13
   as overwhelming vs. empowering, 11
   as talent vs. skill, 9–11, 68
   zigzag, 61–62
   See also analyzing; attack; strategizing;
      and specific items, spaces, and zones
organizing is boring, 19–20
   children's rooms, 181
   traditional office, 75

out boxes, 237
"out" guides, 88
outlets, 54, 93, 100, 108, 204
out of sight, out of mind, 19, 124

packet organizer rack, 198
pagers, 237
Palm Pilot, 224, 234, 235
pantry, 52, 194, 197, 198
   zone, 139
PaperMaster (software), 233
papers, 20
   boxes for archiving, 72
   computerizing, 231
   cubicle workstation, 103, 106
   household, 124, 126, 127–30
   mobile office, 114–15
   piled on desk, 75
   storage, 126
   traditional office, 80–82
   volume control, 82–83
Paper Tiger (software), 233
paperwork zone, 53, 55, 76, 160, 162
Peg-Boards, 140, 146
pencil dot test, 89
perfection, 34–35
personal digital assistants (PDAs), 120,
      224, 233–34
personal files, 84
Personal Information Management
      (PIM) programs, 225, 233, 235
personal item zone, 104
Phirripidus, George, 119
photos
   containers, 147, 208, 209
   purging, 206
   sorting and saving, 127, 142
planner, 223–26, 227, 235
planning/scheduling zone, 94
plan of action, creating, 47–58
pocket bags, 177
pocket files, 88, 133
Post-it Notes, 72, 86, 88
pots and pans, 194, 195, 197, 198
preprinted labels and envelopes, 113
presentation and selling zone, 112, 113
privacy, 20. 109
"problems log," 43
procrastination, 31
"project box," 31, 100, 108

project management programs, 234
property records, 128
proposals, 83
prospect files, 97
Psion, 234
psychological obstacles, 17, 25–34
purging
    attics, basements, and garages, 142–44
    bathrooms, 154–55
    bedrooms, 162–63
    children's rooms, 184–85
    closets, 173–75
    computer and electronic information,
        231–32
    cubicle workstation, 106–7
    defined, 59, 62–64
    home-based office, 96, 97, 99
    household information center, 128–30
    kitchen, 196–97
    living rooms, 206
    mobile office, 116–17
    need for, 16
    shortcutting pitfall, 97
    sprees, 12
    time management, 222
    traditional office, 82–84, 89
    what to do with discards, 63
purse, 118
push technology, 238–39
puzzle trays, 186

Quicken and QuickBooks Pro, 233
quick sort, 61

racks, 140
    battery, 146
    belt, 40
    floor, 176
    kitchen, 198–99
    sports and bike, 146
    wall mounts, 146
reading, while sorting, 84
reading file, travel, 117
reading material
    purging, 116, 240
    sorting, 162
    See also specific types
reading zone, 53, 54, 55, 67, 160, 203
rearranging, 25
receipts

cash, 97–98
files, 88, 97–98, 99
how long to keep, 129, 130, 143
mobile office, 120
sorting, 127, 130
Recycling Zone, 139, 147
reference books, 107, 108
Reference Zone, 76, 104
Relationship Time Zone, 216
reminder system, 19
    e-mail, 235
    planner, 227
    software, 233
remote control caddy, 207
rent receipts, 129
reports, 107
research library, 100
research materials, 83
résumé, 129
retirement, 23
retreat, need to, 30–31, 215
rewarding yourself along the way, 65
road maps, 130
Rolodex, 83, 89
room divider, 95, 204
roommate, 21, 24
rotation box, 185

safe deposit box, 129, 131–32
safety, 64, 118, 197
sales books, 116
Say Yes to Your Dreams (Taylor), 29
scanners, 231, 233
scarf stand, 176
schedule, 129, 213–27
    template, 218
    See also planner; time management
schoolwork, 23, 181, 184, 186
screens, 164
search engines, 238
secretary, 14
sections, organizing by, 61–62
Security First Network Bank, 238
Seinfeld, Jerry, 213
Select One Rule, 63, 223
Self Time Zone, 216
sentimental attachment, 33–34, 138, 196,
    203. See also memory book; memory
    box
serving pieces, 206

shared space, 20, 21, 175
shelf dividers, 175, 177
shelves
    bathroom, 152
    bedroom, 161, 163
    closet, 170, 171, 175
    cubicle workstation, 105
    entry hall closet, 176
    fabric-enclosed, 100
    home-based office, 95, 100
    household information center, 126
    kitchen, 194
    living room, 205
    utility, 140
Sher, Barbara, 29
shoe bags and racks, 176, 186
shoebox containers, 157
shoebox files, stacking, 209
shoes, 41, 174, 178
sideboard, 53
single-function storage, 63
sink, storing under, 152
slatboards, 108
sleeping zone, 160, 181
software, 233–34
    e-mail, 235
    faxing, 237
    upgrades, 240
sorting, time, 57
sorting, 59–63
    attics, basements, and garages, 141–42
    bathrooms, 152–53
    bedrooms, 162
    children's rooms, 183–84
    closets, 172–73
    cubicle workstation, 105–6
    electronic information, 230–31
    home-based office, 96, 97–98
    household information center, 126–28
    kitchen, 194–95
    living rooms, 205–6
    mail and faxes, 237
    mobile office, 114–16
    quick, 61
    shortcut pitfall, 97
    time management, 220–21
    traditional office, 79–82
sources list, 83, 99, 106, 240
space
    gaining, 62, 143

    limited, 24–25
    mapping out, 54–55
SPACE formula, 59
space-stretching ideas
    attics, basements, and garages,
        140–41
    bathrooms, 152
    bedrooms, 160–61
    children's rooms, 182–83
    closets, 170–71
    cubicle workstation, 104–5
    home-based office, 95–96
    kitchen, 193–94
    living rooms, 204–5
    mobile office, 113–14
    traditional office, 77
spare household supplies, 139, 140,
        146–47
spare room, 126
"spark" files, 97
speed of life/technology, 22, 75, 104
spices, 195, 198
sports equipment, 140
    zone, 138, 140, 146
spouse, 21, 151, 161
stationery, 99, 107
    stacker, 101
    trays, 186
stemware, 196
step rack, 89, 199
step stool, storage, 146, 178
stereo, 163
storage, inconvenient, 18
    bedrooms, 159
    children's rooms, 181
    closets, 169
    cubicle workstation, 103
    home-based office, 91–92
    mobile office, 112
    traditional office, 75
storage, off-site, 63, 82, 106, 143–44
"Storage Bin" file, 144
storage space, 16, 19, 64
    home-based office, 95, 96
    limited, 21, 24–25
    See also master storage plan; more stuff
        than space
storage units
    activity zones, 53
    assigning home, 63–64

storage units (*cont'd*)
  attics, basements, and garages, 138–39
  bedrooms, 160
  built-in, 55
  children's rooms, 181–82
  closets, 169–70
  finding spot for, 54
  home-based office, 94
  household information center,
    124–26
  kitchen, 192–93
  living room, 203–4
  rearranging, 55
  time management, 216
  traditional office, 76
  untraditional uses, 53
  See also containerizing; containers
straight-line filing, 87, 88
strategizing, 15
  attics, basements, and garages, 138–41
  bathrooms, 151–52
  bedrooms, 160–61
  children's rooms, 181–83
  closets, 169–72
  cubicle workstation, 104–5
  defined, 47–58, 71
  home-based office, 92–97
  household information center,
    124–26
  kitchen, 192–94
  living rooms, 205–9
  mobile office, 112–14
  time management, 216–19
  traditional office, 75–79
stuffed animal hammock, 186
subdirectories, 232, 239
subject files, 81, 97
supplies
  and activity zones, 53
  attics, basements, and garages, 138–39
  bedrooms, 160
  children's rooms, 181–82
  closets, 169–70
  household information, 124–25, 133
  kitchen, 192–93
  living-room, 203–4
  office, 76, 83, 94, 95, 104, 116
  for organizing, 71–72
  sorting, 106, 116
surge protectors, 93

tab coding, 87–88, 130
taboret, 100
tag sale, 63, 144, 145
Taming the Paper Tiger (Hemphill), 128
tape recorder, 113, 117
Task Masters, 4–5
tax
  deductions, for donations, 143, 144
  file, rotating six-year, 133
  papers, 82, 89, 99, 106, 128–29
Taylor, Harold, 29, 224
technical errors, 17–20
technology, 22, 228–40
telephone
  jacks, 54
  message pad, 235, 236
  stands, 133
  supplies, 80
telephone calls, 222
  scheduling, 227
  software, 233
  zone, 53, 76, 104, 112, 113
telephone company voice-mail, 236–37
television zone
  bedrooms, 160, 163
  containers, 67, 207
  living room, 53, 54, 55, 204
time-stretching ideas, 217–19
time management, 21, 62, 213–27
Time Map, 217, 218, 220–23
time required to organize
  attics, basements, and garages, 141
  bathrooms, 152
  bedrooms, 161
  children's rooms, 183
  closets, 171–72
  cubicle workstation, 105
  estimating, 56–58
  home-based office, 96
  household information center, 126
  kitchen, 194
  living rooms, 205
  mobile office, 114
  time management and schedule, 219
toiletries, 117, 152–54, 156
  bag or case, 118, 120
  travel, 114, 115, 118
tools, 140, 141
  containers, 146, 178
tooth care items, 154

towels, 152, 154, 156, 173
toy chests, 185
traditional office, 73–89
transition, 20, 22–23
trash bags, 72, 147
travel
  documents, 116
  equipment, 115
  files, 98, 131
  light, 113–14
  time, using productively, 117
  See also mobile office
trays, 198
trunk, cedar-lined, 147
trunk of car, 119, 120
tune-ups, 68
  attics, basements, and garages, 148
  bathrooms, 157
  bedrooms, 165
  children's rooms, 188=89
  closets, 178
  computer and technology files, 240
  cubicle workstation, 109
  home-based office, 101
  household information center, 135
  kitchen, 200
  living rooms, 209
  mobile office, 121
  time management, 227
  traditional office, 89
Turbo Tax, 233
turntables, 157, 177, 198

unclear goals and priorities, 28–29
  bedrooms, 159
  home-based office, 91
  time management, 216
uncooperative partners, 23–24
  bathrooms, 150–51
  cubicle workstation, 103
unrealistic workload, 21–22
utensils, 195
utility bills, 129
utility closets, 167, 170, 175
  containers, 177–78
utility shelves, 146
utility zone, 51

vacation planning box, 131
VCR, 163

vertical storage, 140, 182
videotapes, 107, 162, 163, 203, 206, 208
visitors, 25, 92
vital records
  how long to keep, 129
  "map," 132
  safety deposit box, 131–32
  sorting, 127–28
voice mail, 20, 228, 230, 235–37

wallet, 114
wall storage, 77, 100, 134, 108, 157, 171
Wall Street Journal, 57
warranties and instructions, 129, 130
what items are most essential?
  attics, basements, and garages, 137
  bathrooms, 150
  bedrooms, 159
  children's rooms, 180
  closets, 167
  cubicle workstation, 103
  defined, 43–44
  home-based office, 91
  household information center, 123
  kitchen, 191
  living rooms, 202
  mobile office, 111
  time management, 215
  traditional office, 74–75
what's causing problems?
  attics, basements, and garages, 138
  bathrooms, 150–51
  bedrooms, 159
  children's rooms, 181
  closets, 168–69
  cubicle workstation, 103–4
  defined, 46
  home-based office, 91–92
  household information center,
    123–24
  kitchen, 191–92
  living rooms, 203
  mobile office, 111–12
  time management, 215–16
  traditional office, 75
what's not working?
  attics, basements, and garages, 137
  bathrooms, 149
  bedrooms, 158
  children's rooms, 180

what's not working? (*cont'd*)
 closets, 166
 cubicle workstation, 102
 defined, 41–42
 home-based office, 90
 household information center, 122
 kitchen, 190–91
 living rooms, 202
 mobile office, 110–11
 time management, 214
 traditional office, 73–75
what's working?
 attics, basements, and garages, 136
 bathrooms, 149
 bedrooms, 158
 children's rooms, 179–80
 closets, 166
 cubicle workstation, 102
 defined, 39–41
 home-based office, 90
 household information center, 122
 kitchen, 190
 living rooms, 201
 mobile office, 110
 time management, 214
 traditional office, 73
white picket fencing, 186
why do you want to get organized?
 attics, basements, and garages,
  137–38
 bathrooms, 150
 bedrooms, 159
 children's rooms, 180–81
 closets, 167
 cubicle workstation, 103
 defined, 45–46, 65
 home-based office, 91

 household information center, 123
 kitchen, 191
 living rooms, 202
 mobile office, 111
 time management, 215
 traditional office, 74–75
wicker
 basket, 163, 208
 drawer units, 199
 three-drawer chest, 163
 trunks, 163
Windows 95, 232
windows, 93, 205
Windows Explorer, 232
wire "add-a-shelf" products, 177, 198
Wishcraft (Sher), 29
Wizard, 224
workflow rails, 107, 108
working computer files, 232
Working from Home (Edwards and
  Edwards), 92
working parents, 20
working together, 65
 children's rooms, 179
 living rooms, 201
work
 overload, 21–22, 75
 schedule, establishing, 56–58
 time zone, 216
 zone, mobile office, 112, 113
writing supplies, 79, 117

Yahoo, 238
Yo-yo Organizing Syndrome, 3

zigzag organizing, 61–62
Zip drive, 231